BEYOND REAGAN

BEYOND REAGAN

The Politics of Upheaval

The Reporters of
WASHINGTON WEEK IN REVIEW

Edited by
Paul Duke

Essays and Roundtable Discussions by
Charles Corddry, Georgie Ann Geyer,
Haynes Johnson, Charles McDowell,
Jack Nelson, Hedrick Smith

WARNER BOOKS

A Warner Communications Company

Copyright © 1986 by WETA
All rights reserved.
Warner Books, Inc., 666 Fifth Avenue, New York, NY 10103
A Warner Communications Company

Printed in the United States of America
First Printing: April 1986
10 9 8 7 6 5 4 3 2 1

Library of Congress Cataloging-in-Publication Data
Main entry under title:

Beyond Reagan.

   Includes index.
   1. United States—Politics and government—
1981– —Addresses, essays, lectures. 2. Reagan,
Ronald—Addresses, essays, lectures. I. Duke, Paul.
II. Corddry, Charles.
E876.B48   1986   973.927   86-1508
ISBN 0-446-37019-3 (U.S.A.) (pbk.)
     0-446-37020-7 (Canada) (pbk.)

Book design: H. Roberts

ATTENTION: SCHOOLS AND CORPORATIONS

Warner books are available at quantity discounts with bulk purchase for educational, business, or sales promotional use. For information, please write to: Special Sales Department, Warner Books, 666 Fifth Avenue, New York, NY 10103.

**ARE THERE WARNER BOOKS YOU WANT
BUT CANNOT FIND IN YOUR LOCAL STORES?**

You can get any Warner Books title in print. Simply send title and retail price, plus 50¢ per order and 50¢ per copy to cover mailing and handling costs for each book desired. New York State and California residents, add applicable sales tax. Enclose check or money order—no cash, please—to: Warner Books, PO Box 690, New York, NY 10019. Or send for our complete catalog of Warner Books.

Acknowledgments

Many people have made this book possible, contributing time, advice, energy and encouragement. Among them:

Carolyn Shields, who patiently and painstakingly taped and transcribed our panel discussions.

Michelle Harris, who proofread the manuscripts and discussion texts and went beyond the call of customary duty in superbly checking out important facts and data.

Jim Wesley, who assisted in the editing of the manuscripts. Jim has been the producer of *Washington Week* since 1983.

Ricki Green, who, in her role as executive producer of *Washington Week,* supervised many important details and arrangements to assure publication.

Gail Ross and Ronald Goldfarb, who acted as go-betweens in dealing with the publisher and provided much valuable counsel.

Robert MacNeil, Lincoln Furber and Dick Fryklund, whose recollections about the early days of *Washington Week* were particularly insightful and helpful.

Sue Ducat, whose zestful enthusiasm cheered us on at all times.

And last, but hardly least, Gerald Slater, executive vice-president of the PBS Washington station, WETA. It was he who came up with the idea for the book. What's more, he had the persistence to see it through to fruition.

—P. D.

Contents

A Success Is Born, *Max M. Kampelman* 1

Introduction, *Paul Duke* 7

An American Revolution, *Haynes Johnson* 31
    Roundtable discussion of
        An American Revolution 51

The Reagan Legacy, *Jack Nelson* 83
    Roundtable discussion of The Reagan Legacy 116

Congress: Will There Be Realignment?, *Hedrick Smith* 137
    Roundtable discussion of Congress: Will There
        Be Realignment 171

Star Wars, *Charles Corddry* 193
    Roundtable discussion of Star Wars 220

Television Politics: The Medium Is the Revolution,
    Charles McDowell 235
    Roundtable discussion of Television Politics 262

When the Future Becomes the Past,
    Georgie Ann Geyer 285
    Roundtable discussion of When the Future
        Becomes the Past 308

Index 329

BEYOND REAGAN

A Success Is Born

Max M. Kampelman

MAX M. KAMPELMAN, 65, was named chief U.S. arms control negotiator for the American government in early 1985. As such, he has spearheaded efforts of the Reagan Administration to negotiate a reduction in nuclear weapons with the Soviet Union. A native of New York City, he has pursued a career in the law, government service, education and public affairs since coming to Washington in 1949. He served as legislative assistant to Senator Hubert Humphrey in the 1950s, as a senior adviser to the U.S. delegation to the United Nations in 1966–67 and from 1980 to 1983 was head of the U.S. delegation to the European Security Conference. And, with all his many achievements, he takes special pride in having given *Washington Week* its send-off in 1967.

Washington Week in Review was an important part of my life for several years and I take considerable pride in having been one of its founding fathers.

The real beginning was a telephone call one day back in the 1960s from my friend Newton Minow. Newt, a brilliant young lawyer and intimate of former Democratic presidential nominee Adlai Stevenson, had been chosen by President Kennedy to head the Federal Communications Commission, which he was proceeding to revitalize to help turn radio and television into responsible parts of a mature democratic society.

In this connection he wanted me to accept the chairmanship of Washington's new public television station, WETA, and try to turn it into a flagship for the country. Even though I protested that I was too busy in my law practice and knew nothing about television, Newt would not be dissuaded. "I insist, as a favor to me, that you accept," he said.

Public broadcasting was in its kindergarten phase and I soon found there was much work to be done—raising money, building a strong staff and developing appealing new programs. One clear need was for something in the news and public affairs sector, which was virtually nonexistent.

Then, out of the blue, another phone call. This one came from Hartford Gunn, the manager of Boston's WGBH, a pioneer in public broadcasting. He told me his small but sophisticated audience wanted news programs and analyses from Washington. Gunn, who later became the first president of the new Public Broadcasting Service, wanted WETA to start feeding news programs from the capital to Boston and a few other stations. He said he was prepared to hire his own Washington correspondent, but preferred for us to do the job if at all possible. I naturally felt that our future role in covering governmental activities would be crippled if we didn't stake out a territorial imperative. Accordingly, we agreed that Gunn would hold off for a few months while we tried to meet the need.

As it was, I considered public affairs and politics my cup of tea. I had come to Washington originally to serve as Hubert Humphrey's legislative counsel in the Senate. Education was a primary interest since I had taught at the University of Minnesota and Bennington College. While in the Senate, I had become friends with Neil MacNeil, a young *Time* magazine reporter whose book on the House of Representatives, *Forge of Democracy,* I had used as a textbook in teaching. Hence, as a starter, I arranged to put Neil on the air weekly, with a keenly honed, penetrating fifteen-minute report and analysis on Congress. Soon, Douglas Kiker, a feisty *New York Herald Tribune* reporter who later went to NBC News, had a companion fifteen-minute weekly report on the White House. It was a good beginning.

Before long, with public broadcasting taking stronger root, the time seemed ripe for expansion. So we drew up plans for a weekly half-hour program that would feature reports on Congress, the White House, the Pentagon and the State Department. Bill McCarter, WETA's new general manager, gave the idea his loving and enthusiastic attention, suggesting that the journalists cross-question one another to bring out all the relevant facts. Thus was *Washington Week in Review* born in February 1967. Within a few weeks its infancy was shared by Boston, Philadelphia, Pittsburgh and several other eastern seaboard stations.

We settled on four reporters: MacNeil for Congress; David Willis, diplomatic correspondent for the *Christian Science Monitor,* for the State Department; Peter Lisagor, bureau chief of the *Chicago Daily News,* for the White House; and Dick Fryklund of the *Washington Star* for the Pentagon. Fryklund had been one of my students at the University of Minnesota and someone with whom I occasionally discussed some of my television ideas.* After a few weeks he left the newspaper profession to accept a position as deputy assistant secretary of Defense for Public Affairs. His successor was Charles Corddry of the *Baltimore Sun,* whose quiet authoritative dignity still graces the program.

Having lined up our reporters, there was still one slot to be filled—the moderator's chair. McCarter proposed that I try out for the job, even though I had no on-air television experience. I took and passed the screen tests. With a few hiatus periods, arising out of my loyalty to Hubert Humphrey and my belief that I could not serve as moderator while helping him run for President, this lasted for three exciting years.

---

*Fryklund, now with the American Petroleum Institute in Washington, remembers that Kampelman got the idea for *Washington Week* while attending an American Political Science seminar for reporters in Minnesota. "One evening Max and I were sitting beside one of the state's 10,000 lakes—I've forgotten which one, but it was near Brainerd—sipping our drinks and talking about many things. I remarked that there were a number of newspaper reporters in Washington who knew their beats quite well and were ham enough to appear on television and talk interestingly and informatively about events at the White House, State Department, Capitol Hill or federal agencies. I said that it was too bad that TV news made little use of this expertise. Max said it ought to be possible to put together an effective program using those kinds of reporters. He said he would think more about it when he returned to Washington. He did think about it and came up with *Washington Week.*"

Yes, a political scientist/lawyer/politician does occasionally view public affairs differently from the way a journalist does. I saw our main responsibility as that of teachers, to help the public understand the great issues of the day. I had one chief criterion in deciding whether a story deserved attention: Did we think that five years from now history would judge that the event was significant? The headline stopper is certainly no measure of that. The significant story could be discussed and challenged in an interesting and entertaining fashion, which meant some argument and disagreement on and off the air. But it worked. We must assume, I argued, that our viewers saw the evening news on commercial television. What we needed to explore with our audience was why and how decisions were made, with what available options and with what likely consequences. It was also, I felt, essential that we not duplicate commercial television programs. My own role was basically to cajole and challenge the reporters to bring out the pertinent information.

We were good. Our audiences slowly grew as we added stations around the country. *Washington Week* became the first regular program to be fed nationwide to the new PBS system. We won prizes (as I write at my desk now, I look at an Emmy proudly hanging on my wall). It was impressive and startling to walk through airports and be stopped by strangers recognizing my face from watching the program. Indeed, even today, more than fifteen years later, when I am so busily involved in matters of war and peace, there is still an occasional mention of *Washington Week in Review* from an occasional stranger with a long memory. The power of television!

To Bill McCarter, and all the others, thanks for getting us under way. To Paul Duke and his worthy and talented associates, thank you for carrying on.

Introduction

Paul Duke

PAUL DUKE, 59, began his career as an Associated Press reporter in his hometown of Richmond, Virginia. He covered the early civil rights struggles after the 1954 Supreme Court school desegregation decision. Promoted to Washington in 1957 by the AP, he moved to the *Wall Street Journal* in 1959 to report on Congress and national politics. He made the switch to television in 1963 by joining NBC News, where he served as congressional correspondent. Duke went to public television in 1974. In addition to his *Washington Week* duties, he has anchored many PBS news specials and documentaries. He has interviewed almost all presidents and national leaders of the past twenty-five years. He lectures extensively, has written widely for major magazines and has won several awards for his reporting and writing. He says he has never had a job he didn't like but claims *Washington Week* is "best of all."

A funny thing happened on my way out of the glitzy and glamorous world of big-time broadcasting a decade ago. I discovered what real television power is all about.

Not that I was completely ignorant. As an NBC News correspondent I had observed firsthand the rising impact of the frisky new medium on American life, having covered many of the major stories of the tumultuous sixties and seventies—the civil rights strife, the Vietnam debates and Watergate, among others. I was, however, unprepared for the surprise awaiting me upon arrival in the smaller pastures of public broadcasting, where my new duties included running Max Kampelman's half-hour discussion program of the week's top news stories. The title "Washington Week in Review" seemed clumsy and unwieldy, the audience was small and the panelists were unfancy newspaper and magazine reporters. Somehow, though, it all added up to magic for the faithful few who watched.

To a graduate of a powerful commercial network, the devotion of *Washington Week*'s fans was little short of phenomenal. Nothing at NBC had equaled it, including the following for such old institutional favorites as the *Today* show and *Meet the Press*. Most amazing was how far some people would go to show their loyalty, something that soon became apparent during a trip back to my hometown of Richmond, Virginia, for a guest appearance. A spunky little seventy-eight-year-old woman in frazzled tennis shoes came up to extend greetings and, in a gush of flattery, told of getting up early and taking a bus to travel fifty miles from her farming community so she could shake my hand and say how she never missed our Friday night sessions. "I like the way y'all tell it like it is," she enthused.

Now, in its twentieth year, *Washington Week* is still telling it like it is as the longest-running PBS program. From the few thousand who originally watched on a half-dozen eastern seaboard stations in the late 1960s, the audience has skyrocketed to 7 million for 285 stations covering all fifty states.

By all conventional standards of television success, *Washington Week* should have long ago passed into video oblivion. It is an old-fashioned talking-heads program of the kind supposedly passé. It relies on reporters who actually cover the news rather than on more publicized columnist-commentator types. It has spurned the trendy tendency toward electronic razzle-dazzle and gimmickry in news programming. And it has retained the same essential format, emphasizing factual reporting and informed analysis rather than confrontational journalism.

Since the formula has worked so well on the air, we are emboldened to carry it into print. This book represents an attempt to apply the same straightforward reporting techniques to describe and put into perspective a remarkable series of events that have dramatically begun to change American society and the world. Most have occurred in the 1980s, already destined to go down as the decade of Big Change— much of it profound, some of it disturbing, almost all of it exciting and provocative. In six tightly written essays, *Washington Week*'s first-team reporters chronicle the key developments in the same candid style that Americans have grown accustomed to on Friday nights. Only this time, with the luxury of a broader canvas, the story portraits are deeper and more penetrating. As leaders among the capital's corps of 5,500 journalists, Charles Corddry, Georgie Anne Geyer, Haynes Johnson, Charles McDowell, Jack Nelson and Hedrick Smith bring a grand total of two hundred years' experience in covering the major stories of the past twenty-five years. All have achieved national renown; most have written books of their own, including best sellers; three—Johnson, Nelson and Smith—have won Pulitzer Prizes for distinguished reporting. They are, in brief, people who know what they are talking about.

Washington Week has been on the front line of an extraordinarily difficult period for Americans since the original broadcast in February 1967. Those early years saw the country getting a one-two punch, first from the Vietnam War, then from Watergate. Not only did these twin traumas cause a serious sagging of the national spirit, but the revelations that our highest officials had abused the public trust suggested—in Jeb Stuart Magruder's memorable phrase—that somehow the country had lost its moral compass. Nothing so underscored the gathering mood of pessimism in the early 1970s as a satirical bumper sticker: "Honk if you believe in anybody or anything."

Many people expected a turn for the better when Richard Nixon left office in August 1974. The night after his resignation, Peter Lisagor of the *Chicago Daily News* came on *Washington Week* to say that Gerald Ford had been sworn in as the new President in an atmosphere of hope "as though someone had opened the windows in the White House." Unfortunately, the hope soon faded as Ford's modest interregnum did little to dispel the crisis in confidence. Nor did the Christian populism of Jimmy Carter provide much uplift, the Democratic administration foundering on the economic shoals of 16 percent mortgage rates and 13 percent inflation. It was finally sunk by a year-long humiliation to American authority in far-off Iran.

By 1980 the country was adrift. Nothing seemed to work anymore and no one seemed in charge. The bright dreams evoked by John Kennedy's Camelot two decades before were gone; the rising expectations had given way to declining expectations. Moreover, the deepening distrust in the traditional political leadership was accompanied by a new skepticism of government as the principal problem solver, with millions believing the political process was no longer responsive to public concerns. Suddenly, the cry was everywhere, from Democrats as well as Republicans, to curb Uncle Sam's expansionist habits of almost half a century and to begin restraining the federal octopus.

It was a rebellion heavenly made for a veteran California Republican who for two decades had been preaching a sermon of leaner government, lower taxes and less regulation. His time had clearly come, but hardly anyone figured that the disillusionment was so deep that it would catapult Ronald Wilson Reagan into such a surprisingly easy conquest of Jimmy Carter in November 1980.

Three days later I began *Washington Week*'s postelection discussion this way: "The political earthquake that reverberated across America last Tuesday will bring many changes to Washington. A much more conservative White House. A much more conservative Congress. And perhaps a new conservative era. In the process we are certain to have new policies to try to solve the country's long-standing economic problems and to build up American power and prestige abroad." In the analysis that followed, Hedrick Smith called it "a fascinating moment in history" because the new leader had been given a mandate "to try to do something different." Haynes Johnson said the Republicans had been given their "greatest chance in a generation to show that they can put into place programs that will work."

To be sure, the Reagan victory had its nostalgic side, a yearning for easier, less complicated times and a return to a period when America reigned supreme. But fundamentally it symbolized the country's willingness to strike out in new directions, to experiment and to try new solutions for old problems—even if some of them sounded dangerously simplistic. Implicit was the message that the heyday of the welfare state was finally over.

All the same, no one quite knew what to expect when the new Republican Administration took possession of the government in 1981. Washington had long been used to presidential candidates campaigning in one fashion and governing in quite another. Even if Reagan had been delivering the same consistently conservative message since Barry Goldwater's time, he still remained something of a wild card whose course was not always easy to fathom.

But now, in the nation's foremost command post of power, he soon eliminated all doubts. He would go for broke. Moving expeditiously, the Reagan White House mobilized an all-out political press aimed at implementing as much as possible of the radical program on which the new President had campaigned up and down the land. Not since Franklin Roosevelt's days had anyone so boldly attacked the status quo. What no one reckoned with, though, was that a compliant Congress would so willingly embrace the new Chief Executive's call for sharp reductions in social spending, deep cuts in taxes and a massive buildup in defense. Whatever Reagan wanted, Reagan seemed to get. By the end of 1981 it was plain that his first-year record would be the best of any President since FDR and the fabled 100 days of 1933.

The Reagan revolution (or more aptly, counterrevolution) was for real, or so it seemed. Whether for good or ill, the President succeeded in unleashing a stunning tide of social, economic and governmental change unparalleled since New Deal days. And while the pace of that change later slowed—and continues to slow in Reagan's second term—it is nonetheless true that he has transformed Washington in ways that no one would have dreamed possible when he arrived on the scene in 1981.

There is a *new* politics. And a new *style* of politics. Conservatism is fashionable again. Liberalism is in retreat. New, more ideologically committed players are running the old town. The famed Mr. Republican of forty years ago, the late Senator Robert Taft of Ohio, would barely recognize—and perhaps not even approve of—the zealous brand of partisanship practiced by these latter-day conservative apostles.

The biggest surprise, of course, has been Ronald Reagan himself. Reporters knew that the onetime Hollywood actor was a talented political player, having served two terms as governor of California, but there was nothing in his past to suggest that he was a big-leaguer in the FDR style who would so skillfully wield the cudgels of power.* For all of his surprising success, though, Reagan remains one of the most paradoxical Presidents ever to sit in the Oval Office. The contrasts are striking:

> Ideologue and Pragmatist
> Great Communicator and King of Bloopers
> Noncompromiser and Artful Compromiser
> Tough-Talking Hard-liner and Restrained Hawk

Indeed, what has made Reagan hard to figure out—and for the press to cover—has been a penchant for political ambiguity. Take as one example the area of civil rights. The President has repeatedly—and sometimes heatedly—denied charges that the GOP Administration has downgraded civil rights, yet it is unquestionably true that civil rights no longer

---

*Interestingly, the press was wrong about Roosevelt, too. In the campaign of 1932 Walter Lippmann dismissed him as "a pleasant man who, without any important qualifications for the office, would very much like to be president."

enjoys the governmental priority it did during the sixties and seventies. During his first two years in office, Reagan vowed to make no changes in Social Security. But in 1983 he accepted money-saving modifications to protect the system from bankruptcy. Time and again he shifts out of seemingly rigid gear, dismaying skeptics and supporters alike. And now, as he moves through his second term, he is establishing a new reputation as a master of strategic withdrawal after encountering heavy fire on Capitol Hill for several of his policies.

While he may never have won an Academy Award for his acting ability, Reagan deserves some kind of prize for the way he plays the media with a good-guy blend of graciousness and charm. In a White House that emphasizes public relations over public information—and goes out of its way to protect the President from all adversity—it may be understandable that Reagan would escape blame for the Administration's setbacks and mistakes. But this explanation hardly does justice to Reagan's theatrical talents in fending off press assaults. His news conference performances and deft one-liners are an art form rarely impeded by the facts; indeed, Reagan probably has made more straight-faced denials of the obvious than any President in history.

Consider, for instance, the farce that was played out on the Washington stage in October 1985 when Margaret Heckler was dismissed as secretary of the Health and Human Services Department. The action followed weeks of front-page reports that White House aides wanted to remove Mrs. Heckler because they regarded her as a poor manager and that they wanted to send her packing off to be ambassador to Ireland. She resisted and fought back fiercely, even rallying congressional Republicans to her defense. The pressure eventually became too great, however, and she finally accepted reassignment, although it meant a salary reduction of $11,000 and considerably diminished authority. The spectacle had all the trappings of a public hanging, yet there was one incredible climactic scene when Reagan walked into the White House press room to make the official announcement. With Mrs. Heckler at his side, looking as if she wanted to cry, the President made it sound as if she were being promoted after doing a wonderful job at HHS:*

> **Reagan:** I am delighted and happier than I have been in a long time. Margaret Heckler has agreed to my request that she become the ambassador to Ireland.
> ... I'm sorry that I didn't start saying it sooner, that the malicious gossip, without any basis in fact, that has been going on for the last several days about this is without any basis in fact. She has done a fine job at HHS.
> ... Whoever finally replaces her there ... will find that that agency is in great shape as a result of her direction and her leadership.
> And it has been absolutely unjustified, whoever has been leaking these falsehoods and intimating. Well, for one thing, I certainly have never thought of the embassies as dumping grounds, and therefore, if she hadn't been doing as well as she has been doing, I certainly would not have picked Ireland, or any embassy for that matter, but Ireland especially, for her to take that post. ...
>
> **Reporter:** What's the malicious gossip ... you mean the fact that leaks coming mainly from your Administration said that she'd be appointed ambassador to Ireland?

---

*Reagan has never liked to fire subordinates or to make drastic changes in his Administration. He also resisted getting rid of James Watt as Interior secretary and Anne Gorsuch as director of the Environmental Protection Agency, finally letting both go under pressure from congressional Republicans who felt the two had become political liabilities.

Reagan: No, the leaks that we were doing this in some way because we were unhappy with what she was doing where she was.

Reporter: You were not unhappy?

Reagan: No.

Reporter: ... If you're not unhappy with the job that she's been doing, why isn't Mrs. Heckler staying?

Reagan: Because we have a need for an ambassador, and Ireland is getting very impatient, and I thought that she might like a change of pace ... and I think that she will be just great.

Only an old actor can get away with voicing such lines, and Reagan has made it seem easy. His rapport with the American public is astounding. He may be intellectually lazy, inattentive to details and sometimes ignorant of important developments, but most voters don't seem to mind. The image of a take-charge leader more than compensates for the personal deficiencies, even if the script does not always conform to reality. It may not be the stuff of past presidential heroes, but Reagan is assuredly a hero to millions who believe he has moved the country back onto the right track and restored American prestige around the globe. If the seventies were the dark decade of disharmony and self-doubts, the eighties by comparison appear to be the comeback decade for a proud and resurgent U.S.A.—and Reagan gets the credit.

The architects of the new conservatism see themselves as bringing about changes as lasting and significant as those of the New Deal period. Whether that proves to be the case or not, the Reagan presidency has reaffirmed the vitality and genius of the American system. The founding fathers plainly foresaw change and compromise as the building blocks for the struggling young republic, with a flexible Constitution "intended to endure for ages to come and to be adapted to the various crises of human affairs," in the words of John Marshall. Looked at another way, the triumph of Reaganism has reinforced the truism that democracy thrives on diversity, its enduring safety valve. And it most certainly has reminded us that no one political party or philosophy can expect to be dominant forever, no matter how well its policies may be received for a while. This periodic renewal of the country's inherent character was perhaps best explained by historian Daniel Boorstin when he wrote: "Of the many comforting illusions [about the United States] none was to be more seductive than that the American way of government could remain unchanged, or that it could be imprisoned in one generation's conscious purposes."* Thus, again as in the 1930s, peaceful change through involution has made revolution—real revolution—unnecessary.

Nevertheless, the consequences of the Reagan period could be formidable. Is the long-predicted realignment of the major political parties finally at hand? Are the Republicans regaining their nineteenth-century dominance of the political landscape? Is the presidency again restored to political preeminence after twenty years of paralysis, corruption and stalemate? Is the new conservatism an aberrational fad? Is Reagan himself a mere passing meteor, much in the fashion of Canadian conservative star John Diefenbaker, who soared to prominence in the 1950s, only to sink back into obscurity after a few years in the sun? Is television, that marvelous young upstart that has been such an important instrument for Reagan's leadership, permanently altering the rules for governance?

The Big Change has not been limited to the American political arena. There is the military buildup, the biggest ever

*From *The Americans: The Democratic Experience*, Volume 2. (New York: Random House, 1973)

in peacetime. And now the President's push for an expanded defense frontier in space promises to raise the stakes of technological warfare to superhigh levels, making it more probable that Buck Rogers will arrive in the twenty-first and not the twenty-fifth century. Will Star Wars, as Reagan says, change the course of human history by rendering nuclear weapons obsolete? Or will it mark the final stepping stone to an ever-closer Armageddon?

Meanwhile, back on earth, time is marching backward in some faraway places—and a frightening march it is. A rapid rise in fanaticism threatens to plunge parts of the Third World into a throwback period of medievalism when religious fundamentalism served as a convenient cover for despotism. Is this antimodern trend an ominous wave of the future? Should we take it seriously? Could it endanger Western civilization at some point?

All the answers aren't in, but we know enough to make some assessments and judgments. One caveat is in order: In no sense do we mean this to be a recitation of the entire record or the definitive work on the 1980s. Rather, our purpose is to inform and enlighten through the observations and insights of six people who have been on-the-scene witnesses to this important parade of history. We have, however, gone beyond the formal essays and provided a variation of the real thing—a genuine *Washington Week* discussion (everything but the cameras). In sessions that ranged up to two hours, we sat down just as we do in the television studio on Friday nights and engaged in a lively, free-wheeling dialogue on each topic. The idea was to enlarge upon the essays with additional opinions, thereby giving readers an even broader view. The transcripts of these discussions thus serve as an epilogue to each chapter.

In pursuing this *Washington Week* endeavor, we have adhered to the reporting rule laid down by Peter Lisagor, who said the journalist's duty is "to walk down the middle of the street taking potshots at both the windows on the right and the left." Nobody did that better than Lisagor, a poor boy from West Virginia who rose to be one of the top journalists in the country and the first great star of *Washington Week*. More than any single person, he was responsible for the program taking root and becoming a television fixture.

Peter was a reporter with many charismatic qualities. As the Washington bureau chief for the *Chicago Daily News,* he covered the White House for many years and, as one critic said, "could tell us what was going on there as if he had the keys to all the rooms." With his bemused cynicism, he never suffered foolish politicians gladly and loved to pinprick stuffed shirts. Almost every program produced a funny and demolishing line, such as the time I asked him to compare the performance of President Ford's press secretary, Ron Nessen, with that of Richard Nixon's man, Ron Ziegler. "Two Rons don't necessarily make a right," he shot back.

Lisagor was heir to a long line of sage and irreverent commentators of the national scene stretching back to Benjamin Franklin and including Mark Twain and Will Rogers. Henry Kissinger called him "the Renaissance man of Washington journalism." He could move easily through the palaces of the mighty while retaining his warm, common touch—never fazed by the glitter, never too busy to speak to copyboys and stagehands or to help those struggling up the ladder behind him. When Peter became ill from lung cancer in 1976, our office was deluged with well-wishing mail from fans wondering when he was coming back. As he grew worse, I suggested he compose a few lines for me to read on the air and he agreed. On the morning of Friday, December 10, he dictated a statement to his daughter to phone to our office. It was the old Lisagor—witty, self-effacing, musing mischievously that his absence "had improved the program immeasurably . . . some *Washington Week* viewers have felt blessed, others delivered and a few vindicated."

Five hours later he was dead at sixty-one, and that night I had to make the saddest announcement of my broadcasting career. Peter had been on *Washington Week* almost from the beginning, the leader of a trio of regulars that included the *Baltimore Sun*'s Corddry and Neil MacNeil of *Time* magazine. We all had lumps in our throats as we reminisced about Peter—MacNeil calling him "an original . . . who had an astonishing talent for getting to the real heart of a question," and Corddry saying, "We've simply lost the best reporter in town."

The ensuing weeks brought an outpouring of tributes from every corner of the country, more than two thousand letters from people who just wanted to say they shared our grief. The expressions were heartrending: "I feel I have lost a guiding light in the wilderness," wrote a Kansas City man. "I am grateful his kind of integrity can still be found in the world," said a San Francisco woman. Many confessed to crying when they heard the news, a Huntington Beach, California, woman saying: "Except for President Kennedy, I had never wept upon hearing of the death of a public figure, but I did tonight when I heard you say Peter had died." The striking denominator was that these people—people who had never met Peter—knew so well the essence of his character and personality. A writer from Jacksonville, Tennessee, may have put it best when she said, "Mr. Lisagor's remarks stayed on the soft edge of the cutting sword." This fact—that he was never mean or bitter or played favorites—earned him an unparalleled following among Washington journalists while also assuring *Washington Week*'s success.

There was a time when that success was in doubt. Lisagor, in fact, figured in a celebrated attempt by the Nixon White House to kill *Washington Week*. For several years presidential aides had complained of what they viewed as a liberal slant in the fledgling public television system's news programs, and *Washington Week* was singled out as a prime target, primarily because of Lisagor's outspoken and courageous reporting. Although he had been equally tough on Lyndon Johnson, some of Nixon's advisers didn't take kindly to Peter's pungent thrusts, particularly when Watergate came along. The White House, launching a campaign of intimidation, took to calling public broadcasting officials demanding that they "get that guy Lisagor off the air." Failing in that, the Nixon staffers began maneuvering to cut off federal funding for *Washington Week* and almost all other national news and public affairs programming. Faced with the prospect of cancellation, producer Lincoln Furber read a statement just before Christmas 1972 informing the audience that the program's days might be numbered. The public response was overwhelming—fifteen thousand letters of protest, many enclosing donations in the hope that disaster could be staved off. The White House got the message. Before long, with Watergate becoming an increasingly serious distraction, Nixon staffers backed off from their attack on public broadcasting and *Washington Week* was saved.

As it was, Watergate was rapidly becoming *Washington Week*'s biggest story. "It was one of the first places where Americans might have heard about Watergate's true dimensions," recalls veteran journalist Robert MacNeil, who was serving as moderator at the time. "In October 1972 Neil MacNeil [no relation] emphasized that it could grow into the biggest scandal Washington had ever known, a scandal that could bring down the Administration. I thought he was exaggerating."

This kind of solid reporting not only was establishing *Washington Week*'s integrity but also was enabling it to become the premier national program for weekly news analysis. By now, even skeptical public broadcasting executives were impressed. In the early years some had predicted *Washington Week* could not possibly survive because it was, as one complained, "dull, dull, dull." In a 1969 survey of PBS stations, several managers disparaged the program as tedious and lacking in colorful personalities.

The television critics were starting to take notice, too, citing *Washington Week* as a pioneer in the news field. Barbara Ryan, writing in the *Denver Post,* said the program was presented in "an atmosphere of cheerful bluntness that bears about as much resemblance to the decorous quizzing on NBC's *Meet the Press* and CBS's *Face the Nation* as the Rolling Stones do to Mozart." Jack Gould told *New York Times* readers that "a crucial video vacuum" was being filled, and Randall Roe of the *New York Daily News* said that "in an age of superhype and bionic anchormen, *Washington Week* is comforting. It is an uncommon sight to see journalists acting calmly, to find a news show that isn't angling for a page one story the next day." Honors and awards began to come as well, including the prestigious DuPont-Columbia prize for outstanding journalistic achievement.

Many important ingredients went into the *Washington Week* stew—the chummy camaraderie, the relaxed civility, the intimate glimpses of capital life, the feeling that outsiders were tuning in to what the insiders knew. The chief condiment, however, was credibility: The panelists who discussed the news were the people who had been in the trenches all week covering the news, not commentators who sat high above it all in their ivory towers. The result was a program that many felt got to the bottom of things and in its own small way countered Mark Twain's claim that it was hard for ordinary mortals to understand what was going on in Washington.

Washington Week's reporting roster has changed and enlarged over the years, but audience attitudes have remained the same. People still regard us as old friends who drop in on Friday nights and help them to catch up on what's been happening during the week. "It is the next best thing to inviting people in for interesting conversation" was the way a Platte, South Dakota, viewer put it. Stories are legion of those who say they never go anywhere until the program is over, who take the telephone off the hook to prevent interruptions and who get together in groups to watch. "We miss it only under duress," said a Mount Vernon, New York, man. Even the capital's social habits are occasionally affected, Senate Democratic Leader Robert Byrd once holding up an elegant dinner party because he couldn't miss "my favorite television program."* We landed our sponsor, the Ford Motor Company, because corporate chairman Philip Caldwell happened to be a fan. Perhaps the all-time award for loyalty belongs to a young couple who joined a Midwest commune to pursue a more contemplative life, forswearing the ways of the world except for one thing: They took along a radio to listen to *Washington Week*. (A taped version of the program is carried on National Public Radio.)

Much as we might like to swim in all this glory, there is another side. To be perfectly honest, the mailbag does bring pans as well as paeans. Hence, any temptation to smugness is dashed by critics who see us as messengers of darkness who repeatedly confirm Spiro Agnew's indictment of the press as "nattering nabobs of negativism."† A Kalamazoo, Michigan, man, upbraiding us as the voice of gloom and doom, wondered "if the suicide rate is higher on Friday nights after your program." Contending we were too downbeat for his taste, a Jackson, Mississippi, man asked: "Do

---

*Byrd also has said he often leaves the Senate early on Fridays, "and I must admit, at times I've gone a little faster than the speed limit to get home in time for *Washington Week*."

†From a White House–inspired speech delivered in San Diego on September 11, 1970, in which Spiro Agnew attacked the press as being overly negative.

you like this country, or would you rather live in Cuba?" A Bay City, Michigan, writer said we reminded him "of the witches in *Macbeth* bent on causing as much trouble as possible." And a Des Moines, Iowa, woman condemned what she interpreted as the tattletale tone of one session as bringing back memories of "the verandah virgins, a group of small town women who sit in rockers on the porch and gossip about the minister's wife having an affair with the local butcher."

The most passionate protests come from those who think we are politically biased. Any mention of presidential failings, election campaign foul-ups and troubles for one of the two major parties evokes a small flood of vitriol. "With what unabashed glee three of your panelists sailed into the Republicans," fumed a Sarasota, Florida, writer who took exception to one discussion during the 1984 fall presidential campaign. The ensuing weeks, however, brought a volley of accusations from Democrats that we were soft on Reagan and had not given a fair shake to Walter Mondale in our coverage. A Middlesex, Massachusetts, man charged that we had "tossed cotton balls at Reagan and grenades at Mondale."

Some complainants demand to know our political affiliations and voting habits. Others aver that we make it difficult for any President to run the country. "You found fault because Jimmy Carter paid too close attention to detail," griped a Baltimore woman. "Now you find fault because President Reagan doesn't pay enough attention to detail." Reagan partisans sometimes vent their anger by writing the President directly. A Goldsboro, North Carolina, man, upset at what he described as press distortions of the Administration's record, took pen in hand to declaim: "Mr. President, my nomination for the dubious distinction of being the most outrageous is *Washington Week in Review* ... as I approach my 81st birthday, watching this program could be injurious to my health, especially my blood pressure, but like so many my age, I live dangerously these days."

All of this is in keeping with American custom. For two hundred years the press has been under assault in one form or another, always managing to survive the outbursts of those who believe they have somehow been wronged and that freedom has been imperiled. In fact, Presidents and other political notables have generally led in the assaults. Thomas Jefferson felt so vilified by the newspapers of his day that he proposed they set aside special pages labeled "lies." Alexander Hamilton called the press "a wild animal in our midst." More recently, John F. Kennedy became so fed up with the *New York Herald Tribune* treatment of his Administration that he ordered the White House subscription canceled. While criticism can never be ignored, the reality is that most accusations of press bias come from people who really want the press to reflect *their* biases, regardless of the truth.

The brickbats, however, have not been limited to political matters. We have been humbled in other ways. One newspaper critic said it took him three martinis to get through our sober-sided view of things, and another compared our serious demeanor to that of "appliance dealers trying to figure out why refrigerators weren't selling." Others have charged that we are too cautious, too calm and too much of a gray-headed league. One television critic concluded that we offered little more than comic book wisdom, but even this became suspect after a California study found that the few sixth-grade students who watched *Washington Week* scored lower in reading than the sixth-grade viewers of any other program. At the opposite extreme, there are those who believe we are sometimes too highbrow. Fortunately, on this count, we are saved by our good-humor man Charley McDowell, who received a letter from a Niagara Falls, New York, family saying that sometimes they didn't understand what the other reporters were talking about, but that his presence made them feel better because *he* didn't seem to know, either.

Then there are the grammarians, a punctilious and outspoken breed that regards *Washington Week* as a downright hazard to the English language. The slightest slip of the tongue can provoke a torrent of dressing-down letters. My reference to "an old cliché" one night prompted a Concord, New Hampshire, woman to respond, "Please, Mr. Duke, give us 'a new cliché' sometime." Panelist Richard Burt of the *New York Times** heard from the hinterlands after using the word "irregardless," a Philadelphia man admonishing: "Be advised that 'irregardless' is not a word regardless or irrespective of what you may think." After one especially objectionable program, a Mill Valley, California, writer claimed that we were undermining the country's values, adding that "the English language ranks with other things worth preserving these days."

Some of the language custodians keep score of the bobbles. "You had a woman reporter who used 'basically' thirteen times, at which count I turned off the set," wrote a Phoenix, Arizona, woman. That utterly useless phrase "you know" is a particular horror. Two viewers from Kentucky and South Carolina flayed a rookie reporter's performance, counting thirty-six "you knows" in a span of six minutes. A tape check confirmed their count. For a while a Baltimore man kept a chart of weekly offenders, pointing out that the reporters never used the phrase in writing their newspaper and magazine stories. "The words may be acceptable for prize fighters and football pros but not you," he counseled. "Ughs" and "wells" also come in for considerable damnation. Another woman from Phoenix, charging that we were

---

*Richard Burt has since gone on to greater glory, having been named assistant secretary of State for European Affairs in 1982 and currently serving as American ambassador to West Germany.

succumbing to the dread disease of beginning too many sentences with "well," said we nonetheless were in good company because she had clocked White House Chief of Staff Donald Regan uttering fourteen "wells" during a half-hour television interview.

Sometimes the cause becomes a crusade. A few years ago a New Rochelle, New York, man launched a verbal fusillade against Hedrick Smith and me for what he saw as an absurd number of "a number of. . . ." Over a period of months he argued his case with unassailably historic logic: that the Bible did not say that God gave Moses "a number of" commandments; that Columbus did not sail West in "a number of" ships; that Lincoln never said "a number of" years ago our fathers brought forth; that Tennyson never wrote that "a number of" soldiers rode into the Valley of Death. When the inanity didn't end, our reproacher suggested that perhaps Smith and I should be hit over the head with baseball bats to bring us to our senses. Superfluous words, he argued, were causing an enormous drain of energy. "Over the years they destroy forests and ravage other natural resources; first, for the paper on which they are written and produced; second, for the power required for reproduction and dissemination. And think of the ancillary benefits from elimination: smaller newspapers (fewer hernias from lifting Sunday editions); briefer newscasts (more time for deodorant ads), and conceivably improved political speeches!"

Such fervor underscores the most singular characteristic of *Washington Week,* to wit: the intense personal interest and involvement that so many veiwers take in the program and its participants. Hardly any facet of the broadcast has escaped comment, be it the studio set, the hairstyles, the facial makeup, the clothes we wear or the water glasses atop our slate-blue table. A Boise, Idaho, man complained long and vociferously about the studio lighting, saying it was particularly unkind to Jack Nelson by making it appear that he was "aging fast." After a fly buzzed in one evening and audaciously came down on the nose of Lisa Myers of the *Washington Star,** four flyswatters arrived in the following week's mail. All of us have received inquiries about our origins, from those curious as to whether "you are possibly the Geyer girl who grew up down the street" or the "Johnson kid who went to PS 27." A Coronado Island, California, man named Roger McDowell, professing kinship with Harry Truman, wrote Charley McDowell that he had discovered that they, too, were cousins. He went on to say that he was a friend of Ronald and Nancy Reagan and suggested Charley get to know the First Family, adding, "You can get in touch with them at the White House."

Success has brought other by-products as well. Our reporters, once largely unknown outside the capital, have been recognized on the streets of London, Rome, Paris, Tokyo, at the Great Wall of China and in a Dublin pub. A Canadian couple from Willowdale, Ontario, named their second child after Charlie Corddry; in 1985 Charlie received a Toronto Blue Jays baseball cap from his now seven-year-old namesake, Corddry George Taylor, as a token of international affection. We have been featured and satirized in novels, cartoons, comic strips, by Johnny Carson and on *Saturday Night Live.* Poems have been dedicated to our troupe and occasionally courtships and marriage proposals have been received. One West Coast gentleman even sought some advice for the lovelorn, calling the *Washington Week* office in 1982 to ask if we had any inside information as to whether war might break out in Greece, where two friends planned to honeymoon. Sorry, we replied, it was impossible to make any predictions, but we did think a honeymoon in Greece was a terrific idea, war or no war.

It is pretty heady stuff. McDowell, who first came

---

*Lisa Myers later joined NBC News.

aboard in 1977, summed up the impact on his career this way:

> For 30 years I worked quietly on the *Richmond Times-Dispatch* and through sheer durability became almost as well known as 50 other reporters in Virginia. Now, thanks to *Washington Week,* I have been invited to speak to the Detroit Economic Club, the San Francisco Foreign Affairs Forum, the National Association of Universities and Land Grant Colleges, the Institute of Government at Harvard and a hundred more places. In less than a day's time not long ago (1) a young senator held an elevator door for me at the Capitol and called me Sir, (2) a taxi driver turned and said without preamble 'You don't know what you're talking about on tax reform' and (3) a professor at Cornell wrote to say I shouldn't say 'formidable' if I couldn't pronounce it correctly (FOR-midable).

In a time of notable change in so much of the world it is reassuring that many people can continue to find satisfaction and enjoyment in something that has not changed. *Washington Week* may be too young to qualify as an American institution, but after nineteen years on public television it most assuredly qualifies as a broadcasting senior citizen. The hope is that we can go on meriting the approval—and even the criticism, when called for—of faithful friends such as the woman in Fresno, California, who made the case better than anyone: "Thank goodness there is something that works in Washington without people yelling at each other."

An American Revolution

Of People and Presidents in the Eighties

Haynes Johnson

HAYNES JOHNSON, 54, has reported on most of the major news events at home and abroad for the last generation, and on the activities of every president from Dwight D. Eisenhower to Ronald Reagan. He was a reporter, editor and special assignments correspondent for the *Washington Star* from 1957 until 1969, when he joined the *Washington Post*. He won the Pulitzer Prize, as did his father before him, for his reporting of the Selma (Alabama) civil rights crisis in 1965. He has been a network TV commentator, a professor at Princeton University and is the author or coauthor of nine books, including a historical novel of Washington in World War II to be published in 1986. His *Washington Week* appearances date back to the late 1960s.

A few miles from town, under glowering late October skies, the Hollywood people positioned their cameras on the rolling dark Iowa farmland. They were filming an epic about hard times in the American heartland, one that recalled the bleak Depression days of family foreclosures and grim discouraged farmers but was recast fifty years later in the affluent America of the mid-1980s. The film had a great star, Jessica Lange, and a compelling title, *Country,* all of which naturally made it a major subject of conversation among the people of Iowa who lived in the vicinity. It was then that I first met Toni Nies.

She seemed to have stepped full-form from screen into real life without, of course, realizing it. Like the character Jessica Lange portrayed, she was a young woman struggling to save her family farm. The economic circumstances confronting Toni Nies were similar to those facing Lange in the film. Whether fictional heroine or actual American woman of the Midwest, time and fortune were moving against them both.

We talked at length. This was exactly a year before the presidential election of 1984, and I knew instantly Toni Nies was someone to watch. At the time, I was nearing the end of another long reporting swing around America assessing the attitudes of voters who would determine whether Ronald Reagan would be given a second term in the White House. For me, Toni became a symbol of the kinds of voters I kept encountering, and also a clue to the political future. She was a lifelong Democrat who had voted for Jimmy Carter against Reagan in 1980; but despite that background, despite the hardships she and her husband were then experiencing and despite her own specific criticisms of Reagan policies, she was not personally bitter about him. She then remained, in the fall of 1983, a year before judgment on his presidency, undecided about how she would vote.

Exactly a year later, just a week before the presidential election, I again interviewed Toni Nies in Iowa. The ensuing twelve months had been disastrous and heartbreaking for her. She and her husband, Jerome, had lost their battle to keep their 140-acre farm. They had been forced off land that had been in the family for three generations. They were selling off their farm machinery; their livestock would be sold next. I asked Toni how she felt about Reagan now—and how she intended to vote next week. She laughed slightly. "Well, I don't feel better about him," she said. "He certainly hasn't helped us." Then she said: "But, you know, I feel a President can't do his job in just four years. It's like farming: It takes a longer time to get your crops established. That's how I feel about Reagan. He needs more time to do the job for the country. So I'm going to vote for him this time."

And so goes the "Teflon" presidency. That voter, and countless others like her I met, knew full well the record of Ronald Reagan's presidency. They understood exactly where and how his policies had affected them adversely. Yet whether they were unemployed factory workers or sorely beset farmers battling the harshest times since the Great Depression, they voted for him nonetheless. In so doing they were implicitly testifying that something more than affection for Reagan personally, and something more than ignorance of his policies, lay at the heart of his overwhelming victory—and something more contributed to Reagan's popularity than selfishness, the "Me first!" and "I've got mine, Jack" mentality that was said by critics to affect Americans in the mid-1980s.

The behavior of voters like Toni Nies and millions like her suggests there was something deeper, too, behind their support for Reagan than traditional political bread-and-butter "pocketbook" interests. I can cite numerous examples, and so I'm sure can any political reporter, of interviews I've conducted with registered Democrats who formed the heart of that majority political party yet, like Nies, voted for Ronald Reagan and thus sent a chilling message to their party and the party of their parents. Some of them represented a startling shift in allegiance. There was, for example, the self-defined "left-liberal" history professor near Berkeley who had been active in the civil rights, anti-Vietnam, campus Free Speech movements of a generation ago. There was the Hispanic Democratic officeholder active in the nuclear freeze initiative. There was the previously active fund-raiser for liberal Democrats, not long ago a prominent figure in Democratic gatherings in his part of the country. All voted for Reagan; all expressed the idea that they were part of a significant shift in our politics.

They are, if Reagan adherents are correct, heralds of new attitudes changing the nature of politics in America in the Reagan Era. They are the vanguard of the Reagan Revolution. And, to follow that line of reasoning, they offer tangible evidence both that a potentially great political realignment is in the making, one as profound in its implications for the business of government and the values of the society as the dawning of the New Deal half a century ago, and that the Reagan presidency has already left a distinctive stamp on the American people.

If so, this is the stuff of great history and great change and we are in the midst of it. In a moment, I'm going to offer a markedly different interpretation for the current American political environment and suggest that other conclusions can be drawn from an examination of the attitudes that give force and strength to the Reagan presidency, but for now let the other case be made.

Certainly only a fool, or an even more arrogant and insulated breed of Washington journalist than our most severe critics portray us to be, could fail to see these results as evidence that something politically important appears to be happening. It doesn't require the mind of a Machiavelli, either, to understand that some sort of a Republican ascendancy is in the making—or has already arrived. After all, Republican candidates have won four of the last five presidential elections. The only time the Democrats succeeded in breaking that run, in 1976 with the singularly atypical politician Jimmy Carter, their candidate received barely over 50 percent of the vote. This sort of Democratic presidential record prompts some analysts to predict that we have seen the last of Democratic Presidents in this century, that, indeed, the Republicans with their commanding edge in the most populous Sunbelt states with the largest electoral votes have a lock on the White House. In fact, the winning GOP presidential streak looks even more impressive when viewed over a longer time span. In the last nine elections, beginning with 1952, only three times have the Democrats been able to win the White House and only once, in 1964, the year after John Kennedy's assassination, has their presidential candidate's victorious margin been over 51 percent of the popular vote.

And there's more to this political-tides-of-change business than a reporter's selective seat-of-the-pants litany of voter shifts or partisan claims from the Reagan camp about a historic conservative political tide sweeping America in the mid-1980s.

When political scientists examined the voting data from the 1984 presidential election, they came up with two major findings. Both lend support to the great Reagan realignment thesis.

The first involves the way voters identify with the two major political parties. Reagan's reelection brought a noted change. As Professor Martin P. Wattenberg of the University of California, Irvine, writes: "In 1984 identification with the Republican Party increased to the point where the plurality of Democrats over Republicans reached its lowest point since such measurements began in 1952."

Even more striking, and ominous for the Democrats, was the voting behavior of young Americans, obviously the political base of the future. To cite the analysis of another scholar, Professor Helmut Norport of the State University of New York at Stony Brook:

> 1984 was not the year in which George Orwell's prophecy of the all-intrusive state came true, but in which a party dedicated to less government made significant gains in the American electorate. In a historic reversal, the Republican Party has edged the Democratic Party in the allegiance of young voters, a series of recent New York Times/CBS News surveys shows. Among voters 18 to 27 years old, self-identified Republicans now outnumber Democrats by a 6 to 5 ratio whereas Democrats continue to maintain a clear 8 to 6 lead among voters older than that. As a result, the Democratic lead over the Republican Party in the overall electorate has been cut in half.

This evidence led Norport to conclude, in his paper prepared for the American Political Science Association's annual meeting in New Orleans in the summer of 1985:

> The party split along age lines, with younger voters leading the move toward the GOP, offers tantalizing hints

that a realignment of the kind that occurred in the 1930s may be in the making. In the 1930s, according to *The American Voter,* the Democratic Party became the majority party not so much by converting to its side many voters who previously identified as Republicans. Instead, "the Great Depression swung a heavy proportion of the young electors toward the Democratic Party and gave that party a hold on that generation, which it has never fully relinquished." The result was a Democratic edge in party identification over the next fifty years.

So we're in a new era, right? Of course. We always are. So we're not only experiencing historic change in our politics but also witnessing other kinds of dramatic departures from our past? Again, of course. Change is always occurring. It is true that recent years have brought change of such magnitude and at such an accelerated pace that it almost defies understanding. Everything seems to have happened so bewilderingly fast. And it has all taken place amid the most protracted political crisis in the nation's history, a crisis that lasted for more than a decade and nearly destroyed the democratic process. It certainly was a destroyer of illusions. I refer to the long years of division spawned by America's involvement in the increasingly unpopular war in Vietnam abroad and the long painful divisions created by the disintegration of Richard Nixon's presidency, culminating in his forced resignation from the White House.

My belief is that our America of the mid-1980s, Ronald Reagan's America, is not the result of a so-called Reagan Revolution. It is a nation better described as experiencing a Reagan *Reaction.* We are in the midst of a period produced by a historic reaction to the events of an extraordinary generation that altered the face of America and changed the way Americans traditionally thought about themselves and their country. It is that reaction that has provided the surface soil upon which Reagan's presidency flourishes. I would argue further that the real revolution in America is not a political but a personal one. By that, I mean a revolution in personal attitudes and values—sexual and racial primary among them. These changes in behavior and attitudes, startling when compared to the more straightlaced traditional America of a generation ago, also hold significant political implications. We have today, if I'm right, a citizenry that is far more liberal in terms of its social values and personal practices—favoring abortion, much more tolerant about sexual behavior, about divorce, about racial relations and civil rights—and yet also notably more conservative when it comes to fiscal and governmental matters, especially government from Washington.

I say this based on my own experience as a reporter, and buttressed by the public opinion data and polls. For more than a generation, while based in Washington, I have roamed the country seeking to gauge the attitudes of citizens outside the capital that form the political mood upon which policy can be debated and formed by the politicians there. What I have to say here is based primarily on that experience, and I write from that perspective. I don't believe it possible to understand the Reagan Era without examining that history and those changing national attitudes.

Looking back on all that now, even for one who intimately witnessed most of the major events, the America of less than a generation ago is almost unrecognizable. Already, the beginning of the sixties, when the great break in the familiar patterns of our lives began, seems like eons ago.

There were few great debates over issues then, certainly none that tore and divided the country and its citizens. There was no dissent, no marches, no riots, no assassinations. It was even possible to believe—and many Americans did—that there were no problems, except the ever-present but distant one of communism. And we could handle that. We were history's winners. By the middle of that decade, after the Kennedy assassination, after the war in Vietnam had begun in earnest and sparked a poisonous reaction at home, after the racial riots in the Watts section of Los Angeles had flared and spread to our great cities from west to east, north to south, the course of the country had changed irrevocably. It was no longer possible for Americans to be so complacent. For the first time in their experience, traditionally optimistic Americans began to doubt themselves and their country's direction.

Chroniclers of other periods—Mark Sullivan, Frederick Lewis Allen, Eric Goldman—could look back on their times and evoke a sense of nostalgia. No matter how intense or far-reaching the problems then, whether from the stock market crash or the Depression or even the Great World War, they did not seem insurmountable. The sixties and the seventies created another impression.

They were so full of turbulence and terror that it seemed as if America had lost its moorings. Assassinations reminded us that no man, no matter how high or well protected, was safe. Riots raised questions about the survival not only of our cities but of our system. Power shortages and power blackouts and oil embargoes and frightening shortages left a vivid awareness of how dependent society had become on elements beyond the control of most citizens—and then, it seemed, beyond the control of anyone.

Heightening the feeling of dismay was another crucial factor in changing public attitudes: television. With incalculable impact, television carried the dissonance from the streets and distant battlegrounds into American homes. Through television, Americans participated in every moment of triumph and tragedy: from Kennedy's inauguration to the day in Dallas and the murder of Oswald by Ruby before a watching country; from Birmingham to Selma to Watts during the dramatic events that formed the civil rights revolution; from Memphis and Martin Luther King, Jr.'s, assassination to Los Angeles and another Kennedy shot in the head; from the embattled campuses to the mob scenes in the streets of Chicago at the Democratic convention and then on to the moon landing itself; from disturbing pictures of environmental hazards threatening water supplies and nuclear accidents to the seizing of American hostages and the nightly burning of American flags by clamorous foreign mobs—it was all there, all live, all in color, all before our eyes.

Unquestionably, such immediacy contributed to the tensions of the times. It did not create them; it certainly did, however, influence and affect them for good or ill. And, cumulatively, it played an important part in communicating the sense of foreboding and frightening change. It was clear, if you traveled the land often then, as I did, that a great many Americans were becoming increasingly distrustful of a great many things: of government and politicians (an old American attitude, anyway), of institutions that served the public and of the press and television.

After the news media came under increasing public attack (George Wallace, southern sheriffs and the John Birch Society had been doing so with effect for years) by the Nixon Administration's spokesmen, the ground was well prepared. The point was made often, but accurately, that many Americans would rather blame the messenger than the message. It was also true that the press did stress the negative at the expense of the positive. Not surprisingly, what many people wanted was to stop hearing about the problems; the trouble might go away if it weren't reported so frequently and played so prominently.

Looking back on my reporting from that time and examining the papers of the day, an impression emerges that dangerous divisions could be found everywhere. "Polarization" was the byword, and polarization did exist, though it was probably exaggerated. Black and white, rich and poor, blue collar and white collar, student and migrant worker—society was said to be angry or apathetic, afraid or frustrated. The press reported on the presumed phenomenon; the politicians played with people's emotions. "Forgotten" Americans, "troubled" Americans, a malaise in the land, a nervous, restless, previously uncharacteristic questioning of national values. These were the findings. And these were the symptoms: Prices were too high; school and children were a problem; getting to work was an ordeal; crime, corruption, catastrophe, drugs, promiscuity, sexual experimentation. Problems, problems, problems.

The paradox—and it was profound—was that while Americans believed, as never before, that life in general was getting worse, most were better off than they had ever been. When you crossed the country, everywhere you found material progress: families with two cars and two homes, color TV, leisure time, vacations in Europe, children routinely attending colleges, taking for granted astonishing scientific, technological and medical advances, and, inflation notwithstanding, more money to buy more goods. The stores were crowded, the shopping brisk, the bounty unparalleled by any other society at any other time. Even among the most disadvantaged—the poor white, the black, the migrant worker—substantial economic progress was being charted by any statistical measurement. What malaise existed, if indeed it did, was mental, not material.

It was my privilege during those years to see at first hand many of those events that so deeply affected and changed us. In retrospect, the most memorable of those times were not during some political campaign or during those tragic moments of riot or assassination or bloody battleground. It was when you journeyed alone to Coos Bay, Oregon, or Gig Harbor, Washington, to the Mexican-American workers of the San Joaquin Valley in California, to visit the citizens of Wichita, Kansas, or Boone, Iowa, or

Huron, South Dakota, to whites back in the hollows of Appalachia or to the laconic townspeople in Concord, New Hampshire, that the country came into clearer focus.

No silent majorities or rebellious minorities, no great anger or anguish. Just a great many Americans, most of them friendly, most of them still open to a stranger, most of them reasonably contented in their personal lives. They viewed the American problems with bewilderment. As the difficulties continued, the older citizens expressed a desire for a return to the values they had been taught to believe in, values that suddenly seemed so rudely threatened, such fundamental and reassuring touchstones as conceptions about flag and family and country.

There was a period when two contrary strains were competing among Americans. One was the belief that the country was falling apart. It was in the time when cities were going up in smoke, riots were breaking out everywhere, leaders were being slain, the war was escalating, youth was turning on and turning off, and next summer—always the next one—was going to bring the final scorching fire. Persistently, the same dispiriting theme was expressed: America was in danger of following the example of other great powers and finally falling. We had become too rich, too fat, too corrupt, too contented to survive. We would fall like the Romans.

The other belief directly flowed from these gloomy perceptions. It was, in my experience, the single dominant thread that has bound together Americans of all ages and backgrounds from then to now, and one that existed everywhere. From the time of John Kennedy's murder in 1963 to Ronald Reagan's inauguration in 1980, Americans continually and repeatedly expressed a yearning for new and vibrant leadership; some strong, fresh personality who would carry America out of its wilderness. This feeling existed among the supporters of Barry Goldwater, George Wallace, Eugene

McCarthy and Robert Kennedy in the 1960s, and it was fervently voiced by the followers of Richard Nixon, Spiro Agnew, George McGovern and Jimmy Carter in the 1970s.

And it was and remains the greatest source of political support for Ronald Reagan in the 1980s—and the primary reason, in my view, for his success. In Reagan, Americans finally found a president who made them believe our national luck was turning for the better. His presidency has been a great affirmation of the power of personality upon our political life. Almost by force of will, personal expression and jaunty manner, he forces the country to feel better about itself. He radiates optimism and promises a happy ending. His very themes—simplicity, success, security, safety, strength—are the ones for which the country has been searching in its hope for strong presidential leadership. The sense of renewed national pride and patriotism and rekindled sense of competitiveness are a part of his appeal.

Political revolution? Nonsense. Political reaction? Yes, and for good practical reasons: Americans have been hungering for a feeling of success. With Reagan, so far, they've got it.

It's not coincidental that the two events that stirred the greatest emotional response in America during his presidency, and brought hails of praise for him personally, involved the successful employment of military force in expeditions that reversed the long sense of national failure and frustration. The invasion by U.S. forces on the small Caribbean island of Grenada in the fall of 1983 and the dispatch two years later of U.S. jets to capture Mideast terrorists brought waves of exhilaration throughout the country and created an almost fierce sense of redemption in Americans everywhere. These episodes, totally minor from a military standpoint, were nonetheless major in their national psychological and political implications. Americans, after such a run of bad luck and sense of national impotence, at last felt like winners. Which is precisely what gave Reagan's presidency such power, and him such a hold on the public. So long as the country continues to feel successful, his popularity doubtless will continue. Whether politically there's more to his presidency is another matter.

It has been argued by respected scholars that Ronald Reagan is the most ideological President of this century. His most fervent supporters see him as finally bringing a conservative political movement to Washington where it will change the direction and destinies of the nation. They believe Reagan's appeal is ideological not personal, that Americans follow him not because of some deeper emotional hunger and need growing out of the painful experience of the last generation but because of his conservative political approach. I remember one staunch Reaganite predicting, with fire, after Reagan's first election: "This country's going so far to the right you won't recognize it."

That, demonstrably, has not happened. Whenever the Reagan hard-line ideological approach has been employed in such so-called New Right political agenda items as affirmative action and school prayer amendments it has been checked by the Congress. And there is no evidence that Americans today are any more ideological than they have ever been. If anything, they are nonideological.

A political scientist, Professor Leonard Ritt of Northern Arizona University, in a thoughtful recent essay, examined this question of political ideology among Americans. He noted what he described as "a curious paradox in American politics: Observers from the earliest days of the Republic to the present have asserted that Americans are a non-ideological people—that they pay very little attention to consistency and/or abstraction in political thought." Then, as so many others have done over the last century, he quotes the observation of Alexis de Tocqueville:

> I think that in no country in the civilized world is less attention paid to philosophy than in the United States.

The Americans have no philosophical school of their own; and they care but little for all the schools into which Europe is divided, the very names of which are scarcely known to them.

Still, the debate about an American ideology, about whether we are "liberal" or "conservative," whether we are moving to the "right" or to the "left," has raged continually throughout our history—and probably at no time more heatedly than in the present day of Ronald Reagan's presidency where ideology supposedly reigns in Washington and is reaffirmed by the people.

In fact, no such conclusions can be drawn. Scholars such as Ritt who have studied the subject tell us it's all hopelessly inconclusive. For nearly four decades, for instance, beginning in April of 1948, the Gallup Poll has been trying to assess what people mean by the terms *liberal* and *conservative*. The results are wonderfully mixed. In 1948, a presidential election year, 40 percent of the voters were unable to give a description of those terms at all. Of those who did, the basic definition for a conservative was "cautious, go slow, careful." A liberal was defined vaguely as someone "in favor of change." These kinds of generalized responses have continued to the present day. They tend to be nonpolitical in meaning.

"Thus," writes political scientist Ritt in 1985, "we are faced with the following situation: The words Liberal and Conservative are bandied about every day in the real world of politics. And political scientists have spent a great deal of time and effort trying to discover if Americans think ideologically. Yet there has been virtually no direct assessment of whether Americans really know what the two most common ideological terms—Liberal and Conservative—mean. Most of the research has been inferential and experimental."

So much for the true believers. And so much, too, for the Reagan ideological revolution.

I believe, and so do many scholars, that Reagan's strength lies elsewhere than ideology, that in fact if anything Americans are becoming less ideological politically and less interested in political labels of any sort. Increasingly, it is the personal qualities of the presidential candidate, not his political affiliations and ideological stands, that matter most to Americans.

For instance, take other conclusions of those two scholars cited earlier who found some evidence of a potential political realignment in the results of the Reagan landslide. California's Martin Wattenberg:

> For over three decades prior to 1984 the American public had been drifting away from the two major parties. Once the central guiding forces in American electoral behavior, the parties had by 1980 come to be perceived with almost complete indifference by a large percentage of the population. The decline of public affection for the parties was not due to any greater negative feelings about the Democrats and Republicans but rather to an increasing sense that the parties just no longer matter much in the governmental process.

To strengthen his point, he cites the responses of over a third of all voters interviewed in the 1980 National Election Study to four questions:

Q. What do you like about the Democratic Party?
A. Nothing.

Q. What do you dislike about the Democratic Party?
A. Nothing.

Q. What do you like about the Republican Party?
A. Nothing.

Q. What do you dislike about the Republican party?
A. Nothing.

In 1952, when those questions were first asked, only 10 percent of those interviewed answered that way. Which leads him to conclude:

> In the 1950s such indifference usually proved to be part of a more general sense of political apathy and lack of political knowledge; by 1980 it was much more likely to be a specific indicator of apathy and lack of knowledge about the parties themselves.

And New York's Helmut Norport, about the larger political meaning of the Reagan tide:

> Yet aside from the presidential vote tallies, nothing else supported claims of a partisan realignment in the sense of a dramatic shift in the overall partisan balance. Neither the voting for House candidates or statewide offices, nor the split in party identification produced compelling evidence for the thesis of a Republican majority. . . . After the 1980 election, Republican gains in the electorate were reported, but forecasts of a partisan realignment were put forth with great caution. It is nothing short of astounding that, from 1952 to 1980, the Democratic Party has managed to hold on to a majority in the American electorate, even though its candidates lost five of eight presidential elections. During that period of almost 30 years, according to the Michigan CPS/NES surveys, the Democrats have roughly maintained a 4–3 edge over the Republicans. The victories of Republican presidential candidates in those years remained personal triumphs; they did not turn into party triumphs. The moral is that a landslide does not a party realignment make.

None of this means we aren't experiencing a significant shift in our political thinking. Indisputably, the mood among

American voters today (and the politicians who respond to their feelings) is more conservative. A reaction has set in to the national disasters, real or perceived, of the last two decades. People are weary with being asked to continue making sacrifices for others perhaps less fortunate, they are frustrated with a sense of national failure and impotence, they are tired of the burden of heavy taxes and aid programs for others. All this congeals most strongly in the public perception of the Democrats—that is, of the Washington Democrats: It is of a party that represents the minorities (mainly blacks), the poor, and the clamorous, selfish, special constituent interest groups (especially unions) that are believed to infest Washington and work against the best interests of all the people. People are more responsive, whether because of innate self-interest or selfishness, to appeals for less government at any level, to let 'er rip free enterprise actions. And they do seem more inclined to shun responsibility for providing for the common weal of those who are weaker and otherwise unable to provide for themselves.

They have not, however, embarked on an ideological conservative crusade. And there's no reason to think the public mood won't shift away from even so sunny and appealing a political figure as Reagan if people begin to sense the nation's fortunes are again turning downward, whether at home or abroad.

Ronald Reagan has not won his political revolution yet. The country has not been transformed ideologically. The most you can say, as he begins the final years of his second term, is that the outcome of his political course and the policies he espouses might bring about some of that long-term change that could affect the course of the country for years to come.

In the end, the real revolution that shapes the future of the America of the closing years of the twentieth century is not political but personal. Of that future, there are as many forecasters as there are people. Prophets of despair still abound. They warn gloomily of nuclear nightmare or economic collapse from the exponentially rising budget deficits. Yet it is still possible, on the basis of our recent past, to draw a different conclusion. No matter how difficult were the public events that created the political climate that brought Ronald Reagan to power, at no point did Americans succumb to the lure of the demagogues of political left or right. No matter how shattering the impact on the public of such disasters as the assassinations and impeachment process and the Vietnam War, at no point did Americans break and disintegrate into a despair. They kept waiting for better times to come. This leads me to conclude that, for all its seeming disorder, America may well be entering its most mature period, a time when realism finally replaces easy rhetoric, when practicality supplants ideology.

Our revolution is not abating. It is accelerating. In science, technology, medicine, space research, art, and music the future promises to be almost unrecognizable. And the greatest of all the changes is surely in the way we live and think. As the process of change spins ever faster, our writers seem to have been supplanted by our musicians—by sound over sight, as it were. It is all moving so swiftly that few seem able to pause to attempt to place what is happening in perspective. Perhaps it is only a dying society that can afford historians. We have not reached that phase yet.

Years ago, when he finished *The Great Gatsby,* his fable of another vanished American era, Scott Fitzgerald wrote of that "orgiastic future that year by year recedes before us." Race though we did, it always eluded us, he said. "So we beat on, boats against the current, borne back ceaselessly into the past."

He was wrong. It is not the past that beckons us now, but the future, a future forged by and tempered by all the lessons of our recent bitter personal and political experience as a nation.

ROUNDTABLE DISCUSSION

"An American Revolution"

<u>PANELISTS:</u> Paul Duke, *moderator*
Haynes Johnson
Charles Corddry
Georgie Anne Geyer
Charles McDowell
Jack Nelson
Hedrick Smith

DUKE: Haynes, you seem to come down on the side of optimism in the country.

JOHNSON: Yes. We're supposed to be gloomy in Washington and those of us who report on the country are supposed to believe that America is nothing but troubles. But I cannot look at the last twenty years without being optimistic.

The country has survived, it's stronger, it's healthier, people know more, they're not in a trough of despair. Where I think the problem has been, if there *is* a problem, is in the political governance of the country from Washington and the way people look at it.

But if you go back and look at the America of twenty years ago, of a society of segregation and racial hatreds and hostilities, we have survived and moved on.

NELSON: But Haynes, when you look at what's going on right now, isn't there an awful lot beneath the surface with blacks terribly dissatisfied with this administration and the rolling back of affirmative action? Isn't there a terrible dissatisfaction about the income gap growing between the poor and the rich? A majority of the American people may be satisfied, but there are also real pockets of society that are upset and unhappy.

JOHNSON: If you turn it around and take your point of view, what's most disturbing is that we are drawing farther apart, that those who have made it are doing better, and that includes blacks who are doing well, too, I might say. But the poor and the dispossessed feel out of American society all the more.

DUKE: The reality is that we still have enormous problems in this country. Unemployment has remained quite high during Reagan's presidency. There's great suffering these days in the farm belt. Here in Washington there is an impression that officials care less and that government policy is not directed as seriously at many problems as in times past.

JOHNSON: I'm not suggesting we don't have problems. What I am saying is that we've gone through a troubling period and we've come out of it. We haven't caved in. And I think in many ways the society is better off than it was twenty or twenty-five years ago.

McDOWELL: I agree. I think Jack and Paul make excellent contemporary observations in a contemporary context. But the country is in a more optimistic mood, and it seems to me the scale of improvement and correction in our society has been striking.

SMITH: Aren't we really talking about swings in the public's mood? That if one goes back and takes the long view, the time of Harding in the twenties was a comfortable time. The time of Eisenhower in the fifties was a comfortable time, and here we are after another thirty-year gap. This is a comfortable time.

The mood of the country is not rancorous despite high unemployment, despite a trade deficit, despite industries that are going out of business because they can't compete, despite a very high poverty level, despite the problems of the minorities. There is a sense that the predominant majority is comfortable, and that's what takes the sense of national polarization out of the public mood, even though there is a political polarization that goes on in Washington between the President and Congress.

GEYER: I think there is something else, too. I agree with Haynes and Charley. What Americans have not understood before is that each answer to problems causes new problems, which is what civil rights did. We talk about minorities. Are we talking about the Vietnamese minority? They are doing magnificently well.

We've sifted down now to a point where it's cultural values that count in this society. I think what Americans are having—what we're sort of reflecting here—is that Americans have always thought there were absolute answers, and we're beginning to learn that there are relative answers, and I think maybe that what we're seeing under President Reagan is that a lot of Americans are thinking, well, the relative answers aren't so bad.

McDOWELL: I happen to be a citizen who doesn't feel very comfortable in the Reagan Administration as I look around at the kinds of problems that Paul and Jack describe. But in the sweep of time that Haynes has written about, we have been through a remarkable period in which the U.S. has addressed many of its problems and made heartening progress in dealing with race, poverty, health and all these other concerns.

That's not an endorsement of how we're doing today with a given policy.

NELSON: You're saying we're in a period of benign neglect now?

McDOWELL: I'm saying I'm unhappy with what's happening now, a lot of it. But measured against the past we can see astonishing progress the country has made.

JOHNSON: Jack and I covered civil rights throughout the South, and we saw people killed and clubbed when they tried to walk from here to a building across the street to register to vote. I'm not suggesting that all our race relations problems are resolved. But I think they are better and healthier today than they were then.

You can carry it on down the line in a lot of areas. But I think the Reagan presidency, which we're dealing with here, can't be understood unless you put it in that context.

CORDDRY: Hubert Humphrey once said—if he didn't, I'm sure he would have—that the function of government is to look after people who can't look after themselves, and one of the members of the Reagan Cabinet told me shortly after they arrived here the first term that he thought, well, poverty in this country had been got down as far as you could get. I don't know whether these are contradictory points of view, but I suspect they are.

In all our great improvement, has compassion gone out of the system, so to speak? If it has, how long is it going to stay out?

JOHNSON: I don't think compassion has gone out of Americans in their views and their attitudes, but there is a different tone today, which is in part reaction to all the reforms and all the programs of the past.

You can see it in the Congress. No one is speaking for a return to the New Deal or to the welfare programs or to Hubert Humphrey programs of the Great Society and of the New Frontier period.

We're now at the end of the era of reform. But it

doesn't mean that you've thrown away the reforms. They are still there.

DUKE: But if this is true, Haynes, that we're in a necessary pause, as it were—

JOHNSON: That's a good way to put it.

DUKE: —from the great wave of reform, isn't it also true that there are problems in our society today which are certain to smolder and fester and eventually explode? One analogy might be the Coolidge presidency, when the problems began to fester and then overwhelmed the presidency of Herbert Hoover. Even if Ronald Reagan escapes, the next presidency may suffer from today's complacency.

JOHNSON: I had lunch today with a Republican senator, and he got to talking about all this and said: "You can't understand how angry many Republicans are and how really bitter they are at the White House because we're going to be left to clean up the mess, and our necks are on the line." He said he doubted they could hold the White House after '88 because of economic problems and other frustrations.

But he said that Reagan would escape all identification with these problems. Whether that's true or not remains to be seen. I think that if the economy starts to slip further in the remainder of the Reagan period, he *will* get tagged with it. But I think that's an interesting observation, one I rather share.

McDOWELL: I wonder if history won't say—that's a nice pompous thing to say—when we're nice and old that the remarkable thing about the Reagan period was how little the people's Congress was willing to roll back in terms of social programs and other programs.

Reagan has proposed vast rollbacks. Yet we're already seeing that in his second term he can't even get substantial *Republican* support for any fundamental rollback of things that have come to us all the way from the New Deal.

JOHNSON: We are not overturning the past so much as consolidating it. We are not, however, about to embark on a new period of reform, and I think there's a feeling that we've gone about as far as we can go right now to absorb governmental programs.

NELSON: But going back to what Charlie Corddry said, do you think we are a less caring society today than we were before? Are we more racist than we were before? Do we not care as much about poorer people? Do we not think the government has a role to play for people who are handicapped or disadvantaged in some way or another? It seems to me that we are.

JOHNSON: I think the answer is a little bit of both, Jack. People are not rejecting so much as saying they're tired of supporting programs that they don't think work as they're supposed to.

DUKE: Isn't the fundamental point, though, that the social programs which have been woven into the governmental fabric since the New Deal have remained in place? Not a single program has been ended by this Administration.

JOHNSON: That's right, Paul.

DUKE: There is a slowdown and a pause. But as somebody said, what America appears to want today is a conservative welfare state.

JOHNSON: Well, I think that's what they've got: a more conservative approach to a welfare state.

NELSON: But the fact is if you take what this Administration did in the first year, the President's tax cut plus his cut in the growth of social programs, the poor people came out worse and the wealthy people came out better. I mean, there's no two ways about it.

JOHNSON: No question. Absolutely.

NELSON: And the American people endorse that. And so it seems to me that if you look at it, the society today is a little less caring about government's role in taking care of people who are disadvantaged.

JOHNSON: That's true, Jack.

CORDDRY: That was what I was trying to get at, whether we're getting into a kind of permanent division here. I think Reagan got elected because his program was to cut taxes, do something for the middle class and to bolster defense, and everybody who could afford to be was happy, and you have a division in society—what I guess I'm asking you, Haynes, is it a permanent thing, or will the pendulum swing as it always has?

JOHNSON: The pendulum always swings back.

DUKE: Many of the historians contend that what we basically have in the Reagan presidency is a detour and that the steady progression of American liberalism will shortly resume. Whether it resumes, say, in a year or two years or five years or ten years, it will resume.

SMITH: But there's another way to look at it, Paul, and that is if you go back to Arthur Schlesinger, Sr., talking about American history all the way back to Jefferson and then Jackson and then on to the Civil War period and the post-Civil War period. He talks about swings of history, and in some ways there's a natural rhythm, that a society takes on a lot of new social tasks, a lot of legislation is enacted, you have activist Presidents and then after a while, particularly after a war or some trauma, you kind of settle down and go into a period of normalcy. Then the nation becomes aware of new sets of problems, and another period of activism is set off.

JOHNSON: Which is exactly where I think we are, and in answer to your statement and Charlie Corddry's point, about the pendulum: It's always swung in our history. But we've always made enormous progress as a society.

GEYER: Many European thinkers like the late Luigi Barzini have said—he said it to me once—that we are the practical ones, we Europeans, while you Americans are the idealistic ones. We have been a utopian society because we are an abstract idea.

In many ways, the Soviet Union is an abstract idea, too, so it's not accidental that the two countries are up against each other. But now we're changing and becoming more practical, and that's why I do not see us going back. The liberal idea of state control in Europe and many other places hasn't worked. Those countries are just going to fall back and back and back, and this is something that Ronald Reagan understood.

DUKE: Are you saying that we've turned down a new road, a more conservative road, and you think we will continue going down that road?

GEYER: Well, I don't think conservative is the word. I think it's free enterprise, market economy, economic individualism. I think we can use new terms. I don't find the Reagan conservatives very "conservative." I do find them impassioned about economic freedom, if you want to call it that. You can call it a lot of things, but this is the way the world is going. So I can't see people going back to large social welfare.

JOHNSON: I don't buy that. "Conservative" today doesn't mean what "conservative" did yesterday. Reagan people aren't conservatives by any measure of the American past. They're radicals. I mean, they're trying to undo the American government, not only just roll it back but cast it aside. They talk about the free market, but they want the government intruding more and more into the actions that will support their point of view, whether it's on race relations or civil rights or the Supreme Court or even the economy. All of a sudden the Silicon Valley, which was the free enterprise bastion of the new America, they're here in Washington banging on the door saying we need protection. I don't think the American people voted for Ronald Reagan to roll back the clock. They voted for him because they liked him, number one. We'd had a bad run of luck and he promised success, he made us feel good. But there's something deeper than that. People feel that if he, as the symbol of the political system, survives and presides well, the country will rebound. That's an American idea, too: that we are a successful society. We haven't felt very good about ourselves for a long time, and that's what people have been searching for. That's why people support Reagan. But they also don't want the undoing of programs that affect their lives.

DUKE: Isn't it also true, Haynes, that a great many Americans feel an empathy with Reagan as expressing American values? For example, the President wrote a preface to a book about Norman Rockwell in which he said "the values he cherished and celebrated—love of God and country, hard work, neighborhood, and family—still give us strength, and will shape our dreams for the decades to come."

SMITH: That's precisely a period of consolidation, going back to believing in yourself.

I wonder, though, if it isn't worthwhile looking at other changes in our society. There have been a variety. A number of institutions are no longer as powerful as they were before—political parties, organized labor—very different from what they were before. What does that mean? Can you expect a swing back toward traditional liberalism, of the New Deal type or of the Lyndon Johnson type, without the underpinning of organized labor? If government becomes more activist again, it may become more activist for the sake of international competition of American enterprise. It may not be strict free enterprise. It may be a kind of Hoover liberalism, if you will, reconstruction finance corporations, that kind of involvement. A guy like Gary Hart is talking about that now. A lot of Democrats are talking about it, calling themselves neoliberals. It could mean another period of activism but with a very different social and institutional meaning in this society.

JOHNSON: I'll predict right now we're going to see a more active presidency by the end of the 1980s. The President is going to have more powers. It's going to happen because of the economy. We are not competitive, and it's going to take a larger governmental effort, not a smaller one, to change things. Whether it'll be a President that will be described as liberal or conservative, it'll be someone who promises success. And I don't think the parties will matter particularly.

NELSON: But it also depends, doesn't it, Haynes, on who becomes President?

JOHNSON: Of course.

NELSON: I mean, if you have another Jimmy Carter, you wouldn't have a strong President.

DUKE: But won't the parties still serve as the vehicles through which the personalities will emerge?

McDOWELL: The parties don't have to be the vehicle. I would submit that the vehicle could be good old television.

JOHNSON: It's television. Sure. Television has almost replaced the political parties as the agent that embraces all of American life.

DUKE: But nobody's going to be elected President unless he has the party mechanism to achieve the presidency.

JOHNSON: No, I don't even believe that.

McDOWELL: I don't believe that, either.

JOHNSON: I think you could see somebody run "Paul Duke for America" and if you had the right personality and the right money—

McDOWELL: Absolutely.

NELSON: I disagree with that. I agree with Paul. He's got to have the party behind him.

McDOWELL: It took Jimmy Carter about four weeks to muster the Democratic Party as his own.

DUKE: But he was elected President as a Democrat.

McDOWELL: Well, that's right. He was a product of the Democratic Party.

SMITH: He was a rank outsider.

McDOWELL: And he ran against the party.

NELSON: But the party still makes a tremendous difference. Here's a man [Carter] who'd gone around building up IOUs around the country for almost two years. I mean, he had his grass roots very firmly established.

SMITH: That was personal.

NELSON: That's right. But nevertheless, without the party he would have never—

SMITH: Well, sure—

McDOWELL: Now we go around the parties.

DUKE: They're still critical, and likewise, in the case of Ronald Reagan, who had come to represent Mr. Republican to many people, he couldn't even get the nomination of his own party in 1976.

SMITH: He fashioned a national movement, and he became a challenger to a sitting President, Gerry Ford. I find it remarkable he sustained the challenge as long as he did.

DUKE: Well, we had a challenge to a sitting President in 1980 from Ted Kennedy on the Democratic side.

NELSON: And he almost won.

SMITH: I think you guys are making the case that McDowell was trying to make by the examples you're choosing. Reagan essentially assaulted the party mechanism by building a national movement outside it. Jimmy Carter captured the Democratic Party nomination by working outside the party. He didn't make deals with the national party. He didn't come to Washington. He went out to the grass roots, and the party eventually had to—

NELSON: I don't think Paul and I were disagreeing with that. What we say is that the party apparatus and the party's nomination are absolutely essential to reach the White House. You can say that Jimmy Carter assaulted the party mechanism and won, but he did it from very long-term, meticulous work. I'll never forget that I was in Los Angeles at the *L.A. Times* when he was still governor, and he came out for a luncheon one day, and he told the publisher of the paper and all the editors, "I'm going to be running for President," and people around the table sort of snickered. And so, near the end of the lunch, I think it was the publisher, Otis Chandler, who said, "Governor, if you come out here next year, we'd like to have you come by and have lunch with us again." He said, "I'll be out here thirteen days next year." [Laughter.] He had all the dates set up, and as we walked away from the table, Ed Guthman, who was then our national editor, turned to me and he said, "This is a very serious man. He's going to be a serious candidate."

That was when he was still governor, it was long before he was really running. He built up IOUs all around the country. He worked very hard, and he had a lot of people within the Democratic Party. Now you can say he captured the Democratic Party mechanism, but he had a lot of Democrats working with him.

McDOWELL: The whole dynamic is different today. Parties don't produce, promote, angle, deal, play like they used to. They're very different things.

DUKE: Well, sure, we all agree on that.

GEYER: William Schneider, the political scientist at American Enterprise Institute and a brilliant man, calls this antiestablishment populism, and says there were coups within both of the parties, in effect, by their populist outgroups, and it's right in the old American tradition.

McDOWELL: Jack and I attended an elitist lunch the other day where we were the two nonelitists present, and the guest was Ed Rollins, who directed the President's forty-nine-state victory. I was fascinated to sit an hour and a half with the director of one of the great victories in American politics, and I've never talked to a man less interested in political parties. It was almost as if someone had brought up something irrelevant. He said it's the people—the people we care about are people that don't care about parties.

CORDDRY: What do they want to get those people to do?

McDOWELL: Vote for their candidate.

NELSON: Register Republican.

McDOWELL: They don't rush at the word Republican. They rush at the word Reagan, Bush or whatever they—

JOHNSON: Vote for the new face.

McDOWELL: —or whatever they're selling.

DUKE: Anyway, is it your view, Haynes, that the political parties will continue to decline and perhaps eventually go the way of the dodo bird?

JOHNSON: No, I think that the Republican and Democratic parties as we look at them today are obviously not the force in American life that they were twenty, thirty, forty, fifty years ago. The Reagan Republican Party is totally different from the Republican Party of only fifteen years ago, for instance. But you need some kinds of political organization to give direction and shape and force. There has to be a mechanism. But clearly, they're changing. We're seeing the ascendancy of personality over party. People identified with Carter because he was different, fresh, new. They identified with Reagan because he was hopeful, sunny, optimistic, a real American whose values weren't just Republican or Democratic.

When you go down to state and local levels where organizations *do* make a difference, there the parties remain strong.

NELSON: I don't think the parties are anywhere near going down the drain, although they've certainly changed character. All 535 members of Congress are either Democrats or Republicans. And the governors, too. The Republican Party is a helluva lot more powerful today than the Democratic Party, not in members, but in the way it operates. They computerized at least five years before the Democrats. They're much better at getting out and beating the hustings than the Democrats.

McDOWELL: I don't know a candidate below the Potomac River—in other words in the South—who will willingly put the word *Republican* on his campaign literature if he can help it in 1985-86.

NELSON: But they'll take the party's help, right?

McDOWELL: You bet.

NELSON: All right.

JOHNSON: That's a technological, financial matter. What's happening now is a groping toward new political identifications. The Republican Party of today is demonstrably more conservative than it used to be. The moderates are shut out—Nelson Rockefeller, were he alive, couldn't even speak at a Republican convention today. It is a dramatic change. As for the Democrats, it's hard to tell where they are.

DUKE: If indeed the parties are changing in tone

and complexion and makeup, how will the yuppies, today's young people, really affect the politics of the future?

JOHNSON: They are identifying more with the Republican Party, but this is tentative. It's really more with Reagan. They're identifying with a sense of success in the country as symbolized by Reagan. They are clearly more anti-big government than their elder brothers, sisters or mothers and fathers, and the outcome of the Reagan presidency will tell us whether they are a new political force. It's interesting that this group has come to voting age during the first two-term presidency since Dwight Eisenhower. Half of the Americans alive today don't even remember a time when we didn't have one-term Presidents.

NELSON: Bob Teeter, the Republican pollster who has done work for the White House, told me one difference between these young people who've gone for the Republicans and others in the past is that they are anti-government all the way down the line. In other words, they're against loopholes for big business as well as being conservative in other areas. He said when asked who had got too much attention from the government in recent years, the answer was big business and blacks. So they are a little different breed.

JOHNSON: They are far more liberal in the way they view their own lives, whether it's on sex or abortion or power, whatever. They don't want any government interference. They don't want school prayer. They don't want the government telling them what to do or what to think. At the same time, they are notably more interested in entrepreneurship. So you find on the social, personal side that they are more liberal than they would have been twenty, thirty years ago, but more conservative on economic questions.

GEYER: It's an extremely interesting theme, Haynes, and something else that jumps out at me from your piece is where you say the single dominant thread that has bound together Americans of all ages and backgrounds is a yearning for a new and vibrant leadership, some strong, fresh personality to carry America out of its wilderness.

What it's saying to me is Americans are not depending upon institutions anymore. They think that on the horizon somewhere there is a quick fix, but there is no longer any quick fix from a strong, fresh personality.

CORDDRY: Well, for gosh sakes, the search for vibrant new political leaders is as old as history. That doesn't imply that institutions are going to collapse. I don't think Haynes is trying to tell us that, are you?

JOHNSON: No, I just think we're in a different period. That's all. And I think the complexities that we're dealing with are more difficult. It's harder to govern today. There is a problem over size, over displacement of power, not only in our basic industries, but in our political parties. None of them is as strong as they were. I think we're more homogenized as a society. We don't fall so easily into labels anymore. That's all part of it.

SMITH: I want to go back to this notion of a resurgent America, of a self-confident America, an America that believes it can get things done. You cite, quite properly I think, the wonderful feeling that the country had after the invasion of Grenada, that we had won one, we beat the Communists. And then the same kind of feeling reoccurred, though not quite so strongly, after the recovery of the Palestinians who hijacked that ship in the Mediterranean last fall, and although we got into a squabble with Italy and Egypt about it, nonetheless, there was that sense we'd come back.

But I really wonder whether in fact, particularly as

Americans look at the world and look at themselves, they really do see a self-confident America. Go into any used-car lot and try to buy an American car, and every darned used-car salesman will tell you the Japanese cars are better. Go into an electronics shop, and they'll tell you the Japanese or the German electronic equipment is better. Go travel around the country into western Pennsylvania or eastern Ohio, and you find a lot of people who are worried about steel imports, and go into the South—in North Carolina and South Carolina and Georgia—and they're worried about textile imports, and it isn't just textile imports from Japan. It's China, Korea, it's Taiwan.

There is a sense here that some of our well-being is based on what we can get from abroad, and in the economic arguments today, more and more experts are saying that the prosperity and the growth and the continuing recovery that we have had are dependent on foreign capital attracted by our high interest rates.

I wonder whether this is a country that would get involved very much militarily abroad, or is it still traumatized because of the Vietnam experience? I wonder if this isn't a country that is sensitive about its ability to compete internationally and that is not quite so resurgent.

JOHNSON: I don't disagree with that, Rick. But there is a hunger for something that is strong, successful, and I think up to this point people have put their faith and trust in the commanding presence and personality of Ronald Reagan, that he's going to make it okay. It's like Roosevelt, who was regarded as the great father of America if you grew up in the New Deal, someone who would make it okay. There was Dr. New Deal and Dr. Win the War. I think those threads are very much wrapped up in Reagan. Whether they last or not is something else.

NELSON: Are we standing tall, or are we not standing tall?

SMITH: But, see, what I'm hearing and what you're saying is not a feeling of a self-confident nation, but a nation that's not self-confident and seizes on small episodes to get a sense of relief from the frustration and humiliation that we felt over Vietnam and Iran. It's coming back very slowly.

GEYER: Isn't this a "Teflon" resurgence? I feel much as Rick does. I was embarrassed at our crowing over bringing down a small unarmed plane. I was pleased we did it, but it should have been something that in the old days would have been a barely noticeable police action on the part of a great power.

DUKE: Or at least you would take it with grace.

GEYER: Yes, exactly.

CORDDRY: I want you to know that it was not easy to fly out into the middle of the night, in the dark, in a sky that could have been full of airplanes and find an [Egyptian] airplane from the moment it left and to see that it landed without ever touching it and to know what you would have done if it had been resistant and to jam its transmissions to Cairo so that it had no choice but to land. It is a small point, but I assure you, my friends, it is not easy.

Now, the other thing that is very important is we were not crowing over bringing down a little unarmed airplane but a big Boeing airplane. We are not crowing because we caused it to land. We're crowing because at long last some terrorists were brought to book.

JOHNSON: The emotional response had nothing to do with the capability of our pilots or anything else with the military. We sent a mission out and it was successful, unlike the Iranian rescue operation which fouled up in the Carter Administration.

NELSON: All the same, there has been an awful lot of unseemly breast-beating going on around this town.

SMITH: Whether it's unseemly or seemly, to me isn't the point. What I was trying to suggest was that even if we did well in Grenada and dealt effectively with some terrorists, I nonetheless sense an uneasiness, reading the polls, talking to people, talking to politicians about the application of American power, about American involvement in the rest of the world and about American ability to compete, particularly in the economic arena. It's not the same country that we had in the fifties that had a self-confidence born of nuclear supremacy and great power. It is a chastened power that has now come back from pessimism but is still struggling to regain the old confidence.

CORDDRY: It was the universal power in the fifties. That's over.

SMITH: I understand.

DUKE: Are you saying, then, that a great many Americans do not agree with Ronald Reagan when he talks about America standing tall today?

SMITH: No, I think probably people are of two minds or of one mind and one heart. I think in their hearts they do respond, that they're glad we're up from the bottom and that some things are working.

DUKE: But they recognize it's not totally true.

SMITH: It used to be seen very much in pure military power and nuclear supremacy terms. I think our sense of ourselves in the world is now at least partly and significantly defined economically, and I think that has changed enough so that the military stuff is not always paramount.

GEYER: I find people just underneath the surface very apprehensive that we just can't do anything right. The American people do not want their leaders to go too far because they don't have confidence that they know how to handle these situations, and I would add—coming back to what Rick said—that if we're going to be an immediate-gratification society, which we are to a great extent, then we're not going to have the kinds of institutions and organizations that allow us to plan for the long term, and intercepting the plane, which I totally approved of, worried me because if Americans thought that was going to turn any tide, it means we were succumbing to immediate gratification.

CORDDRY: You're probably right, but I don't think you know that yet.

GEYER: I know it absolutely. Because four Palestinians were captured in a plane, that's going to stop terrorism in Iran, which is centuries old and—

CORDDRY: I won't argue with anyone who knows something absolutely. [Laughter.]

DUKE: Let's get Charlie's view here.

CORDDRY: I think that the American handling of foreign policy from the end of World War II up to 1961, just to pick a date, was incredibly good, and it was backed by immense unchallengeable power, and then I think that the Kennedys were really riding high after Cuba and said why not take on Vietnam, and we were off and running. But, of course, there are limits to our power. However, I think there are fewer limits to our power than to anyone else's.

SMITH: Some of the senior military commanders who have retired recently have talked warily about the application of American power unless the people are behind it. The whole attitude that Weinberger has represented.

CORDDRY: We didn't go into World War I and World War II until political leaders educated us to that necessity. In fact, we didn't go into World War II until we got socked. So I don't find it a new thing that Americans are a little hesitant about applying their military ability.

Weinberger says that you can't go to war if you don't have public support. I think he gets this from the military leaders who say never again, fellows. I mean, you sent us out to Southeast Asia and then you just left us there, and you didn't even welcome us home, and the next time you want us to go to war, we want to know that you mean it. I think that reflects just about all the important opinion. I mean, both the military and the defense civilian leadership were extremely opposed to putting the Marines into Lebanon, and I think they turned out to be right.

SMITH: But opposed for military reasons or opposed because they sensed that the American body politic wasn't behind them as reflected in Congress?

CORDDRY: Well, I can't quote a four-star officer involved in it by name, I don't think that'd be fair, but he said we don't want to get into that cat fight. No, no, it was not a question of whether you had public support. It was a question of what could you achieve.

SMITH: That's a sober judgment, and it's much more realistic. It reflected Eisenhower not wanting to go into the first Indochina war in 1954 because as a military man he knew the price of a land war in Asia, which we had to learn all over again fifteen years later.

CORDDRY: We also decided that if we did go we weren't going piecemeal, which is how we ultimately went.

McDOWELL: I don't think there's anything really so astonishing about the unease that everyone senses and feels when the nature of war changed, when the stakes escalated beyond imagination, when everything changed, when the nuclear balance began to assert itself and we got uneasy, and I'm not so sure sitting here that we aren't living in a world now where the military has a more realistic sense of things than we as civilians as we react to our environment. I'm not so sure they aren't the people that understand how we're playing on a whole different scale.

SMITH: This sense of sobered realism about events abroad, this sense of vulnerability may contribute to the strong desire domestically to feel comfortable, to feel good again, to have the kind of leader that Haynes has been talking about. I think these things interconnect.

JOHNSON: Of course, they do. And the whole thrust of what I was trying to write about was you can't understand Reagan's popularity and appeal without looking at the underlying deep divisions, hesitations, fears, concerns, frustrations growing out of a feeling America is no longer a winner, no longer as strong, no longer able to rule the world. I don't mean in the Roman sense, but we just can't do what we used to *think* we could do. It's an understandable reaction. You don't want instability, you want security. You want strength, you want safety, and you want to feel good about your country.

NELSON: And you want to be a winner, and so you've got to make sure you're not in something that you might possibly lose, so therefore you get out of the World Court, or at least you reduce your role in it because you're going to lose a decision over violating Nicaragua's sovereignty. You drop out of UNESCO. I mean, the President has made people feel comfortable about isolationism.

JOHNSON: I don't think we're an isolationist country at all.

NELSON: No, but I think that he wouldn't mind—

JOHNSON: In a sense there's an appeal of Reagan that is going back to the twenties where there were seemingly no problems, but there are concerns about the economic struggle. You talk to people who are auto workers, you talk to people in little towns of the Midwest who are conservative Republicans, and they know we're in a competitive struggle. They know it's different today. Their lives are being impinged upon by Japan, Germany. We're in a frighteningly complex period, and they're looking for some easy answers or something that they can cling to, and I think that explains much of the appeal of Reagan so far, that we're not falling apart.

NELSON: You're suggesting sort of holding things together with bailing wire.

JOHNSON: Well, so far.

SMITH: Wooooo! In a time when there is this sense of vulnerability and competitiveness, where does organized labor fit into the picture? For a long time it was pushing for fatter contracts, higher wages, more benefits and helping price American products, particularly cars but other things as well, out of the market.

JOHNSON: Except for American big business back fifty, sixty, seventy years ago, I don't know of an institution that has been more out of touch with American life than organized labor, a group that was led by old men who were out of touch with their own workers. There also was a great deal of corruption they didn't deal with. These days you don't have as many labor people getting their shoes dirty and leading marches—or maybe the day of marches is over.

GEYER: One power group we haven't talked about is the governors, and many people feel they are the real hope for the future because they have to do more now with the federal government cutting back.

JOHNSON: To a large extent, they have taken on problems that were unthinkable ten or fifteen years ago. They've been forced to. They've raised taxes in recessions. They have regenerated education and other services, not from Washington but from their own states, and that's a positive thing.

DUKE: Isn't this one of the beneficial side effects of the Reagan Administration—that it has given new life and vitality to state government? The governors had a tendency to just buck the problems on to Washington, and now the hardened attitude from Washington is forcing people to face up to problems at the local level which they should have been facing up to all along.

JOHNSON: That's correct. And what's interesting, too, is that for a long period in our national life, we got our presidential candidates out of the state houses, and then we went through this whole period where it was Washington that was the spawning ground. The last two Presidents, I need not remind you, were governors—of California and Georgia. That's not just by accident.

DUKE: Still another group which has become newly reassertive and has made its influence felt in the 1980s is the religious right. In the 1920s we had a great surge of religious fundamentalism that produced, among other things, prohibition. Then it ebbed in the thirties and forties and seemed to pass into history, but now it has come charging back again with the Moral Majority and other religious organizations. Many preachers are on television and even one prominent evangelist, Pat Robertson, is contemplating a run for the presidency. How does all this figure into what's happening, Haynes?

JOHNSON: I don't make too much of it, to tell you the truth. The Moral Majority, for instance, is not a majority of Americans.

I don't think that the country is in a wash of some new great political force that's going to transform its basic political base or the way it thinks. The Moral Majority and other fundamentalists have organized better politically, they have turned out their votes in areas where they are powerful. But I don't think that they are going to sweep into the White House, and I don't think this country is going back again ideologically.

NELSON: But going back to this luncheon that Charley McDowell and I were at with Ed Rollins, they may be a very important factor, however, in both the '86 elections and the '88 elections.

For example, Rollins said that Pat Robertson, who has 10 million listeners or whatever it is—that he is setting up a political action committee that's going to raise $2 or $3 million to influence the 1986 senatorial elections, that he wants to be an important part of the Republican Party. Rollins, who is working for Vice-President Bush for the presidency in 1988, said Robertson may turn out to be the voice for the 10 million fundamentalists that voted for Reagan—at least he said it was 10 million—in 1980 and 1984. Rollins thinks he may represent a strong constituency.

So, in the long run the fundamentalists may not be a lasting force in politics, but in the short run, they could be significant.

SMITH: Haynes was making the point, if I understood you right, that the country was not in a great moral sweep that was going to move it to the right.

JOHNSON: It's not the majority. That's what I was saying.

SMITH: But there's no disputing that this is a very important and powerful factor—

JOHNSON: Absolutely.

SMITH: —within party politics, particularly within Republican politics. There was a battle for the fundamentalist Christians when Jimmy Carter ran in '76, there was another battle in '80, and there also is a relationship between the rise of this organized movement and the kind of thing Haynes was talking about in the beginning—this effort to return to values, this desire for certainty in life, for clarity of judgment after a period of turmoil and confusion, and also, what's interesting is, this has become a vehicle for drawing in the participation and activism of a lot of people who had copped out politically.

JOHNSON: If you marry money, television and evangelism, the ability to reach tens of millions of people is considerable. I'm not minimizing it. I just don't think that we're going to put on our shields and go off with crusaders again. I don't think that's where we are.

McDOWELL: The polls show a heavy majority of Americans don't like preachers in politics. But now the Republican Party seems to be committing itself to a very open embrace of Jerry Falwell, Pat Robertson and others, and there's a tremendous hazard in that for that party.

NELSON: But Reagan did it to his advantage in 1980 and 1984, and Jerry Falwell has already endorsed Bush for 1988, and as Ed Rollins says, Pat Robertson is even more political.

JOHNSON: Americans are troubled by this. They don't want Elmer Gantry in the White House, and they don't want Jerry Falwell calling shots for the White House. Jerry Falwell is one of the most unpopular people, according to the polls.

McDOWELL: He's from Virginia, and he's scary to a lot of Virginians.

NELSON: If the American people are so frightened by this, they all have got to know that Jerry Falwell has been openly embraced by Ronald Reagan, he's had entree to the White House, he's openly supporting George Bush, and Bush is delighted to have his support. Ed Rollins spoke in the presence of about fifteen Washington correspondents and said, "Pat Robertson wants to be a major force in the Republican Party, and I think he ought to be, he's got a great constituency." They don't sound to me like they're concerned at all that there's any reaction from the American public.

SMITH: Even Teddy Kennedy isn't worried about it. He goes down and debates Jerry Falwell.

DUKE: Aren't we really saying that Ronald Reagan was the great hero of the religious right, but with his passing there will be nobody to take his place? Does this mean that their power is now going to ebb?

JOHNSON: In specific areas, they will continue to be powerful, and that's not going to change. But I do not see them growing as a national force, and I noticed that Robertson, for instance, was quick to point out after a recent profile of him in the *Wall Street Journal* that, yes, he's an evangelist all right, but he's also a college graduate, a son of a senator, Phi Beta Kappa.

DUKE: He went to Yale.

McDOWELL: And the London School of Economics.

JOHNSON: In other words, he's not just somebody who found Jesus.

DUKE: Are you saying, Haynes, that he's beginning to downplay his religious base?

JOHNSON: Sure, yeah. He obviously senses that there's a problem if you're seen *only* as an evangelist when you're running for President.

DUKE: We've all covered many of the major stories over the past twenty-five years. What are your opinions about where you think the country is today and are you more hopeful or less hopeful about the United States on the basis of everything we've been discussing?

GEYER: My concern is that we are unable to act in the world the way we once could. In terms of internal democracy, I feel better about the country. In terms of our ability as the leader of the free world to act in the world and protect that freedom, I feel much worse about that.

McDOWELL: Given the incredible technological change, the velocity of that change from the nuclear bomb to television, the fact that in the last twenty-five years the very environment we live in has changed more than it had in a thousand, given the incredible stress placed upon the country in facing change, we should be thankful it hasn't all fallen apart and that the fundamentals of our Constitution, of the Bill of Rights, the things this country was founded on, remain amazingly strong and beloved. In the midst of change we have changed fundamentally far less than I would have imagined.

SMITH: There's no question that we have a system of government and a nation of people which has remarkable resilience, remarkable creativity, and that we have shown tremendous ability to meet the kinds of challenges that we face.

But I am concerned that these strong qualities are going to be sorely tested in the next several years. I don't think that as a nation and as a political system we have decided how much government and what kind of government we're going to have and whether or not we're going to pay for it and how.

We face a wrenching change ahead in terms of trying to maintain our international competitiveness, whether we're talking about old-fashioned industries like steel and textiles and shoes or newfangled industries like semiconductors and high tech. In politics we have seen that the kinds of qualities that gain the presidential nomination are often quite different from the qualities that are needed to run the country and to build governing coalitions.

I'm optimistic about the country generally. But I'm concerned about the menu of problems that we now face.

NELSON: I've seen the country go through a tremendous number of agonies over the last twenty-five years and I think there's no question that we've got a system that works. After all, it survived Watergate and the Nixon impeachment.

I've seen tremendous improvement in civil rights and in race relations. I've seen improvement in people who are disadvantaged, poor people, and I think that a lot of what happened in the Great Society period that's looked back on now as being outdated and too costly has actually helped a lot of people. So I think that overall this country has progressed tremendously, but the future is not all that bright. Our children and our grandchildren will have to pay off the debt that's being incurred during this administration.

DUKE: In that connection, I'm reminded of something that Dickens once said, that it was the best of times and the worst of times, and to paraphrase that, I believe it's the best of times and the most fearful of times. We stand on the threshold of an incredible era of technological progress—and yet, we stand on the precipice of nuclear obliteration as well. The big questions of our time still are about war and peace. Domestically, the most striking thing about the 1980s is that again we have made a fundamental political shift in our society, whether for better or worse, but nonetheless in keeping with the best of our traditions and ways.

CORDDRY: I am optimistic on the whole. I think that when one uses as a base line 1962, when the country was sort of at the peak of its power, and then what it's been through to get where it is now, one has to be optimistic.

You don't have to agree with Haynes, but it's important that he said in his piece that we went through a ten-year crisis when the democratic process was nearly—what was the word, Haynes—destroyed?

JOHNSON: Hm-mmm.

CORDDRY: Damaged. But in the end it wasn't. I agree with Rick that the management of the competition, which is really a semantic term, with the Soviet Union is going to be a bit dicey, but I'm optimistic.

I think that so much of this is perceptual, and in that vein, I tend to answer Jack's question as to whether we are standing tall in the affirmative.

JOHNSON: I'll just try to wrap up. As far as the basic health of the society, the people, their spirit, their attitudes, the way they feel about themselves and their loved ones, I think that they are healthy, strong and vibrant. It's a creative society. In many ways it's a healthier society today.

I do think that the legacy of Ronald Reagan may turn out to be—and this is what troubles me—one in which he has not prepared the country for problems. We are in a very different period economically, politically, socially, in terms of international relations and everything—all the things that have been said here—and Reagan has created an illusion that we don't have to do anything to change. I think that's a false illusion, so it comes back to a governmental leadership question: Just smile and do nothing, or prepare the country for dealing with complex educational, scientific, technological problems that are now before us.

We have long-term problems, and we're dealing with them on the short term.

Before I came over here tonight, I was searching for something to cite in a column, and I went back and read a speech of Woodrow Wilson's in 1912. Let me read you what he said:

"There is one great basic fact which underlies all the questions that are discussed on the political platform at the present moment. . . . We are in the presence of a new organization of society. Our life has broken away from the past. The life of America is not the life that it was twenty years ago. We have changed our economic conditions, absolutely, from top to bottom. . . ."

Wilson goes on and on and on in that vein. That could have been written in 1985.

The point is we're always changing. We've made progress, but we have some long-term problems still ahead of us.

DUKE: But your feeling is that the legacy of the Reagan administration could be a lot more troubles down the road?

JOHNSON: It hasn't prepared the country and the citizens for difficult choices ahead.

DUKE: We'll let that be the final word.

The Reagan Legacy

Jack Nelson

JACK NELSON, 56, has covered every presidential campaign and every Democratic and Republican convention since 1968 and has regularly covered the White House and politics since becoming Washington Bureau chief of the *Los Angeles Times* in 1975. He began his career as a reporter for the Biloxi, Mississippi, *Daily Herald* in 1947 after graduating from high school. In the 1950s he studied economics at Georgia State College while working as an investigative reporter for the *Atlanta Constitution.* He won a Pulitzer Prize in 1960 for exposing irregularities at a state mental hospital in Georgia. A Nieman Fellow at Harvard in 1961–62, he has written one book and coauthored three others. He joined the *Los Angeles Times* as its Atlanta bureau chief in February, 1965, and covered the civil rights struggle and other major developments in the South before joining the *Times'* Washington Bureau in 1970. His *Washington Week* appearances date to the Watergate days of 1973; his Washington coverage has included the Watergate scandal, the Nixon impeachment hearings, and major political and White House developments during the 1970s and 1980s.

Watching Ronald Reagan bound up the steps and onto a stage at the Tampa convention center one September day in 1985, I was reminded of the time five years earlier when I was in the same city covering Reagan's campaign for the Republican presidential nomination. At the time he was the darling of the conservatives, hustling for delegates in a conservative state. But some of his strategists were concerned about a statewide poll showing 40 percent of the respondents believed the sixty-nine-year-old former California governor was too old to take on the physical and intellectual demands of the White House. L. E. (Tommy) Thomas, Reagan's state campaign manager, was especially worried. He told me he thought age was becoming a significant issue, one that could spell real trouble for Reagan in Florida, where he was counting on a decisive victory over George Bush to help propel him toward the nomination.

"And you know where it is the worst," said Thomas, pointing across the bay from Tampa. "Right over there in St. Petersburg, where there are so many old people. You know what they tell him? They say, 'Hell, I'm sixty-nine and I don't feel good,' and the only thing Governor Reagan can say is, 'I'm sorry, but I do feel good.' And they'll ask where he found the fountain of youth and he'll give 'em that old line about not really being that old, about how they mixed him up in the hospital when he was a baby."

The age issue was being debated nationally, too, and shortly after my Tampa visit it was raised when I addressed an audience in Biloxi, Mississippi, where I grew up and began my career as a journalist. During a question and answer session, someone asked me whether Reagan's age would hurt him in the campaign. I cited Tommy Thomas's comments and said it probably would be an issue. My mother, who is Reagan's age, was in the audience and she jumped to her feet and yelled, "Well, it ought not to be and I don't think it will be!"

My mother never pretended to have any political expertise, but she was a lot closer to the mark than either Tommy Thomas or I. Reagan's age was immaterial—he not only carried Florida and almost every other state in thrashing Bush for the 1980 GOP presidential nomination, but went on to sweep President Jimmy Carter out of the White House, roll over Congress with a string of quick legislative victories early in his first term, and then win a second term with an overwhelming victory over former vice-president Walter F. Mondale, the Democratic nominee in 1984.

So here was Reagan at seventy-four—twice elected president by overwhelming margins, survivor of an assassination attempt and a bout with colon cancer—regaling 2,500 senior citizens in Tampa with more jokes about his age. He was glad to be back in Florida and "happy to have a few kids my own age to play with." Urging support for his plan to overhaul the federal tax system, he noted that while the modern tax code runs to four volumes and 4,000 pages, there were just 15 pages when the law took effect in 1913—and "I may have been the only two-year-old to read it cover-to-cover."

Ronald Reagan had good reason to feel buoyant. He was immensely popular. He had established himself as one of the most resilient men ever to occupy the presidency by surmounting an array of economic and foreign policy problems. And on at least one important count he had already earned a significant place in history: After more than a decade of weak chief executives, he had reestablished the presidency as an office of commanding power, leadership, and initiative. Reagan's success in revitalizing the presidency seemed certain to earn him high marks from historians no matter what happened in his second term.

At the same time, it was clear that to go beyond this accomplishment, to enter the ranks of truly exceptional presidents, Reagan had to do more: He had to retain at least a semblance of the old magic during his second four years. A lackluster performance would not negate the historic accomplishments of the first term, but would inevitably diminish his final record as well as the political legacy to his party. More important, a lapse into the stalement with Congress that had humbled his four immediate predecessors could leave the nation foundering in confusion again.

As it was, the second term soon proved to be a time of testing as critical as any in Reagan's career. He had achieved almost all his major goals early in the first term. But now a combination of events, and the unwanted consequences of some of his own earlier triumphs were converging to threaten much that he had achieved. In foreign affairs, but even more on the domestic front, a series of unusually difficult problems were crowding in on the nation and challenging Reagan's stewardship. Even in his own party, which had stood so solidly behind him, there was rising resentment over White House handling of several crucial issues—even a feeling that the president and his staff might be losing touch with the country.

Thus, as 1986 arrived, the central question was whether the formidable assets and advantages he still possessed would be enough. Would his pluses continue to outweigh the increasing minuses? Like an aging boxer seeking to stay on top through one last fight, Reagan faced a crucial test: Would the reserves of skill and cunning that he had acquired over a lifetime in the public arena prove sufficient to carry him through his final years in the White House?

The answer to that question would determine the final judgment about his presidency.

The gathering problems were plain to see. Unlike his first four years, Reagan's second term had got off to a distinctly slow and stumbling start. The months following his second inaugural were marked by setbacks in Congress and failure to lay down the kind of clear-cut agenda that paved the way for the first-term triumphs. As 1985 wore on, Reagan's advisers became increasingly concerned, convinced that he desperately needed a major goal—preferably one that would lead to a signal victory in Congress—around which to rally the country and regain momentum as the nation's preeminent leader.

In part, Reagan's second-term troubles stemmed from the political atrophy that goes with being unable to run again; even the most masterful presidents had been less successful in their final terms. Also, while Reagan's pluck and good humor in the face of personal adversity had won public admiration, his encounter with cancer had inevitably underlined the mortality of the oldest man ever to sit in the Oval Office.

More important, a series of new problems had arisen to test Reagan's authority and political acumen. His response to these developments would determine whether he could regain the dominance which he exercised over the national agenda in his first term or if he would be swept to the sidelines by the force of events.

The new challenges stemmed primarily from four factors:

- difficulties in setting a well-defined agenda for the new term;

- lack of a realistic strategy to control runaway federal deficits;
- failure in the first term to address in a positive way U.S. relations with the Soviet Union, the one issue overlaying almost all of the Reagan administration's foreign policy; and
- shifts in public attitudes that signaled trouble for Reagan's goal of continuing to shrink the role of government in American life.

In his first term, Reagan had concentrated on a tightly limited set of goals, chiefly cutting taxes, strengthening the national defense, and reducing the role of government in domestic life. That narrow agenda proved to be a source of strength in the early years, but now other issues were surging to the fore and the administration's failure to develop a broad policy framework had put the president on the defensive and made him politically vulnerable.

Budget deficits vastly bigger than any in the nation's history were roaring out of control, fueled in large part by Reagan's cutting federal revenues while sharply raising defense spending. Those deficits, in turn, confronted members of Congress and millions of American voters with a highly disturbing series of political and personal realities: proposals to cut Social Security, stubbornly high interest rates, and an overpriced dollar that made imports cheap for American consumers and exports too costly for foreign buyers, thereby crippling U.S. industry and costing hundreds of thousands of U.S. workers their jobs.

On such issues as trade protectionism, subsidies for embattled farmers, and imposition of economic sanctions against the racist government of South Africa, some of the president's own advisers and staunchest Republican supporters in Congress told me they felt he was out of touch with political reality. They complained that he was devoting too much attention to his plan to overhaul the tax system, which had generated little enthusiasm. Instead, they contended, he should be working harder to lower the deficit because this was the issue that was really provoking the country.

In fact, while the polls showed Reagan's popularity remained at a high level—in the 60- to 65-percent range—those same polls also showed that Americans now opposed his policies on most domestic and foreign issues by substantial margins. A sampling by pollster Lou Harris showed Reagan with a 61- to 37-percent positive rating in inspiring confidence in the White House, but with a 64- to 34-percent negative rating for the handling of the deficit, with substantial negative ratings also on defense spending, women's rights, nuclear arms, South Africa, Central America, and U.S.–Soviet relations.

During the first three years of his presidency, Reagan delighted his far-right supporters with harsh anti-Communist rhetoric, denouncing the Soviet Union as an "evil empire" and predicting it would end up on the "ash heap of history." Not since the Cold War period following World War II had relations been so strained. In November 1983, the Soviets—for the first time in fourteen years—broke off all arms control negotiations to protest the deployment of U.S. missiles in Europe. Critics repeatedly pointed out that Reagan was the first president since World War II who had not met with his Soviet counterpart.

Reagan's foreign policy revolved around the biggest peacetime military buildup in history and the president's own drum-beating for an America that would "stand tall" against Soviet threats from Nicaragua to Afghanistan. Even so, the president could not point to a single foreign policy achievement. There was nothing to compare to the reopening of relations with China by President Richard Nixon or the Camp David peace accords hammered out by President Jimmy Carter, Israeli Prime Minister Menachem Begin, and Egyptian President Anwar Sadat.

In fact, during his first term Reagan suffered significant setbacks in foreign policy, most notably in Lebanon and South Africa. After a terrorist bomb left 241 marines dead in Lebanon on October 23, 1983, Reagan vowed to keep the marines on duty in that war-torn country and warned that a withdrawal would call into question "the resolve of the West to carry out its responsibilities to help the free world defend itself." Scarcely four months later, in a humiliating reversal, he pulled the marines out, tacitly conceding that even the massive military power of the United States has its limits. And there was no "swift and effective retribution"—the term Reagan had used in 1981 in vowing to strike back at terrorists—because there seemed no practical way to punish the shadowy forces behind the suicide squads. Similarly, Reagan's "constructive engagement" policy toward South Africa collapsed when public and Congressional pressure forced him to impose limited economic sanctions against that country.

Two days after the bombing in Lebanon, Reagan ordered U.S. forces to invade the tiny Caribbean island of Grenada for the stated purpose of protecting about 1,000 Americans, including some 800 medical students, and restoring order and democratic rule after a Marxist coup. Acting in conjunction with Grenada's neighbors in the Organization of Eastern Caribbean States, the administration had another—unannounced—objective: to oust Cuban advisers who were exercising growing influence on the troubled island.

Eighteen Americans, as well as forty-five Grenadians and twenty-four Cubans, were killed in the invasion, which was carried out under cover of a highly controversial news blackout. But the operation was deemed a military success; the medical students were rescued and the surviving Cubans sent home. Once American forces had secured the island, the administration lifted the news blackout and moved quickly to exploit the invasion as an example of how the United

States was prepared to meet the Communist threat in this hemisphere with renewed willpower and firepower. Reagan credited the military operation not only with saving American lives but with stopping what he called "a potential threat to all the people of the Caribbean." Trailed by network television camera crews, Vice-President Bush and Defense Secretary Caspar Weinberger inspected masses of Communist bloc weapons seized in Grenada and put on public display at Andrews Air Force Base, Maryland.

Although Reagan was severely criticized abroad for ordering what many saw as an unprovoked attack, the invasion was a political plus at home. It distracted the public from the disaster in Lebanon and in the eyes of many Americans gave credence to Reagan's claim that the nation was regaining its military edge.

There was a strong belief that the administration meant the Grenada invasion to be a warning to the Sandinista government of Nicaragua that the U.S. would not tolerate an expansion of Soviet influence in that country. Invasion fears swept Nicaragua, and in early 1984 the administration fed those fears with a CIA operation that mined its harbors, endangering the ships of friend and foe alike. The mining was widely denounced by both Republicans and Democrats. But Reagan seemed unperturbed by either the mining controversy or press disclosures that the CIA also had assisted in the preparation of a manual that advised the Nicaragua contras (rebels) to kidnap, blackmail, recruit criminals, and selectively "neutralize" Nicaraguan officials. Reagan contended that "neutralize"—a CIA term for elimination or assassination—meant merely that "you just say to the fellow who's sitting there in the office, 'You're not in the office anymore.'"

Not until early 1984 did Reagan put aside his preoccupation with the Communist threat. Then, facing a reelection campaign and growing public concern over his anti-Soviet policies, he finally adopted a more conciliatory approach and began to send signals that he was interested in a dialogue with the Soviets. The opening to Moscow came at an opportune moment for the Kremlin. It faced severe economic problems at home, and relaxing tensions with Washington could provide greater freedom to address those problems. By early 1985, the president, who showed no apparent discomfort in the odd role of suitor, had lured the Soviets back to the arms control negotiating table in Geneva. And—much to the consternation of his most conservative followers—the president arranged a two-day summit meeting in Geneva on November 19-20 with the dynamic new Soviet leader, Mikhail Gorbachev, who at age fifty-four was twenty years younger.

While the meeting produced no breakthrough on arms reductions, it did reduce some of the tensions between the superpowers, opened up new lines of communication and people-to-people exchanges, and established a foundation for what Reagan called a "fresh start" in U.S.-Soviet relations.

Throughout their eight hours of talks, including an extraordinary five hours of one-on-one sessions, Reagan and Gorbachev engaged in spirited exchanges. Gorbachev himself later described some of the sessions that dealt with Reagan's "Star Wars" space-based missile defense plan, officially called the Strategic Defense Initiative, as "very, very sharp." Reagan defended the controversial research project as a purely defensive effort while Gorbachev denounced it as a U.S. attempt to gain a nuclear first-strike capacity, arguing that it would doom arms control negotiations. Nevertheless, a final statement signed by the two leaders contained no mention of "Star Wars"—a significant omission. Two U.S. officials later told me they were convinced that in private Gorbachev did not feel as strongly about "Star Wars" as he indicated in public and predicted that he would eventually modify his opposition and not let it stand in the way of an arms-reduction agreement.

That newfound optimism was evident immediately upon the president's return home. He first addressed a joint session of Congress at the end of a twenty-hour day which included the final summit ceremony in Geneva and a briefing for Western allies in Brussels. I watched him closely as he entered the chamber. He was bleary-eyed, but smiling, standing straight and talking energetically. I could not help but marvel at the stamina and physical appearance of the president as he neared his seventy-fifth birthday. The scene reminded me of a remark by Dr. Joseph Giardano, the trauma specialist credited by Reagan with saving his life after the assassination attempt on a Washington street back in early 1981. Shortly after giving Reagan emergency treatment at George Washington University Hospital, Giardano told me: "I had always heard that physiologically the President was much younger than seventy. He is. His skin is tight and there's good substance to it. His muscles are well developed. He looks like a man of fifty or fifty-five."

The next day he met with about twenty journalists in the White House theater. Reagan was eager to talk about the "arguments" at the summit. When I asked about Gorbachev's concern over Star Wars, the president made a sweeping circular motion with both arms and declared he was convinced that the Soviet leader "really believes" that the program would lead to development of "offensive nuclear weapons circling the earth." The expression of confidence in Gorbachev's sincerity was a sharp departure from the president's past rhetoric about Soviet leaders as cheats and liars who could not be trusted.

Reagan's attitude that morning reflected more than a change in language; it appeared to mark a signal shift in his priorities. In the first term, Reagan had concentrated most of his time and efforts on the economy and other domestic issues and gave short shrift to foreign affairs. But the new dialogue with the Soviets clearly was taking up much more of his time now. In conversations with aides he talked enthusiastically about reaching an arms agreement and his hopes for other accomplishments in the foreign field, including the international economy. Ultimately he wanted the Reagan era to be remembered as one of peace and prosperity—of restoring the economy and the powers of the presidency, improving superpower relations, and reducing the risk of nuclear war.

Shifting the focus of his administration from domestic to foreign policy would not be easy, however. The immediate result of the Geneva conference was to reinforce the image of a strong and effective national leader; the president had, after all, confounded not only the Soviets but also those critics who had said he would get nowhere unless he first abandoned the Strategic Defense Initiative. And as in Lebanon and other overseas crises, the public's abiding faith in him as a sincere, trustworthy leader doing his best to cope with the burdens of office had given Reagan his "Teflon" coating—a shield that was reinforced just before the summit meeting when navy fighter jets boldly intercepted a plane carrying Palestinian terrorists who had captured an Italian cruise ship and killed a crippled American citizen. Yet, the new venture into foreign affairs was fraught with problems.

First, Reagan's inexperience in foreign affairs meant that in formulating policy he was much more dependent than most of his predecessors on advisers and officials with stronger backgrounds in the field. Policy divisions between two of his most powerful Cabinet secretaries, George P. Shultz of State and Caspar Weinberger of Defense, subjected Reagan to internal battles that went beyond the normal feuding among department heads. The Weinberger-Shultz struggle, and a number of lesser contests, reflected profound ideological disagreements within administration ranks. And in this area at least, Reagan demonstrated so little capacity for imposing discipline that administration policy often drifted incoherently.

In arms control, deep disagreements among policymakers were a major factor in bogging down negotiations with the Soviet Union. Weinberger led a faction of hardliners while Shultz led a more moderate group that seemed willing to make significant concessions to reach some accommodation with the Soviets.

The Defense Department was accused by Reagan's first Secretary of State, Alexander M. Haig, Jr., of deliberately drafting the initial U.S. offer at the arms talks in Geneva in such a way as to guarantee no progress.* Noting that the offer was a compromise between State and Defense recommendations, Haig said the president "gave each supplicant half the baby." He went on to say that the half contributed by the Pentagon "required such drastic reductions in the Soviet inventory as to suggest that they were unnegotiable."

In the past, presidents often relied on powerful national security assistants to help resolve disputes among Cabinet officials and to hammer out a united policy. Henry Kissinger performed that task for Nixon and Zbigniew Brzezinski for Carter. But Reagan, always a firm practitioner of Cabinet government, appointed weaker national security assistants and gave policy rivals in the Cabinet free rein to wrangle over their differences. Moreover, the prestige and authority of the office was further diminished by an unusually high rate of turnover among the national security assistants. Prior to Reagan, only four men had occupied that position in the preceding twenty years.

In contrast, Reagan began the second year of his second term with his fourth national security assistant—Adm. John M. Poindexter, appointed December 4, 1985, to replace

---

*From *Caveat*, by Alexander M. Haig.

Robert C. McFarlane. In his two years as national security assistant, McFarlane actually had brought a measure of discipline to the foreign policy process. But he resigned after growing weary of friction with Reagan's top policy advisers. Although publicly insisting that the internal battling played no part in his resignation, McFarlane told colleagues he had tired of dealing with Donald T. Regan, Reagan's chief of staff, and of trying to settle the policy disputes between Shultz and Weinberger. Administration officials told me McFarlane bitterly resented what he considered Regan's meddling in foreign policy matters.

The emergence of Regan as the most powerful chief of staff since Eisenhower's Sherman Adams, and the promotion of Poindexter, who had served as McFarlane's assistant, did not bode well for a coherent foreign policy for the rest of Reagan's presidency. For one thing, both men had little experience in foreign affairs. Also, Poindexter, who was not considered a strong leader, was beholden to Regan and Shultz for his promotion. The appointment left Shultz as the administration's chief formulator of foreign policy and opened the way for Regan to expand his interest and influence in the field. All in all, it appeared to be a formula for the kind of foreign policy disarray that had marred much of the Reagan presidency.

Moreover, beyond these difficulties on the foreign policy front, massive new problems confronted Reagan at home.

A shift in public attitudes spelled trouble for the drive to reduce the role of government in American life. Even conservative commentators conceded the limits of tolerance had been reached.

What worried some conservative strategists was that the continued pruning back of federal services might eventually trigger a backlash against the Republican party. Kevin Phillips, the astute conservative political analyst, suggested that the American mood had begun to shift back toward a more affirmative role for government. Writing in the *New York Times Magazine* of May 12, 1985, he declared: "An Administration whose insistence on the marketplace and diminished government was valid five years ago now suffers from ideological hardening of the arteries." At its extreme, Phillips argued, "leaving national affairs to the marketplace was as out of kilter with the realities of interest groups, nationalism and human behavior as liberal regulatory utopianism was in its own self-indulgent heyday."

For his part, the president maintained his characteristic serenity in the face of such criticism, but his advisers conceded that he was isolated from the concerns of many voters.

Nothing so exemplified Reagan's growing political problems as his first meeting with Republican leaders of Congress in August, 1985, following his cancer surgery. Ordinarily, the president's arrival at such a gathering would have touched off applause, and one might have expected an especially warm reception on this occasion. When Reagan entered the Cabinet Room of the White House, however, he was confronted by stony silence and an unusually grim-faced circle of congressional leaders.

So marked was the lack of cordiality that Reagan tried to disarm the Republican leaders with a joke, reaching back as he often does in such situations to a line or scene from an old Western movie: "Maybe I should have thrown my hat in first."

The image was particularly appropriate because if indeed he had tossed his hat in first, it probably would have been shot full of holes. Republican sources who later described the session to me said the president's comment prompted no more than a faint chuckle or two. The faces in front of him remained unsmiling.

The grim atmosphere sprang from the fact that most of

the GOP's congressional leaders felt their president was ignoring the ever-rising deficit and, in fact, had double-crossed them by abruptly turning against a budget reduction plan worked out by Senate Republicans.

Reagan wanted a chance to explain his flip-flop. It was an especially awkward moment for the president, and when he noted that Senate Majority Leader Robert Dole could not be on hand because he was holding a press conference, several of the Senators smiled wryly. Everyone knew Dole had been so angered by the president's switch that he had boycotted the meeting.

Reagan, who had campaigned in 1980 on a pledge to balance the budget during his first term, told the delegation that he could not accept their package because it would violate another pledge from the 1984 campaign he considered even more important—that he would not raise taxes or reduce Social Security benefits, both of which were features of the Senate Republican plan.

The president's words did not assuage his angry audience. Sitting across the table from him, Senator Pete V. Domenici, chairman of the Senate Budget Committee, put the president on notice that he would not tolerate being toyed with on the budget again; that he would insist in the future that any White House budget reduction ideas recognize the need to increase taxes and cut defense spending as well as social programs. Domenici was blunt: "Mr. President, you can add up all those programs you like to talk about and it comes to $6 billion or $7 billion and that's not enough. We're talking about $200 billion deficits!" Then, glancing at Chief of Staff Donald Regan, who had brought a confrontational style to congressional relations in the second term, Domenici said, "I want you to know, Mr. President, it's the last time I'll do this. I want to make it clear to you and all your advisers in the room that I will not go through with this cover-up again of the fact that you can't get enough out of the domestic accounts to deal effectively with the deficit."

Rep. Richard Cheney of Wyoming, who had served as chief of staff during the Ford administration, described the session with Reagan as "one of the most tense meetings I've ever been to at the White House." The Republicans came away feeling Reagan had blown his best—and perhaps last—opportunity to take the initiative in dealing with the runaway deficit that threatened to engulf his presidency and ultimately wreck the economy.

Indeed, the unhappy Senate Republicans a few weeks later came up with a second deficit-curbing plan—the Gramm-Rudman bill—that in some ways was even more unacceptable to the White House. This plan, endorsed by Congress at the end of 1985, called for a series of automatically phased spending reductions that would ultimately bring the budget into balance in the early 1990s. There would be deep cuts in some domestic programs, but also substantial scaling back of the Pentagon's five-year, one-trillion-dollar buildup. This time the White House reluctantly went along, a tacit acknowledgment that it no longer could resist the congressional tide for budget austerity.

The radical action by Congress was more than a rebuke to the White House for its deficit dawdling. It also was a clear signal that the legislators were now seizing the initiative on important issues. As if to emphasize the point, House Republicans handed Reagan a stunning pre-Christmas drubbing by voting decisively against tax reform. It took all of the president's vaunted powers of persuasion—plus a personal trip to Capitol Hill to plead with the rebels to reverse their stand—to save the day in the House and keep the tax reform issue alive.

Hence, 1986 seemed to portend much trial and turmoil for the Reagan team. As political scientist Norman Ornstein said: "The basic fact is that we're going to have the final two years of the Reagan White House being a period of drift. There is nothing achievable that Reagan wants for his final two years. There's no momentum. And he's going to have a lot of things stacked against him."

If prospects for Reagan's second term seemed gloomy from the outside, it did not necessarily seem that way from the inside. Reagan retained more than a few assets, including his demonstrated skill as a political counterpuncher. His vulnerabilities might prove easier to identify than to exploit. Likewise, for all the difficulties, his enemies had formidable problems of their own. True, the newly reorganized White House staff lacked the political agility and savvy that characterized the first-term staff headed by James Baker. Nonetheless, the president and his men were holding to a strategy which might cause them short-term problems—even substantial embarrassments—but which, given a bit more of Reagan's fabled luck, still could bring them out ahead. The name of their game was to conserve Reagan's most notable asset: his image as a strong leader who had restored the White House and the nation to a renewed position of authority and respect—what Reagan called "standing tall."

The president and his advisers had approached the second term on the basis of some cold-blooded decisions. The budget deficit was judged to be a "no-win" issue for Reagan. So, too, the farm crisis, the trade troubles, and South Africa. All of these issues involved unavoidable minuses, no matter what was done; any action stood to hurt or anger substantial blocks of voters.

Thus, it was decided that the no-win issues should be consigned to "damage control." The administration would not take the lead in proposing solutions. Instead, it would leave the burden for action to time and events, and most of all to Congress. There would be criticism, of course, especially from the press, and there was the risk that events could leave Reagan looking weak and irrelevant. Still, there was the instructive memory of Jimmy Carter to remind them of what could happen to a president who was too quick to grasp nettles he was not strong enough to pull out.

Reagan had taken the same kind of hard-nosed approach in his successful first term when aides were building his image as a winning chief executive. As Jim Baker told me in a conversation after he left the White House to become secretary of the treasury: "The president's got an ideological and pragmatic side, and he's clearly pragmatic enough to know it's important to succeed. He has said many times he would take seventy-five percent or eighty percent of something because it was better than nothing. He realizes that one of the most important things about the presidency and governing is succeeding. . . . We were always conscious in the first term of not going to the Hill with something that was a sure loser. I can remember any number of times when we wouldn't go up with something if it didn't have a good chance to win."

That kind of calculation might not win Reagan a prize from civics teachers, but one of the keys to his long political life had been a keen understanding of the things that would hurt him with voters. He had always recognized that—outside the sometimes fevered confines of Washington—most Americans held a commonsense view that major problems such as the deficit and trade gaps were not created in a day and could not be solved in a day; they were prepared to give a president time and elbow room as long as he seemed to be doing his best and the issues at play were not wreaking havoc with their own lives. Moreover, with his self-deprecating humor and personal courage, his Jimmy Stewart way of shuffling around political potholes and aligning himself with traditional American values, his eternal optimism and pride in the country, Reagan had gained a position of considerable admiration, even affection, in the minds of many voters; so far as his own standing as president was concerned, he already held the high ground. Thus, on the no-win issues, the White House was convinced Reagan could afford to make his enemies come to him.

The president also had demonstrated skill in playing the Washington game. Unlike Jimmy Carter, who despised the nitty-gritty of negotiating with legislators and did relatively little personal lobbying, Reagan understood that drafting policies was only half a chief executive's job; the other half was winning approval from the legislative branch. In his first year as president, Carter once complained to me that when he invited members of Congress to the White House, some of them wasted his time because they were not as well prepared to discuss the issues as he was. His time was "extremely valuable," he said, so people who expected to meet with him "had better know the subject because I know it."

As one who had followed Carter's career from state senator to Georgia governor to president, I had not found it surprising that immediately after taking office he ran into serious problems on Capitol Hill even though both branches of Congress were controlled by Democrats. As governor, Carter had shown contempt for some of the legislators, having a stormy relationship with the Georgia legislature as a whole. Shortly after the 1976 election, Peter Bourne, a Georgian who became a White House aide, told me he was worried that Carter would "treat Congress like it's the Georgia legislature, and Congress will treat him like he's the Georgia governor." Bourne's fears were well founded.

By contrast, the first thing Reagan did after the 1980 election was to come to town and personally visit the barons of Capitol Hill. He lavished attention on individual members and leaders of the House and Senate. During his first hundred days in office—despite being out of action for several weeks while recovering from the March 30, 1981, assassination attempt—Reagan held meetings attended by 467 senators and representatives. Instead of treating them brusquely, he often kept the lawmakers beyond their scheduled time, regaling them with jokes and old Hollywood stories. Rep. Charles W. Stenholm of Texas, a leader of the "boll weevils," a band of conservative Democrats that provided Reagan with crucial support for his economic program, told me he had never set foot in the White House while Carter was president; Reagan, on the other hand, quickly invited him to the Oval Office and turned on the charm during a meeting that went well beyond the scheduled fifteen minutes.

Reagan's handling of the press was equally masterful and again the contrast with Carter was striking. During an interview with Carter in 1980, he answered questions with clipped precision, glanced impatiently at his wristwatch and cut off my questioning precisely at the end of the allotted thirty minutes. I had another interview with Reagan one raw, wintry day in 1981, almost a year after he entered the White House. He was relaxed, greeted me and two other *Los Angeles Times* reporters warmly, answered questions expansively, and as the half hour ended, ignored frantic "time's up" signals from press spokesman Larry Speakes. The president insisted that my colleagues and I ask two or three more questions. It was a small gesture that spoke volumes about Reagan's understanding of how a president communicates with the people and thus shapes public opinion.

Reagan's success was not simply a matter of charm. Contrary to popular myth, he often worked hard, especially when one of his pet projects was at stake. Typically, less than a month after he was shot, he met with senior aides to discuss lobbying for his economic program. The aides were worried about overtaxing the president, still weak from his slowly mending lung. But he was worried about his program and quickly made the tactical decision to adopt as his own the budget-cutting plan of conservative House Democrats. Then he wanted to know which congressmen needed stroking. "Fifteen soft Republicans and twenty-six Democrats," came the answer. Reagan, with a determination that astonished the aides and the members of Congress he called, began to work the presidential telephone.

If he courted individual members of Congress assiduously, Reagan never hesitated to stir up the public against Congress as a whole when it balked at his proposals. He also proved to be a tough negotiator. His friend and political adviser, Sen. Paul Laxalt of Nevada, called Reagan "a consummate poker player in dealing with Congress. He has a wonderful quality of keeping people off balance and that's invaluable in dealing on Capitol Hill. You always think there will be conciliation in the end when dealing with him, but you're never sure." As Democratic Speaker Tip O'Neill remarked ruefully, the problem with negotiating with Reagan was that "every time you compromise with the president, the president gets 80 percent of what he wants." Reagan's response when he heard about O'Neill's quip was, "I'll take 80 percent every time, and I'll go back the next year for the additional 20 percent."

Moreover, as opponents learned to their chagrin, forcing Reagan to back down was not always the same as beating him. After a deal was struck, members of Congress— especially Democrats—were often dismayed to find the president trumpeting victory. In the budget battle of 1982, for example, Reagan had to accept a congressional product quite different from his original proposals, yet as one of Reagan's chief legislative strategists said in a candid moment: "Sometimes there's a fine line between winning and losing or being perceived as winning and being perceived as losing, and I think we were able to portray it as a victory for the president rather than having our back against the wall and compromising when we didn't have any cards left."

In September, 1985, circumstances also forced the president's hand on South Africa and trade protectionism. In a major reversal of both administration policy and his own long-held views, Reagan buckled to congressional pressure and ordered limited economic sanctions against South Africa to protest its apartheid system. Faced with a whirlwind of protectionist sentiment in Congress, he publicly accused Japan, Brazil, South Korea, and the European Economic Community of unfair trade practices and threatened to take countermeasures if they failed to open their markets to American goods and services. In this, he acted just days before the release of Commerce Department figures indicating that the U.S. had become a debtor nation for the first time since 1914. In each case, however, he did his best to turn defeat into victory by taking action to cut the ground out from under his opponents and make it difficult for them to reap any political dividends.

Reagan's approach to economic policy was similarly revealing. He sloughed off warnings from his economic advisers that cutting taxes while engineering an historic boost in defense spending could increase deficits to dangerous levels. In fact, egged on by Edwin Meese III, his ultraconservative White House counselor and second-term attorney general who also distrusted economists, Reagan tended to make light of their forecasts. As the deficit began to take hold as a major national issue in the spring of 1985, Reagan regaled a meeting of the American Business Conference, declaring: "It's been said that if you line a thousand economists up end to end, they still won't reach a conclusion."

"Ronald Reagan simply doesn't believe economists know what they are talking about when they are forecasting deficits," a White House official told me. "For one thing, you don't have to scratch beneath Reagan's surface to find an eternal optimist. And people like Meese rationalize and support everything he says."

The annual budget ritual illustrated this disregard for expert opinion. As each year's budget fight developed, Reagan took to insisting that the deficit figures would turn out to be lower than the dire projections of forecasters. Actually, they usually were much higher; though the administration predicted deficits of $45 billion and $92 billion for fiscal 1982 and 1983, for example, the actual deficits for those years turned out to be $111 billion and $195 billion.

Deficits of that magnitude had all-too-real consequences for interest rates, the dollar, trade, and jobs. Yet the Democrats found it difficult to turn their criticism into solid political gains. The U.S. economy remained the strongest in the world and continued to provide a high standard of living for the vast majority of Americans, seemingly buttressing Reagan's conviction that holding down taxes and curbing government would redound to the nation's benefit, even if the deficit did soar. Not all voters might share that conviction, but absent a disastrous downturn, it was far from clear that they would turn against the president.

Whatever the clouds threatening Reagan's second term, he already had made an enormous impact on the institution of the presidency. It seemed plain that his successors and the nation would be affected for years to come.

In concrete terms, Reagan presided over a period of dramatic policy change, pushing legislation through Congress that substantially reduced taxes, slowed the growth of the government's domestic programs, and brought about the biggest defense buildup since the Vietnam War. In curbing the growth of social programs, he had waged war against a half century of Democratic philosophy, a philosophy often supported by Republicans. During the interview at the end of his first year, I found Reagan unusually buoyant about his achievements. "I believe that we have started government on a different course," he said, "different than anything we've done in the last half century and since Roosevelt began with the New Deal, and that is the recognition that there is a limit to government—must be a limit to government size and power—and that there has been a distortion of the relationships between the various echelons of government—federal, state, and local."

For better or worse, Reagan's early assessment of his presidency has remained correct. The more contemporary functions of government have been reduced dramatically. Spending for most domestic programs declined directly in absolute dollars and as a proportion of the budget, and political scientists predict that this reduced role for government could be a fact of life for a long time.

As Norman Ornstein observed, there will be tremendous constraints on Reagan's successor. "The next president is not going to have money available—for many reasons—to come out with a set of new initiatives to do new things to expand the federal government, at least in the domestic arena. And of course if you look at the tax program, the budget program, elimination of revenue sharing and some of the other changes, the new federalism is terribly destructive of the ability of states to pick up more of the slack. So it means less discretion in government, less money going into these areas of spending."

Reagan also will leave a lasting mark on the federal judiciary. Leaving aside the Supreme Court, on which Reagan ultimately could have a truly historical impact, he almost certainly will have a wide influence on the U.S. district courts and federal circuit courts of appeals. Already, of the 168 appeals court and 575 district court judges, he has appointed over 200; assuming normal rates of turnover,

Reagan is likely to have named a solid majority of all such judges before his second term ends—a level not equaled since Franklin D. Roosevelt and Dwight D. Eisenhower. And the sheer numbers only begin to tell the story.

As he did in California, Reagan has generally earned high marks from legal scholars and the bar for the professional quality and competence of his judicial appointees. But Reagan and his aides have also paid far more attention than other recent administrations to the philosophical views of their prospective nominees to the federal bench. Justice Department officials have closely questioned them in advance on everything from their views on the death penalty to the Supreme Court's decision legalizing abortion in *Roe vs. Wade.* Bruce Fein, a former Justice Department official who aided in the selection of judicial candidates during Reagan's first term, conceded that the administration was being "more meticulous" than other administrations have been in its "concern about judicial philosophy" and said, for example, he knew of no Reagan judicial appointees who agreed with the Supreme Court's abortion decision.

Again, the Carter administration offers a clear contrast. Carter gave high priority to appointing women and minorities to the bench, but his Justice Department paid little attention to whether the candidates supported Carter's policies or were strict constructionists inclined to interpret the law narrowly. In the Reagan administration, according to a study by University of Massachusetts law professor Sheldon Goldman, if there were many minorities, women, or non-Republicans among Reagan's original prospects for the judiciary, few survived the screening process. Of Reagan's first-term appointees, 93 percent were white; 92 percent male; and 98 percent Republican. Almost one-fourth were millionaires.

Although there has been no systematic review of how Reagan appointees have performed on the bench, the conservative Center for Judicial Studies monitored the performance of sixty-two judges appointed in the first two years and concluded that half exercised "judicial restraint" in all their cases and another one-quarter did so in nearly all their opinions. "The conclusion is inescapable that the Reagan judiciary, so far, has lived up to expectations," the center declared.

Apart from the spending restraints and the judicial shift, Reagan has done much to restore the authority and vigor of the presidency itself.

Before Reagan assumed office in 1981, a series of failed presidencies that cut across party and ideological lines had steadily diminished the power of the office. Lyndon B. Johnson, discredited by the Vietnam War, chose not to run for a second full term. Richard M. Nixon, disgraced by Watergate and all its ramifications, resigned rather than face certain impeachment. Gerald R. Ford, with no mandate of his own and burdened by his pardon of Nixon, was defeated by a little-known Georgia governor. And Jimmy Carter, perhaps more than all the others, personified the decline of the office. Unable to command the public's respect or rally his own Democratic Party in Congress, he anguished over his lack of power. Despairingly, he once told me during a dinner at the White House that special interests had become the most powerful force in Washington—"even more powerful than the presidency."

In his farewell address, Carter put his finger on the central problem that had plagued the office ever since Johnson: "The president is given a broad responsibility to lead. But he cannot do so without the support and consent of the people expressed formally through the Congress and informally through a whole range of public and private institutions."

Against that background of diminished presidential power, few political observers gave Reagan much chance of exerting strong leadership. Moreover, while Americans disdain weak leaders, they paradoxically seem uncomfortable with the idea of presidents becoming too powerful. In fact, Americans are so tough on their presidents that, of thirty-nine presidents prior to Reagan, twenty-three served one term or less. (The pattern of one-term Presidents becomes even clearer when one considers that five of those reelected were among the first seven presidents.)

Yet, Reagan managed to emerge as one of the strongest leaders of our time in his first term and to carry forty-nine of fifty states in winning reelection to become the most dominant figure on the American political scene since Roosevelt. He strengthened the presidency during a time when political scientists and other observers were saying the system no longer worked.

Major factors in Reagan's victories were his style and the image he projected as a strong leader possessing great self-esteem and self-confidence. Presidential scholar Thomas E. Cronin, a political science professor at Colorado State College, described Reagan as "an interesting combination of John Wayne and Mr. Rogers of TV. As John Wayne, he talks tough on foreign policy and threatens to send in the marines, but as Mr. Rogers, he talks in a neighborly way that people understand. He has a wonderful capacity to simplify things and say the kind of thing the guy down the street would say."

On the basis of Reagan's first-term achievements alone, Cronin believes "historians, despite any liberal bias, will rate his presidency at least above average and maybe even above that because he made the presidency work." He cautions, however, that the second term may cancel out "some of the rather spectacular successes of the first two years because the second-term agenda is unclear and the Reagan administration is mushy on one of the most critical issues it faces—reducing deficits."

Despite the second-term troubles, many old Washington

hands believe Reagan will be remembered for redressing the balance of power between the executive and legislative branches. Ken Duberstein, a presidential assistant who directed much of the successful first-term strategy on Capitol Hill, observed that when Reagan came in, "everybody was talking about our system of government no longer being able to function very well, that problems weren't being addressed, that our executive and legislative branches were by and large at loggerheads. It was gridlocked. . . . The president's victories on the Hill and the strength of his leadership put the presidency back to where it was before Vietnam and Watergate."

Reagan's popularity and skills as a communicator have been rightly credited with contributing to his success. But there also was meticulous advance preparation and attention to finer details to help him make the most of the golden opportunity that each new president has when he first assumes office.

In lining up a staff and mapping plans for the first 120 days, Reagan's top strategists studied recent presidencies, with special emphasis on the Carter administration. They set up an office of planning and evaluation inside the White House designed specifically to avoid past mistakes, in particular, the Carter trap of having several key appointees who were neither personally loyal nor ideologically sympathetic. Reagan and such longtime associates from California as Meese and Michael K. Deaver set about carefully selecting a first-term team made up of loyalists who were ideologically compatible with the conservative president; not only did senior appointees have to demonstrate their commitment to such things as "Reaganomics," but with rare exceptions Cabinet secretaries had to settle for deputies with closer ties to Meese and the White House than to the secretaries themselves.

Moreover, once empaneled, the Reagan Cabinet marched in virtual lock-step, with no one challenging presidential policy once it had been established on top priority issues. In previous administrations, incessant Cabinet bickering plagued even such strong chief executives as Franklin D. Roosevelt. And weaker presidents such as Carter often found themselves ambushed by loose-cannon Cabinet secretaries with political ambitions or policy agendas of their own. No such disloyalty undercut Reagan as he laid the foundations of his presidency, even if serious disagreements did later erupt over national security and foreign policy matters. Whatever internal problems there were, however, did not seem to detract from the president's commanding image.

Reagan's initial action plan setting forth the general direction for the administration's first 120 days was drawn up by Richard Wirthlin, who did polling for the 1980 presidential campaign and became the regular pollster for the White House. His findings had persuaded Wirthlin that, while Americans expected a lot from their president, they also would give him considerable latitude if he was viewed as an agent of positive change.

Many Americans did view Reagan as a force for positive change when he took office in 1981, an attitude that he reinforced by moving swiftly to score early successes. This was done mainly by zeroing in on his well-defined goals. Again, the contrast with Carter was striking.

Carter had started early in his administration pushing for an energy bill in an all-out campaign he called "the moral equivalent of war." Failing to recognize the need for political planning, he had permitted energy secretary James Schlesinger to work in almost total secrecy, drafting a measure so controversial that it led to a long and bitter battle with Capitol Hill. The bill that finally passed eighteen months later bore little resemblance to the president's original plan.

After spending an enormous amount of political capital, Carter himself concluded: "It's complicated. It's contentious. It's very difficult to understand . . . and politically, I don't think anyone could win from it. It was not something that's politically attractive."

There were no such Pyrrhic victories in the early days when Reagan and his crew were establishing his presidency. Understanding both their strengths and the political realities, the new team set out with deliberate design to build a record of trip-hammer accomplishments. The emergence of Reagan as a strong, effective president who could dominate the national stage was a development steeped in irony: The whole idea of a strong presidency is something liberals have traditionally supported and conservatives have customarily opposed. From the 1930s through the 1960s, liberals worked to strengthen the presidency because they believed a president elected by all the people would tend to be more liberal and cosmopolitan than a conservative Congress dominated by Southern Democrats and Republicans. Conservatives long opposed a strong presidency as part of their "small government" dogma. But now the concept of the strong presidency had been revived by one of the most conservative presidents in the nation's history.

Nothing so underscored these ironies as the moving tribute to Reagan in June 1985 from his longtime Democratic critic, Sen. Edward M. Kennedy. At a dinner attended by Reagan at Kennedy's McLean, Virginia, home to raise funds for the John F. Kennedy Memorial Library in Boston, the Massachusetts Democrat lauded his old opponent for restoring the presidency as "a vigorous, purposeful instrument of national leadership on issues." While his brother and Reagan would not have always agreed, Ted Kennedy said, "I know he would have admired the strength of your commitment and your capacity to move the nation."

In the end, this could turn out to be Reagan's greatest legacy. He disproved the notion that the presidency is too big for any one man and that the president and Congress are destined to be constantly at loggerheads. He may have hobbled his successors for years to come by piling up huge federal deficits, but he proved anew that presidents can succeed. Regardless of how he fares in his final years in office, Ronald Reagan's record of strong leadership will make it hard to argue that the presidency has become an obsolete institution.

ROUNDTABLE DISCUSSION

"The Reagan Legacy"

PANELISTS: Paul Duke, *moderator*
Jack Nelson
Charles Corddry
Georgie Anne Geyer
Haynes Johnson
Charles McDowell
Hedrick Smith

DUKE: How much of the Reagan revolution is attributable to the president personally?

NELSON: A tremendous amount of it. And one big reason is that this is a presidency based more on personality than many previous presidencies. Reagan came into office with strong convictions. And he has used his personality—he's not known as the Great Communicator for nothing—to pursue his goals.

The case can be made that there are people in this administration who are more ideological than the president. A good example is Ed Meese, his attorney general. That also may be true of other people who've served on the White House staff.

But you have to say the president is a true believer in what his staff promotes. At the first Cabinet meeting after his reelection, Reagan pulled out a copy of his speech nominating Barry Goldwater at the 1964 Republican convention, and quoted parts that dealt with cutting back the growth of government. He said his words were as true now as they were then. In a way, of course, he's the Barry Goldwater of the 1980s, only this time the man and the moment met whereas in the 1960s the country was not ready for Goldwater.

JOHNSON: Let me be a devil's advocate and say that I'm not sure there has been a Reagan revolution. He has not cut the growth of government, for example. The government actually has expanded under his administration.

NELSON: He's certainly slowed the pace of growth.

CORDDRY: While you probably are right, Haynes, perception is important, and there is a perception that we've had a revolution just the same.

JOHNSON: I use that phrase myself—the Reagan revolution. I may have been the first one to use it. And perhaps in the long run it will prove to be true.

All I'm saying is that the jury is still out and what happens in the second term will determine how many of the changes are lasting.

SMITH: The word revolution suggests a turnaround, and I don't believe there's been a turnaround. But I do believe that Reagan has bent the path of history, that even to slow the rate of growth and to shift the priorities of government from domestic to defense represents a significant change. At the very least there's been an historic pause.

GEYER: Reagan will go down in history as having brought a kind of corrective movement to American democracy. And the effect has been tremendous.

DUKE: One of the important things is a change in tenor and tone. Whether it's a revolution or not, Ronald Reagan is quite different from the Republican presidents that we've had in the recent past, and he has certainly changed the whole philosophical atmosphere in Washington.

SMITH: It's interesting he's been able to do that when he has actually reflected what the public wanted. There's no question that there was an accumulation of public frustration with the growth of government, a belief that too much money was being thrown at problems. This view buttressed Reagan in 1981, and enabled him to hold down spending and to cut taxes. But four years later, in speaking for tax reform, the president did not create a public groundswell and has run into a great deal of trouble with Congress, with his own Republicans, on this top domestic priority of his second term.

NELSON: One of the main reasons is that people are scared to death of the huge deficits that are being rolled up. The public is much more interested in solving that problem than they are in tax simplification.

JOHNSON: And that suggests that unless there is a resolution of the deficit issue, Reagan's legacy may not be very significant.

NELSON: But in some areas he may leave a real imprint. One place could be the federal judiciary, which is now being loaded up with conservative judges, many with a strong ideological bent.

DUKE: Critics say the stumbling block for the Reagan presidency is that he has put forth an agenda to minimize government's role that is too broad, and cannot be implemented because it just will not be accepted by a majority of the public.

So we have the paradox of a president who is terribly popular, but whose program is not. And one reason is many average Americans are not convinced some of the things advocated by the president will benefit them.

NELSON: When his tax-cutting bill first came up in 1981, my son, who was an insurance man making about $30,000 a year, called me up and said, "Dad, what's the president's tax program going to mean for me?" And I said, for you, not much. For me, quite a bit. I was sorry to say that, but it was the truth.

CORDDRY: I would argue, though, that doing something for the middle class was one of his basic objectives.

SMITH: I don't agree. I think that Ronald Reagan planned essentially to leave the middle class alone, leave its programs largely untouched. That's one of the reasons they didn't fiddle around much with Social Security and Medicare and other programs benefiting many middle-class people. The whole notion of freeing up business from heavy taxes, of bringing down the maximum tax rate for individuals, of stimulating venture capital—all of this was aimed at helping the upper class so they would have more incentive to invest.

The tax reform package was a dead giveaway. Here the goal was to do something for those on the bottom rung, to look populist while primarily helping those at the top by substantially lowering top tax rates. The middle class was not greatly affected.

GEYER: They like Reagan anyway, and one reason is that the American people got tired of liberal guilt and being told that we were responsible for all the ills of the world. Ronald Reagan doesn't feel guilty about anything. Maybe the American people feel good because he's relieved that terrible tension.

NELSON: It's been a difficult administration to cover, the most difficult in the fifteen years I've been in Washington. Even the Nixon White House was not locked up as tightly as this one. I think we've done the best we could to paint Reagan, warts and all. But the fact is that he mesmerizes the public. He can say the most outlandish things and nobody seems to care.

I can give you a perfect example. I covered him not long ago in Tampa, Florida, where he spoke to a group of senior citizens on his tax simplification plan, and anybody who got there a few minutes early heard Jeb Bush speak. Jeb Bush is Vice-President George Bush's son and chairman of the Dade County Republican committee. He got up and quoted a Treasury Department study to deny charges that the simplification program would be harmful to most people. "That's absolutely wrong," he said. "The facts are some would lose, some would gain, some would come out even, 58 percent would benefit, 22 percent lose, the rest would remain neutral."

And yet President Reagan came in thirty minutes later and said: "Every group in America would be better off, and anybody who tells you otherwise doesn't understand or deliberately does not want to understand."

Now he wasn't talking about Jeb Bush, and he wasn't talking about his own Treasury Department. He was talking about Governor Cuomo of New York. But the president was totally wrong, and nobody gives a damn. We've written about his falsehoods and mistakes so much we've stopped because people don't pay attention.

JOHNSON: He's one-half of a great leader. In a public, ceremonial sense, Ronald Reagan has all the attributes that make people feel that there's someone in control. He's comfortable with himself. Richard Nixon was always looking at his navel and telling you how bad he felt. Lyndon Johnson was profane and paranoid. Jimmy Carter was so earnest and self-righteous but couldn't command respect. Reagan may not be a good president, but he's a real person and people like that.

McDOWELL: Incredibly real. I sat at the head table of the Gridiron Club banquet—the longest dinner in town—and talked with the president off and on for five hours. I wasn't bored for one minute. I heard every Hollywood story ever conceived, and they weren't the ramblings of a doddering old man at all.

NELSON: Wasn't it Senator Packwood of Oregon who came out of the White House one time and said all the president wants to do is tell old Hollywood stories?

McDOWELL: I got him started by telling him my hometown was Lexington, Virginia, where there's a little school called VMI. He responded immediately, "Oh, yes, that's the school in *Brother Rat*"—a movie he made in the late 1930s. I said I remember when you came to our town, Mr. President, on location with Priscilla Lane and Wayne Morris and Eddie Albert to make that movie. He said, "You do?" I said, "Yes, sir, I remember it well because we had only one taxi in town, Pete's Taxi, and you all hired it for the whole week, and no one could get around. I also remember seeing you in McCrumb's Store." He nodded, he listened courteously, and then he said, "Now, Mr. McDowell, don't take this hard. But I was the only lead in that movie who did not go to Lexington." I was just slayed, having told that story for thirty years. He put his hand on my arm, and he said, "Now what you saw, son, was Wayne Morris, and over the years, you've just gotten to think it was me, and you've gradually convinced yourself it was me, and you believe it was me. Don't you feel bad? I do things like that all the time." [Laughter.]

JOHNSON: Wonderful story. That explains why he's so good with the political people.

DUKE: Everybody who goes to see him at the White House remarks about how charming he is and how he loves to tell Hollywood stories. But there's a downside to this as well. Congressional leaders criticize him because they can't get him to focus on legislative issues. Indeed, many of them think he's not all that interested in governmental affairs. Speaker O'Neill told of being at a White House dinner party one night and sitting at the same table with the president and a couple of others. For about fifteen minutes the president was silent. Finally, to bring him into the conversation, the Speaker asked the president a question about his old Hollywood days, and he said it was like turning on a lightbulb, that the president just lit up and proceeded to entertain everybody for the rest of the evening. But it was all about Hollywood, not Washington.

CORDDRY: Does he know what he's doing? Is he somebody who's string is pulled, and if so, who pulls the string? I think that the man knows what he's doing.

NELSON: I think that most of the time he knows what he's doing. And even though he lacks details on a lot of issues, something that's apparent at his press conferences, he's not a puppet being yanked around by Ed Meese or Jim Baker or someone else. He makes major decisions by himself. One example was the choice of career diplomat Walter Stoessel to be deputy secretary of state, even though the president's top aides all wanted a political appointee in that job because traditionally it had been one. In this case, Secretary of State Haig wanted Stoessel, precipitating a big fight. Lyn Nofziger, the White House political officer, said he got a call to come over to help other assistants argue the president out of the appointment, so he went to the Oval Office where they tried to convince the president. Vice-President Bush and Jim Baker and all the rest told him he was wrong, that he needed a political man in the job. Reagan sat there listening for forty-five minutes of argument, and when they got through, said, "Well, I'm sorry, but I've made my decision, and Walter Stoessel is my man."

JOHNSON: It makes you realize how wrong some of the perceptions have been—that he was stupid, lazy, an old hack of an actor. The fact is, this is a president who knows exactly what he wants to do and is prepared to take some risks.

I thought Ronald Reagan was the most ignorant major candidate I'd ever seen running for president. I did not think he'd be effective. Traveling with him, listening to him, having lunch with him; the man's lack of knowledge was astonishing. I misjudged him. I was wrong. He has been a far more successful political figure than I gave him credit for being.

DUKE: His success has been mind-boggling. I read somewhere that Reagan's old football coach said he thought he'd just be a radio announcer—that he never dreamed he'd wind up in politics.

JOHNSON: He was terribly underrated at first. I remember Tip O'Neill saying contemptuously when he came to town, "Welcome to the big leagues, Mr. President." And then telling me two years later, "Hey, he's better than my Jack," Jack Kennedy.

SMITH: He's turned out to be a complex figure like FDR and other presidents who made major changes. He's both stubborn and a compromiser.

GEYER: Or is he a person who's really quite simple? He goes by certain maxims in his life, and they're repeated over and over—hard work, individual responsibility—things that I was raised on and feel strongly about, too, and yet, a lot of them don't really carry through in Reagan's life or in the lives of people around him. And I must say, for all his talk about America being strong once more, he has been close to a disaster in foreign policy.

If we look at what he has accomplished, it is virtually nothing. We've made progress in Central America, but the Middle East is a disaster. The Russians have not been handled with any deftness at all. The Philippines could blow up anytime. And we've had no arms control agreement. Where is the brilliance?

CORDDRY: I don't think it's all that bad. He may understand the Russians better than any president we've had.

The Soviet Union, for whatever reason, has been

very well behaved for the last four or five years, and they take him utterly seriously. So on that score, I think that he's done quite well. I tend to believe that the insistence on arms-control agreements is a great academic enterprise, and I'm not sure that the people of this country are as keen on new agreements as they are on seeing that the Russians abide by the ones we've already reached. I don't think they trust the Russians. Reagan represents a majority of the people in that respect.

SMITH: I simply don't think the case can be made that Reagan has made a difference. The Russians had basically absorbed about as much as they could handle before Reagan came in. That is, they'd run up gains for their side in Afghanistan, Angola, and Cambodia, in Vietnam, in South Yemen, in Ethiopia, and they had a lot of trouble digesting what they'd already taken.

I don't see any evidence that since Reagan came in and we've stepped up our aid to the Afghan rebels that the Soviets are any more inclined to get out of that country. Or that our support for the Contras in Nicaragua has made the Russians any less inclined to continue pouring in material to Central America.

DUKE: Jack and Rick—you were at the Geneva Summit Conference last November. Did the meeting with Gorbachev change the president's perceptions about the Soviet Union?

NELSON: If you listen to what the president himself says, it did change him because he said in an on-the-record session at the White House after the summit that he sincerely believed that Gorbachev meant exactly what he said, that his fears about Star Wars were genuine. He talked about having respect for Gorbachev and so did the other U.S. officials, by the way.

DUKE: Somebody said the big benefit of the summit meeting was that it brought Ronald Reagan face to face with reality.

SMITH: There's no question Reagan for the first time had to confront somebody who was really arguing hard against Star Wars with him face to face, toe to toe, darned near at every meeting they had for two days solid.

Secondly, that they were arguing about the basic question of trust—can we trust you, do you think I'm going to launch a first strike? I mean, they were saying things like that to each other.

DUKE: The summit meeting raised hopes for at least a minithaw in East-West relations.

SMITH: We've seen that happen with other summits. In 1955 there was the spirit of Geneva between Eisenhower and Khrushchev, and it went out the window with the Soviet invasion of Hungary in 1956. In 1959, there was the spirit of Camp David between Eisenhower and Khrushchev again. It went out the window in May of 1960 because of the shooting down of the U-2 spy plane.

So there's always the potential in Soviet-American relations that things can be quickly thrown off track. But this summit last November did get the two countries engaged with each other again, to start back with little agreements on civil aviation, consulates, cultural exchanges.

NELSON: Paul, you and I were at a background briefing a couple of days ago with one of the summit participants—a Russian embassy official—who said privately the Soviets do not regard Star Wars as the stumbling block that they claim publicly. He held out, I thought, considerable hope that they may give on that question.

SMITH: Gorbachev himself has said research is tolerable because you can't monitor it. And I've heard people on both sides talk about ground testing being permitted.

The difficulty is that Reagan and Gorbachev never got into that. The two leaders stood very firmly on their basic positions. Presumably in the spring and summer of 1986, before the next summit, there could be movement on this issue. Whether or not they can close the gap and strike a deal is another question.

DUKE: There were a lot of stories about the president preparing for the conference, that his advisers wanted to be sure he didn't make any gaffes.

The question I'd like to put to you is: Was Reagan Reagan in Geneva?

NELSON: Reagan was Reagan in Geneva, although I thought it was rather interesting that at the sessions with the press he seemed uptight. I gather he was advised not to say too much openly or it might somehow screw up the summit. Gorbachev, on the other hand, was loose and even humorous, talking a lot.

At the private sessions, though, Reagan was pretty much himself. He was tough in criticizing the Soviets on Afghanistan and human rights. Reagan was prepared. At one point he even noted that one Soviet official had talked about his movies being B grade. He told Gorbachev he should know that they weren't all B grade. Gorbachev said, well, he understood that because he had seen one movie where Reagan played a fellow with no legs, and Reagan said yes, that was *King's Row*. So, you know, there was a little bit of Hollywood talk. They got along extremely well. That was obvious.

GEYER: I think we saw Ronald Reagan not only being Reagan but Reagan at his very best.

If you look at the pictures of those days, Reagan was extremely graceful. I've never seen him more consciously generous. I was really stunned at how well he did.

Something else that Richard Pipes, the hard-liner Sovietologist, has pointed out was the extraordinary civility of Gorbachev. We've never seen Soviet leaders be that human, that civil in their discourse. And without going too far, I think we can see the beginning of a new generation of Soviet leaders a little less paranoid, a little less accusatory.

NELSON: Gorbachev is somebody very much in control. I went to his press conference, and I thought he was a dynamic guy. He's one helluva speaker. He started speaking from notes in the beginning. He wound up speaking extemporaneously. He talked for about an hour and then he took questions, and he was extremely impressive—and I thought he was throughout the summit, from what you could see of him anyway.

DUKE: Rick, as an old Moscow correspondent, how formidable do you regard Gorbachev?

SMITH: There's no question that this is a guy who has taken hold of the reins of power decisively. American officials said that when they discussed the joint communiqué that Gorbachev would listen and respond immediately. He operated self-confidently, and there's every reason to believe that he's operating that way at home.

He still has to worry about keeping the military happy and keeping the civilian sectors happy. He has a huge establishment where he's got to play off different factions and different constituencies. But when people know that the number-one guy is going to be around for a long time, since he's only fifty-five, they pay a lot more attention to him.

JOHNSON: We don't know the answer to the big question—what impact all this has had on Reagan. Has he changed? Will he now take the lead for arms control?

DUKE: Many see that as the issue—whether he goes down as a peacemaker or a warmaker.

NELSON: One of his close advisers told me he didn't see how Reagan could ever achieve a meaningful arms control agreement because he's so distrustful of the Soviets and has such contempt for them.

On the other hand, Senator Laxalt told me that he thought that his most lasting legacy might well be in the nuclear control area. He said he told him shortly after the assassination attempt, "You know, Ron"—and he calls him Ron—"Ron, the Lord didn't let you survive to save the economy. He let you survive to save the world."

Laxalt said Reagan didn't disagree, that he's going to do his best to achieve a breakthrough on controlling weapons. There's also Nancy Reagan. Many people at the White House say she's more conscious of his place in history than he is and that she wants an agreement with the Russians. So, you can't rule it out. After all, Reagan is the consummate poker player who never reveals his hand until the last minute.

DUKE: Mike Deaver, who was the deputy White House chief, has said: "Behind the hard line there is much flexibility. You don't see a lot of pride expressed by Ronald Reagan, but in the area of negotiation, he does take pride. He thinks of himself as a negotiator, and he knows when to compromise."

SMITH: That's why he's a complex figure. If you take certain basic beliefs that he has, such as getting government off your back, cutting the budget, cutting taxes, mistrust of the Russians, building up defense, appointing his kind of people to the courts, then he pursues a definite course.

But then you look at the other side, and he says at one point "I'm against sanctions against South Africa," but within a couple of weeks he's flip-flopped. He got an enormous tax cut in 1981, then accepted one of the largest tax increases in American history in 1982 and additional hikes in '83 and '84.

That to me is a complex figure, in the way he operates and the way he thinks politically.

NELSON: Lyn Nofziger was with him all the time he was governor, and for a while at the White House. And he claims Reagan is essentially a reasonable man, that he's not a zealot or fanatic who closes his mind to the other side of the argument. Right-wing critics within his own party have fought Reagan for soft-peddling Soviet violations of the SALT II treaty and for failing to retaliate after the Beirut hostage crisis in '85. He knows what he can do and what he can't do, and he always has.

GEYER: What you're saying is that Ronald Reagan is a political animal and a good negotiator who knows when to cut his losses. That's fine. I still believe he's more simple than complex because he doesn't possess well-rounded knowledge.

CORDDRY: I don't know whether this is simplicity or complexity, but he strikes me as a man with a few ideas that he won't deviate from, and he just keeps his eye on the top targets.

He may not understand all the details of Star Wars, but he knows one thing. He knows that the idea of mutual extinction is not a particularly sound one, and he says, All right, maybe we can figure out a way to prevent ourselves from being extinguished; and he gets one or two people to agree with that. He says, Go get it. And we're going to have arguments for forty years at least on whether this can be done.

SMITH: Reagan understands that politics is emotional and symbolic. Politics is not rational and logical, it doesn't come out of some kind of ledger.

McDOWELL: The people look at Ronald Reagan when he makes a mistake or is ignorant about something and they ask, "Did it really hurt us, was he venal, was he bad, was he trying to trick us?" And their answer to all those things is no, and they forgive him because the good heart of him is clear to them.

JOHNSON: Americans are not looking for a philosopher king. But if the record finally is one of failure, I think they will remember the president's mistakes all too well. This is the risk.

SMITH: We don't know the final judgment because the Reagan legacy is unfinished on the two most critical issues of the day: the economy, and war and peace.

JOHNSON: I would add a third potential legacy and that is as a political campaigner. He has set an example, which may be bad, because he has won with simplicities, but nonetheless many politicians are now looking at Ronald Reagan as the guy to emulate.

McDOWELL: Reagan has taught the political world that to be effective on television you have to seem to communicate with people right out of your own authenticity, even if it be full of flaws and ignorance. The fundamental effect is in the practice halls and sound stages of political commercials where people are being taught relax, man, just be yourself, just be how you are, don't sit so stiff, don't hold up a sign, don't have a visual, just talk to the folks. That's a profound change in how people politic.

NELSON: Yeah, and the irony is he got his polish not from television but from the thousands of after-dinner speeches and lectures over the years.

SMITH: Reagan has patented a new art form in politics in the visual press release. When he wants to say the economy is improving and housing starts are up, he goes to a housing development somewhere to emphasize the point, and the impression gets across to the guy and his wife sitting home watching the television set at night that indeed the economy is getting better.

That's what we mean by the Great Communicator. It is not just some artful makeup, it is the effective communication of a political message. Politics is a lot closer to acting than a lot of us want to admit and having been an actor is not a liability, although many people in the Republican Party were worried that that was going to be an issue in the 1980 campaign.

But there is a real risk, too, because what works in campaigning doesn't necessarily work in governing. One of the things that was most effective in Reagan's campaign for reelection was his theme that, "It's Morning Again in America." He was able to get away without clearly defining a second-term agenda, and one of the results is he is finding it much harder to govern in the second term.

NELSON: There was no mandate.

JOHNSON: What he's promised is a happy ending, and that remains to be seen.

SMITH: But they knew there was going to be an unhappy beginning with Walter Mondale, who promised higher taxes. Hence, the landslide.

DUKE: Has the presidency changed Reagan?

NELSON: I don't think it has. I remember when he named William Ruckelshaus to replace Anne Burford as EPA administrator, somebody asked whether it meant he was changing his policies on environmental control. And he said, "I'm too old to change."

CORDDRY: And yet he's shown an amazing capacity to go after the things he wants. I gave a lecture at one of the war colleges after he was elected and before he became president, and I told the mid-career students not to expect all that they obviously were expecting because the Congress would never approve whopping increases in national defense at the expense of social programs.

Mr. Reagan had been in office less than twenty days

when I asked one of his officials what they were going to do, and he quite calmly and casually told me they were going to go to Congress and get thirty-two extra billion dollars. This was *before* many in the top layers of the Defense Department knew what the president's intentions were, and I was absolutely astounded at the way he was able to sell Congress on the defense buildup.

McDOWELL: If somebody had told me in 1979 that Ronald Reagan by common consent would be ranked with Franklin Roosevelt as one of the two most important presidents of the century I've lived in, I would have walked away from such a trivial person, shaking my head and saying there's no hope for any of us if anyone thinks that, and I now think that.

SMITH: We all like a good story, and I have to admit near the end of Jimmy Carter's presidency, I was looking out my office window one day across to the White House, and I began thinking, My God, am I fated to be a journalist in Washington during the twentieth-century equivalent of Millard Fillmore, Zachary Taylor, Franklin Pierce, or James Buchanan, the nineteenth-century nonentities? Is there going to be a Lincoln during my tenure here in Washington?

I'm not saying we have a Lincoln but we have had one helluva story. And interestingly, the Reagan crowd set out to capture the press and have done a much better job than the Democrats in getting their message out, even though this is a rather inaccessible White House.

We have to admit that we are captivated to some degree by somebody who's likable, by somebody who relates to you, and Reagan has been enormously effective at personal press relations.

NELSON: The first time I interviewed Reagan was in Charleston, South Carolina, in 1968 when he was governor of California. He landed in a small plane, and

Lyn Nofziger got out with a jar of jellybeans and handed them around to reporters. Reagan impressed me then as he does today by the way he handles reporters. He gives you the answer to whatever he is thinking about, not necessarily to your question.

SMITH: I've interviewed him several times over the years and almost every question I asked got answered by a human cassette recorder. There was a programmed answer that came out, and he translated the question into a trigger for things he wanted to say. We had no dialogue, there was no discovery. Contrary to what some say, the storytelling does not let you get to know him. It tells you about the old Reagan but not about his conduct of the presidency.

It's a mechanism for avoidance rather than direct communication. But when you're sitting there by the fire in the Oval Office, six or eight feet away, and tossing him a bunch of questions, he leans into the answers the same way your neighbor does. At least you get a sense that, hey, this is a particular issue about which the president cares. And if you're reading the text of the interview in the newspaper, you simply don't get that feeling.

DUKE: I once interviewed Reagan for Public Broadcasting, and I tried to be different in my approach—pursuing his Hollywood days and whether he felt his training as an actor had enabled him to become a better politician. He wouldn't take the bait. As we've all discovered, he just won't be led down any primrose paths. In my case, he took off on how the governorship had prepared him and cited all the things about welfare reform and other accomplishments that we've heard hundreds of times. It's just impossible to get beyond the outer edges, to get him to be reflective or philosophical. He's going to go where he wants to when you interview him.

GEYER: Psychologically, I think he shuts out. He doesn't seem to understand suffering and injustice in the world. He doesn't want to know.

NELSON: There's an awful lot of truth in that. People have suffered under his presidency in my opinion. Blacks have suffered, low-income whites have suffered, farmers have suffered.

SMITH: And it's a more divided society.

DUKE: One in which the rich are getting richer and the poor poorer.

NELSON: No question. Most of his life he has been in California, mainly around the unreal world of Hollywood, where some multimillionaires took him in tow. They were the ones who engineered him into politics.

CORDDRY: We've all heard those stories about how he's also ignored his own grandchildren.

NELSON: And Jim Brady, his press secretary, who took a bullet for him. I know that Sarah Brady is upset because they're almost never invited to the White House. One day the White House called a number of people to come over for a little ceremony to give Brady a mug with Reagan's likeness on it. The idea was to use the mug as a gift to raise money for the Jim Brady Foundation to take care of people injured in the line of duty. Brady was sitting in his wheelchair, and Reagan came in and said, "Hi, Jim," stepped up to the microphone, pulled out his index cards, read from them for about a minute, turned around and went back into the Oval Office. He never even talked to Brady. I stood there dumbfounded.

DUKE: Is the president insensitive to unpleasant things?

NELSON: Well, on the one hand you have to say that at times he shows real compassion when people have suffered personal tragedies. After a plane crashed in Newfoundland just before Christmas, 1985, killing

250 paratroops of the 101st Airborne Division, Reagan attended a memorial service for the victims at Ft. Campbell, Kentucky. It was a typical gesture; he's probably spent more time than any president of recent times personally consoling relatives of servicemen killed in the line of duty. When a nephew of mine, Ronald Nelson, a member of the Special Forces, was killed in a training accident in Panama in 1983, the president telephoned not only my brother and his wife in Canton, Georgia, but also called me in my Washington office. He emphasized that Ronnie had died in the service of his country. It was a gesture that deeply touched us.

On the other hand, he does seem to be insensitive to some of the injustices and other unpleasant aspects of society. And that may be due to his lack of a broader life experience. For example, when he talks about civil rights he harks back to his Illinois youth, suggesting blacks weren't treated so badly. I don't think he understands the truly heinous crimes that have been committed against blacks in our society. He doesn't seem to understand that we're still a racist society. I'm sure he thinks the problem has been licked here just as he thinks it's been licked in South Africa.

CORDDRY: You raise a new question here. Was John Kennedy the last president who made it his business to go out and find out things for himself?

NELSON: No, most presidents have understood what the civil rights struggle was all about. Jimmy Carter did. By God, he'd been out in it. LBJ did. And when he said, "We shall overcome," I think he was probably serious about righting a lot of wrongs.

CORDDRY: Kennedy was always leaping out of his car and buying newspapers, reading them and calling up officials wanting to know why some problem was not being dealt with.

GEYER: Kennedy could do what Reagan cannot—that is, empathize on a realistic level with people and their problems. Reagan doesn't even begin to understand the forces at work in the world.

SMITH: What you're talking about is intellectual curiosity in a president. Does he want to know more about the world than when he came into office?

That's not the hallmark of Ronald Reagan. But the irony is that you had a president like Jimmy Carter who was obsessed with details, who wanted to know everything but wasn't effective. Here you have a president who is not curious, but whose political strength is that he doesn't change. And yet that's a weakness in dealing with the rest of the world.

JOHNSON: What we're all saying is that a lot of caveats and qualifiers and reservations must be attached to the Reagan record at this point. He could go down as a failure like Warren Harding, who was the most beloved president of his time until events caught up with him in the 1920s.

SMITH: We don't know whether it comes out B-plus or D-minus or A-plus or B-minus.

NELSON: We have a strong president who has succeeded in getting a lot of the things he wants and has proved the institution of the presidency is alive and flourishing, but we still don't know whether it's good for the country or bad for the country.

Congress: Will There Be Realignment?

Hedrick Smith

HEDRICK SMITH, 52, has been with the *New York Times* since 1961. He represented the newspaper in Vietnam and the Middle East and has served as *Times* bureau chief in both Moscow and Washington. He was a member of the Pulitzer Prize-winning team that wrote *The Pentagon Papers* in 1971, and won a Pulitzer Prize for International Reporting in 1974 for coverage from Moscow and Eastern Europe. His book *The Russians,* which won an Overseas Press Club book award and was an international best-seller, was reissued in 1983. Since 1975, Rick Smith has concentrated on American politics, the presidency, Congress and national politics. He was born in Scotland and has been on the move ever since. He has been appearing regularly on *Washington Week* since the mid-1970s.

It dawned cold and damp in Washington on January 4, 1985. By afternoon, some reporters wrapped in overcoats and stamping their feet in the cold had gathered on the sidewalk outside Blair House, the official government guest house just across Pennsylvania Avenue from the White House. Not only is Blair House often used for visiting chiefs of state, but newly elected presidents like Ronald Reagan and Jimmy Carter have perched there during the transition period before they enter the White House. In short, Blair House is an important political site with historic overtones and symbolism of the presidency.

But the reporters huddled under their umbrellas in a freezing rain that day were not awaiting a new president or a foreign statesman. They were waiting for the new Senate Majority Leader, Robert Dole of Kansas, who had daringly summoned President Reagan's top White House aides to a high-level strategy meeting on the budget at Blair House. It was barely two months since President Reagan's stunning landslide reelection in November 1984, and here was Dole, acting like something of a usurper practically under the president's nose.

With him were twenty-six Senate Republicans. They had gathered to hear David Stockman, the Reagan budget director, spin a gloomy report on the spiraling federal deficit. It was a familiar litany and a familiar tactic for Stockman, who found over five years in that office that it took the cold shock of pessimism about the federal deficit to ignite serious action from Congress. He was not above using such scare tactics on President Reagan himself. On that day, however, Stockman was preaching to a band of believers. For instead of being discouraged, the Republican senators were fired up by his sour sermon. They gave each other pep talks about freezing the budget and slashing popular programs.

After several hours, Dole emerged bareheaded and coatless and was immediately engulfed by the reporters. He stood tall and trim, head tilted a bit to one side, his good left arm wrapped around a limp right arm, still crippled by wounds from World War II. The reporters asked Dole about a budget freeze. "We've got a freeze already," he wisecracked, brown eyes rolling at the leaden skies. Then he set a bold target—to produce a Senate Republican budget package by February 1, that would cut the federal budget deficit by $50 billion.

I remember thinking at the time that even for Dole, who has a reputation for assertive independence, this was brash. For here he was in his first few days as the new Majority Leader, setting the monumental goal of bringing the deficit under control. Dole was well aware of the difficulties that lay ahead. First, his ambitious strategy meant challenging his party leader, the president, who felt strongly that defense spending should be off-limits to serious restraints and who resolutely opposed any tax increases to trim the deficit. Second, Dole would risk the ire of millions of voters if he tampered with the sacrosanct Social Security system, including the annual inflation adjustment which more than thirty million elderly recipients counted on. Finally, this meant taking on the Democrats, who had cast themselves as the holy protectors of Social Security.

But if the risks were great, so were the stakes. For in Dole's eyes, Republican control of the Senate was riding on the deficit issue. It had taken the Republicans twenty-six long years to break the Democratic monopoly control in Congress, dating back to 1954. Riding Ronald Reagan's coattails in 1980, they finally scored the breakthrough that gave them control of the Senate. And though the Democrats extended their long reign in the House of Representatives—the longest in history—the Republicans held the Senate through the 1982 and 1984 elections.

But Dole knew that the real test lay ahead in 1986. Twenty-two Republican Senate seats would be contested in 1986 and some of those Republicans were dangerously vulnerable to defeat, especially if the economy turned down. In Dole's view, it was imperative for Republicans to tame the deficit. While the White House leaned toward making tax reform its number-one priority for the 99th Congress, Dole's political soundings persuaded him that voters were far more worried about snowballing deficits.

This was the flip side, the hidden risk in the Reagan economic program. For while the president had won a landslide reelection in 1984 and polls showed the public credited Reagan and the Republicans with bringing about economic recovery, there was now a danger that Republicans would be saddled with the blame—or much of it—for the perilous deficit. Thus, Dole argued that only by some drastic budget-cutting could Republicans keep economic recovery going and save their political skins and their slim fifty-three to forty-seven Senate majority. Otherwise, their precious gains would be lost. Privately, he told me: "If we fall flat on the deficit, we're in deep trouble."

The deficit issue had even broader implications for the long-term future of the Republican Party. For in recent years, many politicians, pollsters, and reporters had detected shifts and undercurrents among the electorate favorable to

Republicans. The stunning Reagan victory of 1984 had stirred hope among Repulican leaders that the party could go on to greater gains. They hoped to produce a national political realignment that would firmly end the long Democratic domination dating back to Franklin Delano Roosevelt and make Republicans the nation's majority party in the final decades of this century. Ever since Dwight Eisenhower broke into the Democratic West and the once Solid South in 1952, Republican strategists had been predicting such a watershed. The dream took hold in the Eisenhower presidency, twice under Richard Nixon, and after both the Reagan victories, in 1980 and 1984.

That string of Republican presidential triumphs, four out of the last five elections, had persuaded many of us that a dramatic shift of political allegiances had taken place at the presidential level. But it is my view that the Republicans cannot yet claim to be a new majority party because they have insufficient strength in congressional races and further down the ballot at the grass roots. Each time, their hopes of a grand realignment has been dashed by the split-ticket voting habits of millions of Americans who keep putting Democratic majorities back in control of the House of Representatives as well as in most governorships and state legislatures.

Now, once again, after the second Reagan sweep and after retaining control of the Senate, Republicans dared to believe they were riding a new crest. After the 1984 election I visited with Senator Paul Laxalt, the silver-haired Nevadan who is the president's closest friend in Congress and whom Reagan had installed as the general chairman of the Republican Party. "We're on the threshold of a golden era of Republican politics," Laxalt said exuberantly, luxurious leather cowboy boots showing fashionably beneath his well-pressed suit trousers. "We've got Ronald Reagan and the economy, plus a solid Sun Belt base, while the traditional coalitions in the Northeast are crumbling." His lieutenant, party chairman Frank Fahrenkopf, echoed that optimism. "The prospects and outlook are perhaps the best we've had in fifty years," Fahrenkopf boasted. He was pointing, he said, toward a steady Republican buildup at the grassroots aimed at a Republican takeover of Congress in 1992.

Indeed, the dimensions of President Reagan's forty-nine-state landslide had shaken Democratic confidence. But within months, Democratic leaders felt they had rebounded enough to call the Reagan victory of 1984 the high-water mark of the conservative tide rather than the springboard toward greater Republican strength. In 1986, both parties sensed an important test for these long-term trends. For more than a year, their maneuvering has been driven by the question of whether the political pendulum will continue to swing toward the right or begin to swing back toward the center. And in this struggle, the deficit and the economy are the key issues. Other issues may claim attention—trade, taxes, South Africa, Nicaragua, defense, social issues. But this is preeminently the era of deficit politics.

For Bob Dole, the Republican confrontation with the budget has special significance for his dreams of running for the presidency in 1988. I could not help but think what a remarkable turnabout it was for him to be taking the lead on that bleak day in January at Blair House. Twice before he had seemed on the skids politically. Arriving in Washington in 1969 as a freshman House member from Kansas, Dole had quickly established a reputation as a down-the-line supporter of the Nixon White House. His loyalty won him a choice plum two years later as Republican national chairman. But this job revealed Dole's brash and sometimes abrasive independence, and in 1973 he was unceremoniously dumped by President Nixon. That turned out to be a lucky break because it distanced him from Watergate and left him untainted.

To the surprise of many, he was drawn into the limelight once again in 1976 by landing a spot on the Republican ticket as President Gerald Ford's running mate, replacing Nelson Rockefeller. But once again Dole was upended, for he developed a hatchet-man image in that campaign. Some Republicans felt that his cutting attacks on the Democrats boomeranged badly and helped Jimmy Carter to squeak through to a narrow victory. The next winter Dole joked ruefully that the only person he had really hurt with his tongue was himself. It was a bitter lesson that seemed to transform Dole and soften his partisan edge. He learned to turn his sharp wit against himself and to turn his mastery of substantive issues and political acumen to the cause of legislative leadership on a range of issues from civil rights and food stamps to tax law.

By late 1984, Dole had reestablished himself as a major force in Republican ranks with a strong record of achievement. The Senate Finance Committee, which he headed, became a bastion of his personal power. His position and leadership experience made him a logical choice to succeed Howard Baker as the Senate majority leader when Baker retired to prepare his own run at the presidency in 1988. A majority of Senate Republicans viewed Dole as the kind of independent-minded pragmatic conservative who would stand up to the White House and take the heat for fellow Republicans facing reelection. "He can work with the administration and not cave in to the administration" was the way Missouri's John Danforth put it in his nominating speech.

Elected the most powerful Republican on Capitol Hill, Dole gained a platform for his presidential ambitions and a chance to shape the economic debate. As a traditionalist from the midwest heartland, he believed the deficits mattered deeply and the country could ignore them only at future peril. As the leader of the Senate majority, he took seriously his responsibility for making government work. Often, he chided Young Turk Republicans in the House as a minority who had the luxury of political guerrilla tactics and airy theorizing. Specifically, he cast barbed aspersions at the Republican New Right theology of supply-side economics, which downgraded deficits in favor of growth-oriented strategies. Quite openly, he showed his disdain for Representative Jack Kemp of Buffalo, the leader of the Young Turks in the House and a vigorous apostle of the supply-side creed.

At fifty, Kemp has the blow-dried telegenic handsomeness of the new, media breed of politicians and the raw energy of an athlete-turned-politician. A former professional football quarterback, he proudly wears the heavy gold championship ring of the Buffalo Bills. Without the levers of power that the Senate Republican leaders can command, Kemp has taken his case to the hustings and to the television talk shows. He has underscored his serious concern for economic policy-making in speech after speech and as a cosponsor of an international conference on monetary reform last fall. His personal vigor and the populist thrust he has given his supply-side philosophy have made him the darling of the Republican right wing, including both some of the oldest, staunchest Reagan partisans as well as young bloods. Watching him in operation, I have long felt that Kemp stirs more excitement around the country than in Washington itself.

As the dynamic leader of the Young Turks in the House, Kemp has risen to become Chairman of the House Republican Conference. He has used that platform to preach the need for carrying on the optimistic Reagan gospel. Quite openly, he has derided Dole's approach as a replay of the old-fashioned fiscal conservativism that has bored or alienated important groups of swing voters and kept Republicans a minority party for decades. "The Republican Party lost this country economically with an almost obsessive concern with a balanced budget," Kemp told me during an interview in his congressional office.

In Kemp's scheme of things, the key to the nation's prosperity and to bringing budget deficits under control is cutting taxes, especially for those in the top brackets and those at the very bottom. By revamping the old tax system to help entrepreneurs with lower corporate tax rates and longer depreciation schedules, he sees a way to help raise capital for new business that would both power economic growth for the nation and conquer the ballooning deficits. "My priority is preventing recession and getting the economy to a higher rate of growth," he is fond of saying. Kemp pitched his own tax plan, a prototype for the eventual Reagan plan, to try to cement the support of blue-collar, middle-class voters and thus insure their party the new recruits to achieve a long-term political realignment. His constant refrain in early 1985 was: "Tax reform is a realigning issue."

Dole and Kemp, then, are natural rivals. Their rift is a classic battle full of personal sniping and the rivalries of different generations, different regions, different interests. At bottom, it reflects a fundamental divide over Republican philosophy, strategy, and priorities. It pits the New Right against the traditionalist wing of the Republican Party. Their first dramatic confrontation came during the Republican National Convention in Dallas in 1984 when Kemp succeeded over Dole's opposition in getting much of his economic growth philosophy written into the party platform and used for the Reagan election campaign. And once President Reagan had been reelected, they fell again to arguing over Republican priorities in 1985 and gearing up for their personal competition in 1988.

For the Reagan White House, and indeed for Republican hopes of realignment, this open rift poses problems. I remember Ed Rollins, the Reagan campaign manager who became the White House political director, remarking to me sadly: "The post-Reagan era began the morning after his reelection." What he meant was that the scramble to succeed

Reagan four years hence haunted him even before he was inaugurated in 1985 and plagued the White House effort to manage Congress all last year and this.

Quite naturally, Reagan's sweeping reelection victory had awakened expectations that in Congress his second term would begin with the kind of legislative blitzkrieg that had marked his first year in the White House. Back in 1981, Republican unity had been the hallmark of his success. But in 1985, the deep Republican divide made for a stuttering start to the second term. For eventually, Republicans broke with the president both on the budget and on other issues like the military buildup, on sanctions against South Africa, on farm price supports, and on trade legislation, forcing him to reverse some of his policies. Even where he won some votes, on aid to the Nicaraguan rebels, on the MX missile, and on programs of research into space defense, the split in Republican ranks was a factor in forcing the president to settle for less than what he wanted.

In short, the Senate Republican rumbling over the budget that cold January day in 1985 was the first clear signal that despite one of the most stupendous election landslides in modern American history, Ronald Reagan was being treated by Congress as something of a lame duck even as he took his second-term oath of office. To me, it was an ironic lesson in the ways of Washington. In 1981, both Republicans and Democrats were under the spell of the Reagan victory in 1980. His election coupled with Republican gains of thirty-three seats in the House and the takeover of the Senate loomed like a political Matterhorn over Washington. The ease with which Reagan had swept through many southern districts made many southern conservative "boll weevil" Democrats eager to strike deals with the new president.

But in 1984, Reagan won a far bigger landslide numerically and yet one of the most striking political surprises of

1985 was how quickly many politicians discounted that enormous personal victory. Very rapidly they turned their eyes on the election of 1986. For Democrats who had survived both 1980 and 1984 knew they had weathered the worst and were far less cowed than four years previously. And Republicans sensed that they would all too soon be doing battle without their incredibly popular president at the head of their ticket. The choice of a new campaign was under way.

On the budget issue, the White House seesawed between Kemp and Dole. Initially, back in February, the Reagan inner circle publicly welcomed Dole's budget initiative but privately some officials made it plain the President himself was rankled at being upstaged so openly. And when Dole missed his own deadline for action and assigned the deficit headache to the Senate Budget Committee, I heard White House aides chortling their I-told-you-so's, delighted that Dole had stubbed his toe. But they underestimated Dole's tenacity and when he got the process rolling again, the new White House chief of staff, Donald Regan, threw in his lot with the Senate leader. With some difficulty, Regan got President Reagan to swallow Dole's budget prescription, even the unpleasant medicine on cutting the Pentagon budget and freezing Social Security benefits for a year. White House lobbyists helped Dole corral wavering Republican votes and Vice-President George Bush dramatically cast the tie-breaking vote that gave Dole's ambitious budget for $50 billion-plus in cuts a precarious fifty to forty-nine majority. When that ran into trouble in the House, the Dole group began pushing President Reagan to accept some tax increases as part of an even bolder plan to reduce the deficit.

But by then, the Kemp counterattack was fully under way. Like House Democratic leaders, the Kemp Republicans wanted no part of freezing Social Security benefits—for fear the Democrats would use the issue to club them in the 1986 campaign. They had no enthusiasm generally for deep budget cuts and they adamantly opposed any tax increases. In short, they wanted to sidestep the risks of Dole's painful austerity politics in the belief that a surge in economic growth would bring down the deficit. Secretly, in late June, Kemp and his ally Trent Lott of Mississippi, the House Republican whip, carried their opposition to the Dole plan to Don Regan at the White House.

The pressure from the Kemp zealots paid off. The president soon caved in and parted company with the Senate Republicans, joining forces with House Republicans and—surprisingly—also with House Speaker Thomas P. O'Neill, Jr., in favor of a less drastic budget-cutting plan and against freezing Social Security benefits in 1986. Dole and his Senate Republicans, rejected and undercut by their own president, erupted in fury. "The president has sold us down the river," acidly protested Senator Slade Gorton of Washington. "The agony of getting a budget" and "walking the plank" on Social Security has been wasted, complained Bill Cohen of Maine. Bitterly, Dole himself accused the president and Tip O'Neill of "surrendering to the deficit."

Indeed, the final budget package approved by the legislators some months later lacked the cutting edge of the president's original proposals. He had recommended eliminating more than twenty federal programs to force structural changes in government, and he finally accepted a budget that killed only one major program—revenue sharing with state and local governments. It was a crushing disappointment to those who saw the first months of the Reagan second term as their most favorable opportunity for a major attack on the deficit. "We've lost our best shot," worried Representative Dick Cheney of Wyoming, a traditional-minded House Republican leader. "After seven months of blood, sweat, and tears, we have come to this sorry state," groaned Senator

Warren Rudman of New Hampshire, a leader among the thirteen freshman Republicans who had ridden the Reagan tide into office in 1980. The Democrats crowed. "It is now obvious that the administration has no plan whatever for dramatically cutting the federal deficits," chirped Speaker O'Neill.

After years of being on the defensive about federal spending, the Democrats now hoped they could pass this political albatross to the Republicans. After all, it was the Republican economic program that had precipitated the immediate trouble: the president's rosy belief that taxes could be dramatically lowered, military outlays vastly increased, and the budget still brought into balance by a flood of new revenues cascading into the treasury from expanded business activity. Howard Baker had called it "a riverboat gamble" in the 1980 campaign, and by the autumn of 1985 many Republicans were fearful the gamble would not pay off.

Some felt that they must make yet another assault on the deficit to regain the political initiative and to restore their political credibility. Two freshmen senators, Rudman and Phil Gramm of Texas, took the lead, using as their device a simple bill requiring that Congress raise the ceiling on the national debt to an astronomical $2 trillion, twice what it had been when Reagan came into office. The debt ceiling had to be raised to permit the government to pay its bills, otherwise there would be financial chaos. Gramm and Rudman saw a chance to compel Congress to act on the deficit by attaching an amendment calling for five years of forced budget reductions. It was a calculatingly daring strategy.

With public opinion polls showing the deficit as the voters' number-one worry, the idea took hold. Democrats joined Republicans in passing the measure by a lopsided seventy-five to twenty-four majority. Senator Fritz Hollings, a

South Carolina Democrat, even became a cosponsor, and liberal Democrats such as Ted Kennedy and John Kerry of Massachusetts broke ranks to vote for it in the hope that the Gramm–Rudman formula would lock President Reagan into deeper cuts in military spending and force him eventually to accept a tax increase. Rudman argued that the measure was needed "to insert some backbone and accountability into the budget process" and to break the "fiscal gridlock" that was crippling Congress.

The Republican maneuver initially caught Democratic leaders off guard, but they sensed its popularity with the voters and their own members. Chris Matthews, a spokesman for Speaker O'Neill, ridiculed the idea as "government by vegematic, a device that slices, dices, and cuts" government programs without regard to need and priority. Senator Bill Bradley and Representative Pete Rodino, both from New Jersey, warned that it would involve an unconstitutional grant of congressional budget authority to the president, who was charged with carrying out mandatory cuts if Congress did not meet the yearly deficit targets. But to avoid being trampled in the stampede to get on the right side of the deficit controversy, the Democratic leaders decided not to oppose the measure but to try one-upmanship against the Republicans. House Democratic Whip Tom Foley teamed up with shrewd younger Democratic leaders such as Dick Gephardt of Missouri, Leon Panetta of California, and Dave Obey of Wisconsin to craft an alternative plan that was more ambitious than the Republican version.

For weeks, both sides engaged in political brinksmanship. President Reagan and Republican conservatives promoted the Gramm–Rudman formula as a lever for eventually forcing Congress to lop off domestic programs and to carry out the long-term Reagan goal of shrinking government. The Democratic strategy was to embarrass the president and seize the high ground politically by requiring forced budget cuts more quickly—in early 1986 rather than after the 1986 elections. The Democrats wanted to put the White House and Republicans on the spot by making them cut domestic programs in time for voters to feel the pinch before November. Both parties agreed to exempt Social Security from the budget-cutting machine. The Democrats also exempted several programs for the poor and put limits on how much could be cut out of health programs like Medicare.

And they maneuvered shrewdly to increase their future leverage against the president. They bargained the Senate Republicans into compelling the Pentagon to accept at least half of the proposed budget cuts. And they wrote extremely tight provisions to insure the ax fell widely on many military programs. Privately, Gen. P. X. Kelley, the marine commandant, warned Mr. Reagan that this pinch could eventually bring back the military draft, and Robert McFarlane, the outgoing national security adviser, cautioned that it would halt the Reagan military buildup, echoing congressional warnings. In spite of this, the president kept airily insisting that his military programs would move ahead on schedule. But repeated pleas from Defense Secretary Caspar Weinberger for flexibility for the Pentagon showed that he understood that Congress had fashioned a budget vise to squeeze the Pentagon and that there would be only limited flexibility. It had become obvious that the intent of both party majorities on Capitol Hill was to use the threat of military cutbacks to force the president's hand on a tax increase.

In short, the Gramm-Rudman bill merely pushed the budget battle into the 1986 political year and raised the stakes on the still unresolved clash over national spending priorities, on taxes, and on the future of the political revolution that President Reagan had begun in 1981 against the federal government.

The Democratic tactics in last fall's deficit battle epitomized their effort to head off the dangers of political realignment and to set the stage for Democratic gains in Congress this year. For this grand contest of strength has shaped much of the latest legislative maneuvering. And while the Democrats have failed so far to produce a cohesive party program or a new leader who clearly ignites popular passions, they have found that a cleverly cast "go-along" strategy in Congress has largely neutralized Republican initiatives and deprived the president and his Republican legions from grasping the levers of realignment.

Coming out of the Democratic defeat of 1984, there was grumbling, even insurrection, among Democrats in Congress. In the House, a new generation of moderate leaders reached for power. Richard Gephardt, a sandy-haired forty-four-year-old, fifth-term congressman, was easily elected the new chairman of the House Democratic Caucus. Tony Coelho, a Californian who at forty-three was only in his fourth term, positioned himself for a shot at becoming the next Democratic whip, the number-three post in the House. Les Aspin, a former Pentagon whiz kid in the early 1960s under Defense Secretary Robert S. McNamara, staged a revolt in the House Armed Services Committee and jumped over seven more senior Democrats to win election as its chairman. All three were middle-of-the-road, new-breed Democrats, anxious to give the party a new image of greater fiscal responsibility and concern for national defense.

The senior leaders concluded that the party's best tactic was to lie low politically. Speaker O'Neill made the bow of the vanquished to the victor when Reagan came to Capitol Hill to give his annual State of the Union message in late January 1985. "In my fifty years of public life," he told the president, "I've never seen a man more popular than you are with the American people." Quite openly, he was signaling that he did not intend partisan confrontation with such a popular president.

Privately, Democratic leaders were assessing the political wreckage. They commissioned pollster William Hamilton to do a postelection analysis, and he came back with a diagnosis that the Democrats were in extremely bad shape on four points: They were seen as the party of tax and spend; as weak on defense; as the captive of special-interest groups; and in such disarray that the country lacked confidence in them. That helped persuade O'Neill that the best tactic would be a laid-back approach that permitted the Republicans to take the spotlight.

"I set an agenda within myself," the Speaker disclosed during a private chat some months later. "I told my policy committee and the whip organization: We are not going to go forward with a tax bill. We need a tax bill, but if a tax bill is to come, it is to come from the president of the United States. We are not going to come out first with a defense bill. We are going to force the Senate to come out first on a defense bill. And we are not going to be weak on defense. The president is committed to Social Security, and if he tries to change his policy on Social Security, we'll hold his feet to the fire."

Behind this approach lay some infallible political arithmetic. For the Democratic leaders knew that even though President Reagan had won a smashing personal victory in 1984, he had not carried enough Republicans into Congress on his coattails to revive the predominantly conservative coalition that had pushed through his program in 1981. For that, he had needed a Republican gain of at least twenty-five House seats in the 1984 election and got only fourteen. "Reagan won a great personal vote in the 1984 election but he did not get a party mandate," Tony Coelho told me one afternoon as we sat talking in the Rayburn Room, one of the men's club chambers of the Capitol where lobbyists like to corner members of Congress. "If the White House had not been so selfish and had not worried about trying to carry fifty states and if they had gone out after key Senate races and key House seats, we would be in much worse shape. Reagan did not win a party landslide and that is what his party needed. We have kept our voice."

Moreover, despite his show of bowing to the president, Speaker O'Neill claimed that the electorate had purposefully preserved the Democratic majority in the House to keep a check on President Reagan. "We got clobbered by Reagan," he admitted, tilting back in his favorite swivel chair. "He won by 16 million votes. But when there were 435 Democrats running against 435 Republicans for the Congress, we beat the Republicans approximately 53 to 46 percent, by a little over 5½ million votes. The Democrats lost only a few seats because of the fact that the Americans want them as a watchdog over the policy of the president."

Beyond that, the Senate Republican challenge to the White House gave Democrats their best chance for recovery because it meant the Republicans had to tackle the Pentagon budget and the Social Security issue. And it meant headlines focused on Republican feuding rather than on Democratic disarray. "It was perfect for us," said Coelho. "It was the White House vs. Bob Dole. I keep making the point with our own folks that the Republicans are the government. We have to make them govern and if they can't govern, the public will come back to us."

So in 1985, the Congressional Democratic leaders adjusted to the Reagan agenda and then trimmed it at the margins, gradually fashioning an image of success and denting the president's earlier reputation for invincibility. They adopted the slow, patient, unglamorous line-play of legislative maneuver, which frequently required them to bend in the wind. On the budget, Representative Bill Gray, a colorful, likable former preacher from North Philadelphia who ran the House Budget Committee, deflected White House attacks by promising to match Republican cuts in the budget. When Senate Republicans protested that many of his cuts were subterfuges done with "smoke and mirrors," Gray outflanked them by quietly working deals with House Republicans and the White House. Meanwhile, other Democrats attacked the administration for insensitivity to farmers because of its proposed cuts in farm programs.

On defense issues, the Democrats joined forces with some Republicans and imposed a ceiling of fifty MX missiles. More significantly, with a drumbeat of charges about $600 toilet seats and $450 coffeepots, they turned public debate over welfare fraud into public worry about defense contractor fraud. Indeed, the defense consensus that had backed president Reagan's five-year, $1.6-trillion buildup evaporated so dramatically in 1985 that Congress wanted overwhelmingly to freeze Pentagon spending.

By fall, the Democrats went on the offensive politically, pressing economic sanctions against South Africa, pushing increased aid for farmers, and offering a slew of bills to protect U.S. industries from competitive imports. The Democrats saw a chance to use all those issues to their advantage in the 1986 election. Amid forecasts that the annual trade deficit could reach $150 billion, Dick Gephardt called the trade problem "the Achilles heel of the Reagan economic program." With many parts of the country from the steel regions of Western Pennsylvania to the textile country of the Carolinas to the high-tech centers in California, Massachusetts, or Texas reeling from imports, the trade problem enabled Democrats to strike a "macho" patriotic image of protecting American business and jobs from foreigners.

The president tried to take some heat out of the issue by approving administrative measures to curb imports, and the Treasury Department mounted a campaign to drive down the price of the dollar to make American export prices more competitive. But those steps did not still the politics of protectionism. By whopping majorities, both the Democratic

House and the Republican Senate challenged President Reagan by passing a textile bill to reduce import quotas for several countries. "The problem with the president's plan is that it has no teeth," growled Speaker O'Neill. "Instead of sending a loud roar to our trading partners, it sends nothing more than a whimper."

Democratic aggressiveness last fall also reflected a growing confidence that the party had neutralized the potential political impact of the president's major legislative priority, his proposal for revamping the nation's tax system. Historically, the Democrats claimed paternity for the concept that the nation needed a simpler, fairer tax code, with fewer brackets for average taxpayers and fewer loopholes for the wealthy. Jimmy Carter had tried to push tax reform in 1977 but got nowhere. Ronald Reagan seemed in a much stronger position when he launched his own campaign for reform in the spring of 1985, and Democrats feared that he might build a prairie fire of popular support both for his tax package and for the Republican party, as Jack Kemp kept saying.

But on this major issue, just as on the budget, the Democrats adopted a strategy of bipartisan cooperation rather than partisan confrontation. With many congressional Republicans unenthusiastic about the Reagan tax package because they feared it would hurt corporate America and special interests such as the insurance and banking sectors, Speaker O'Neill and Representative Dan Rostenkowski, chairman of the House Ways and Means Committee, cast themselves as the president's allies.

It was Rostenkowski, a gravel-voiced veteran of the rough-and-tumble Chicago school of politics, who answered President Reagan when he unveiled his tax plans on national television on May 28. Without taking on the president directly, Rostenkowski pitched his appeal at the same northern, urban, blue-collar workers that the Republicans were trying to bring into their ranks with the tax legislation.

Obviously needling other Republicans, Rostenkowski warmly praised Reagan for "bucking his party's tradition as protector of big business and the wealthy" and moved to claim tax reform as a Democratic issue by reminding his audience that thirty years before Harry S. Truman had used language identical to Mr. Reagan's to attack the existing tax code. And identifying himself personally with the working middle-class, Rostenkowski recalled his own roots in a Polish neighborhood on Chicago's north side. "Every year politicians get up and promise to make the tax code fairer and simpler, but every year we seem to slip further behind," he said. "Now most of us pay taxes with bitterness and frustration. Working families file their tax forms with the nagging feeling that they're the country's biggest chumps. Their taxes are withheld at work, while the elite have enormous freedom to move their money from one tax shelter to another."

Moreover, the Democrats grew bolder as President Reagan proved unable to rally the public behind tax reform during his forays into the country last summer and fall. They gradually lost their fear of being badly wounded by the tax issue and moved to exploit it themselves. With the Democrats solidly in control of the House, administration strategists such as Treasury Secretary James A. Baker and his deputy, Richard Darman, calculated they had no choice but to work with the majority party. Otherwise, they felt there was no chance for President Reagan to achieve his goal of revamping the tax code. As a result, Rostenkowski was able to keep the tax bill under his thumb politically for nearly seven months while the administration bided its time and held its tongue. That arrangement, insisted upon by Rostenkowski, ensured that House Democrats would eventually share the credit with the President on tax action and would deprive Republicans of their best realignment issue. Ultimately, the tactic worked to Democratic advantage far more than either the Democrats or the White House anticipated.

For it eventually touched off massive mutiny among House Republicans that shattered all pretense of Republican unity on the tax issue and threw the president on the defensive with his own partisans.

Rostenkowski's tactics were canny. Working from the basic framework of the Reagan tax plan, he maneuvered the Democratic-controlled Ways and Means Committee into rewriting the bill to give it a decidedly Democratic stamp. The Reagan framework gave most individuals a tax cut, dropped the top tax rate from 50 to 35 percent, reduced the number of tax brackets from fourteen to three, took several million poor people off the tax rolls, and increased the personal exemption for everyone from $1,000 to $2,000. It paid for these changes largely by increasing business taxes by about $120 billion over the next five years—by closing some corporate tax loopholes, ending the investment tax credit, and somewhat reducing other business advantages such as oil and gas depletion allowances. The Rostenkowski-Democratic variation tilted more new tax cuts toward the middle class, took as many poor off the tax rolls, and was tougher on the wealthy and on business. The Democratic version imposed a stiffer minimum tax on corporations and wealthy individuals. It upped the corporate tax and capital gains above Reagan levels. It added a fourth individual tax bracket at 38 percent for the wealthy. Very significantly for many corporations, it stretched out depreciation schedules on business. And for individuals, it restored the deductibility of state and local taxes and provided the $2,000 exemption only to lower-bracket, nonitemizing taxpayers.

House Republicans were furious at Rostenkowski's action. Soon their frustration and resentment exploded, nearly derailing tax revision and threatening to cripple President Reagan politically for the rest of his term. For weeks, the probusiness Republican leadership in the House had warned the president and his aides that they opposed the emerging tax bill (some had opposed the original Reagan version, too) and had told him they felt shut out of the tax-writing process by the administration. Even so, the Republican revolt came as a shock to the White House on December 11 when only 14 of the 182 House Republicans voted even to permit debate on the tax package. Trent Lott of Mississippi, the House Republican whip who organized the mutiny, ignored personal appeals from Mr. Reagan and urged fellow Republicans "to kill this snake before it gets out of the hole." Bob Michel of Illinois, the House Republican leader who had been a Reagan loyalist, said it "causes me great personal trauma to take on my president," but added that the tax bill would hurt businesses in his district so much that he had to oppose it. The Republican defection was rancorous and almost total. Dick Cheney of Wyoming, the head of the House Republican Policy Committee, laid the blame squarely on the president. "I don't think he can pass the blame off to his subordinates," Cheney declared. "In the final analysis the president bears the responsibility for what his administration does."

From the Democratic side came Speaker O'Neill's taunt that the Republican rebellion would make the president a lame duck unless he came up with fifty votes for the tax bill, even though it was no longer the Reagan bill. The White House strained to rope in converts. When all else failed, President Reagan made a personal pilgrimage to Capitol Hill for votes and endured nearly an hour of respectful but tense criticism from his own Republicans. But his appearance reinforced his repeated appeals to keep the process of tax reform alive and to let the Republican Senate work on the bill in 1986. In the end, the tactic worked: 70 Republicans finally joined 188 Democrats in bringing the bill to the floor. A final Republican effort to kill it failed, and in a tumult over procedure, the tax bill passed on a voice vote. The president had rescued a pet priority but that was little solace to the riven Republican ranks. For the episode made clear that the White House and congressional Republicans were not only on divergent tracks but had different political priorities. The congressional wing of the party was growing increasingly independent of a president who would never again head their party's ticket, though the members backed off from totally crippling their leader at the last moment.

"The tax bill did not pass on its merits," Henson Moore, a Louisiana Republican remarked to me in the Speaker's Room just off the floor as the votes were tallied. "It is moving to the Senate not by any mandate from the people but because of the twin personalities of Ronald Reagan and Danny Rostenkowski and the twin politics of their parties. Rostenkowski is popular with Democrats and he carried them, and Reagan is popular with Republicans and he carried enough of them. The twin politics are that the Democrats didn't want to be the ones who killed tax reform and the Republicans didn't want to cripple their own president. But that's all it was."

In sum, the political maneuvering since President Reagan's landslide reelection has cast doubt on the Republican hopes for becoming a dominant majority party. The president's personal popularity remains high, but so far his popularity has not brought realignment. And none of the issues that Republican strategists counted on most last year has provided the decisive engine for a mass change in voter allegiances. Nonetheless, something important has been taking place around the country at the grass roots. For the polls show that voters identify with the Republican Party more strongly than they did in 1981 during the high tide of what Republican partisans like to call "the Reagan revolution." But it will take another round or two of elections to test just how significant this is.

One thing is clear: A half century of Democratic domination of American politics is over. What is unclear is precisely what has replaced it. Pollsters and political strategists debate how deep and lasting a change has occurred and precisely what to call it. Republican enthusiasts and some academicians such as Everett Carll Ladd, director of the Roper Center for Public Opinion Research at the University of Connecticut, contend that a major, historic realignment has definitely taken place, at least at the presidential level. Since 1968, Ladd points out, twenty-three states have gone for the Republican ticket all five times, demonstrating steady Republican strongholds, especially in the West but also in the South and New England, while only the District of Columbia went for the Democratic ticket five times in a row.

Many other experts agree there have been important currents of change, but not the kind of clear-cut, classic political watershed that brought the Republican Party into long-term dominance in 1896 and the Democrats in the early 1930s. These experts say the nation has had "half a realignment" or "dealignment," and from my travels to such diverse states as Texas, Massachusetts, Florida, Pennsylvania, Illinois, and California, I would agree. There is now a real question whether the nation has a majority party today. Even Richard Wirthlin, the polltaker for President Reagan and many important Republican candidates, prefers to talk of the Republicans not as a majority party but as "a parity party" that can finally battle the Democrats on equal footing. What is in doubt is whether the Republican strength will hold once President Reagan leaves office and whether even with Mr. Reagan on the scene for two more years, Republican strength will bloom at the grass roots.

What is not in doubt is that the old Democratic hegemony established by Franklin D. Roosevelt in the New Deal is over. The New Deal coalition has been eroded over a couple of decades by defections of two important streams of voters, white southerners and ethnic blue-collar Catholics. In short, the Democrats can no longer be called the nation's majority party, largely because they have lost a substantial portion of their conservative wing.

The breakup of what Democrats used to call the Solid South was the first major jolt. The southern break-away movements first surfaced in the late 1940s and 1950s with the Dixiecrat revolt against the national party's civil rights policies. They gained momentum during the Vietnam period of the late 1960s and early 1970s with disaffection over what many southerners felt was the party's weak stance on defense and foreign affairs. The impact of those double losses, Ladd has observed, was that "no Democratic presidential nominee since Lyndon Johnson has won majority support among white southerners" as they once did so handily.

The Reagan presidency, following Jimmy Carter's legacy of high unemployment, high inflation, and high interest rates, set in motion the second major stream of defections among blue-collar Catholics in northern cities. This phase "has been much more devastating because the party has lost its credibility on economic issues," according to William Schneider, a resident fellow at the American Enterprise Institute in Washington. "These had always held the Democratic Party together, even when race and Vietnam were tearing it apart. Since the 1930s, the Democrats have defined themselves more than anything else as the party that protects people against economic adversity. That's what kept white working-class voters in the party despite their mistrust of its racial and foreign policy liberalism." In the old days, people felt the Democratic Party was the most likely to assure prosperity. The Republicans now get that nod in opinion surveys.

Beyond those defections, the Democrats have fallen far behind the national Republican Party in the modern technology of campaigning: massive fund-raising primarily through direct mail, extensive development of friendly voter lists, targeted registration drives, and slick advertising campaigns. At the congressional level, the Democrats have found protection in maintaining score upon score of safe districts, in the power of incumbency, and the tradition of split-ticket voting, especially in the South. But they worry about finding new sources of strength with popular moods changing. "For half a century, we have been living on the Civil War, Franklin Roosevelt, gerrymandering, and incumbency," Don Edwards, a senior California congressman, remarked to me last summer. "After the landslide of 1984, we'd better turn to something new."

While there are still substantially more registered Democrats than Republicans, the Democratic advantage just about disappears when people are asked simply which party they most identify with. That is a remarkable change. The Eisenhower victories of 1952 and 1956 gave Republicans broad new appeal in presidential voting but not until the Reagan era did this translate into a real shift of declared party allegiances among voters. What the experts have been watching since the 1984 Reagan landslide is whether the Republican surge at the time of that election holds up or fades.

Over the past half century, the Democrats have enjoyed substantial advantages over Republicans in party identification. Even a decade ago, when some Democrats were abandoning their candidate in presidential races, the party had a 15- to 20-percentage-point edge over the Republicans. The 1980 Reagan victory excited Republican strategists because that gap narrowed dramatically to the point where the two parties were close to even. But six or seven months later, by the summer of 1981, the Democrats had regained a substantial 6- to 10-point lead in party identification. Last year, however, that pattern changed, most strikingly among young people.

In the immediate aftermath of the Reagan landslide of 1984, a *New York Times*/CBS News poll found the Republicans actually ahead of the Democrats by 47 to 44 percent among people who either identified with or leaned toward one of the two major parties. The margin was so thin, given the sampling errors in opinion polls, that most experts regarded it as a virtual dead heat, and they watched to see whether the Republican support would thin out as it had in 1981. By last fall, however, the numbers had changed only slightly. The *Times*/CBS News poll and other samplings found the Democrats with 47 percent and the Republicans with 45 percent, again a virtual dead heat. The figures reflected an unprecedented gain for the Republicans since the 1930s.

Two developments in particular have stirred hopes for longterm change among Republican strategists: first, the young; and second, the trend of recent conversions. With party switches by outspoken Democrats such as former-Representative-now-Senator Phil Gramm of Texas, the Republicans have tried to stage rallies of political converts. They have generally fallen short of their ambitious goals, but can nonetheless claim some progress. One survey taken last fall for the Republican Congressional Campaign Committee by Robert Teeter, head of Public Opinion Research, reported that only one in eight Democrats reported being converts from the Republican Party, whereas one in three Republicans claimed to be fallen-away Democrats. "That keeps the theory alive that things are moving in our direction," commented Joe Gaylord, executive director of the Republican Congressional Campaign Committee.

As for the young, GOP strategists are quick to point out that in both Reagan victories, the president drew lopsided support among the under-thirty crowd. Many surveys suggest that the young are the prime prospects for future Republican gains. A Teeter poll last September, for example, found Republicans leading by 51 to 39 percent in party identification among registered voters under twenty-five, while the national breakdown of all ages gave the Democrats a 2-point edge.

But there is a debate over whether the young are a good political barometer for future trends. "Young people are seen as a 'forecaster' group, a kind of electoral weather vane," asserts Everett Ladd. "Since they have relatively little experience, they are especially susceptible to currents of the day." The theory is that their Republican leanings reflect the strong influence of the Reagan presidency. By this logic, the GOP benefits from the fact that younger voters have known only two presidents, Ronald Reagan and Jimmy Carter. Not surprisingly, Democratic leaders challenge how stable their loyalties are and whether their current allegiances foreshadow a long-term trend. "Those young people are fickle," argues Tony Coelho, the Democratic congressional strategist. "They'll switch to the Democratic Party in '88 if we come up with the right nominee and the Republicans don't."

More broadly, there are reasons for wondering just how firm is the party loyalty of voters in general, regardless of age. In my experience, the past decade has been a time of great political fluidity, of floating allegiances, and of increasing numbers of voters who call themselves political independents. What I have heard again and again from people is, "I vote for the person, not the party label." Indeed, some political scientists concede that for the time being there has been a surge in Republican identification but that this may amount to no more than what Martin Wattenberg of the University of California at Irvine has called a "hollow realignment" because many people lack firm opinions about what the parties stand for.

In practice, the acid test of whether the Reagan victories provided a springboard for the Republicans will come in the 1986 and 1988 elections. One well-respected Republican strategist and student of American politics, Kevin Phillips, a former Nixon White House aide and author of several books on the conservative surge in America, believes that the Republican era really began with Mr. Nixon in 1968, was blunted by Watergate in 1974 from achieving a full realignment, and may now be peaking. Pointing to the speed with which the rivalry between Dole and Kemp surfaced after the Reagan landslide of 1984, he commented that this may very well be "the last united hurrah" of a Republican Party that is "poised for fratricide" between its New Right and traditional conservative wings.

Equally telling was Phillips' observation that for all President Reagan's personal popularity in 1984, he showed remarkably little ability to help bring other Republicans into office on his coattails. Except for the Senate, the 1984 election left the Republican Party with fewer members of the House of Representatives, fewer governors, and control of fewer state legislatures than at any time in three decades in a winning presidential election year (183 members of the House, 16 governors, and 11 states where both houses of the legislature were in Republican hands). "In short, the Republicans—now in the process of launching a rebuilding plan—are not doing so from anything resembling grass-roots strength," Phillips asserted. "Actually, they were stronger at the state level during the Eisenhower and even the Nixon years."

There is limited value to political predictions made months before an election, when the state of the world and the state of the American economy are uncertain. Even so, the exuberant Republican optimism has faded from a year ago. After his reelection last November, New Jersey's Governor Thomas Kean worried about Republican fortunes "when we lose Reagan as a candidate and the inevitable (economic) downturn comes." In 1986, the party's top political experts no longer talk of important gains in the congressional elections; they anticipate modest losses of two or three Senate seats and ten to fifteen House seats, assuming the economy remains on a fairly even keel. However, they are braced for larger losses if the Reagan recovery turns downward toward recession—meaning, the Democrats might reclaim control of the Senate.

American history provides ample precedents for such losses in the sixth year of a two-term presidency: Under Eisenhower in 1958 and again under Nixon in 1974, the Republicans lost forty-eight House seats; the Democrats under Franklin D. Roosevelt lost seventy-one seats in 1938. Indeed, the best the Republicans have done after being in the White House for six years in a row was losing just ten seats back in 1926. This year, the Democrats are targeting the hard-hit farm-belt region and southern states such as the Carolinas and Texas for gains. On the Republican side, Joe Gaylord acknowledges: "It's a real question whether we can hold our gains in the South. There's been a pattern of our gaining seats in presidential years and then losing them in off-year elections. And if we get many people retiring, it's going to be tough holding those open seats."

But the battle royal in 1986 will be for the Senate, where the Republicans hold a fifty-three to forty-seven edge and where a net loss of four seats would bring a Democratic takeover. Because the Reagan tide brought in so many new Republican senators six years ago in 1980, the Republicans have more to lose this year. Of the thirty-four seats to be contested, twenty-two are now in Republican hands and four of the incumbents have decided not to run again. Democrats sense Republican vulnerability in farm-belt states such as North Dakota, South Dakota, Wisconsin, and Oklahoma; in other states with freshmen Republican senators such as Alabama and Pennsylvania; and in open seats in Maryland, North Carolina, and Nevada. The Democrats have mounted particularly strong challenges with two very popular governors running against Republicans Steve Symms in Idaho and Paula Hawkins in Florida, both of whom won very narrowly in 1980. On the other side, the Republicans are hoping for pickups in seats left open by retiring Democrats in Missouri and Louisiana as well as in California and Vermont, where Democratic incumbents appear vulnerable.

Even though many Republicans expect some net loss in the Senate, other strategists like Dick Wirthlin contend that the party has a new cushion because of the voter realignment. Wirthlin contends that the Republicans have a "51-percent chance" to keep control of the chamber, contingent upon a healthy economy. Actually, it would set a historical precedent for the Republicans to avoid a recession this year. For over sixty years, every Republican administration has suffered a recession around the midterm elections—in 1926, 1930, 1954, 1970, 1974, and 1982.

There is, finally, one other political perversity that could foil the Republican dreams of building their realignment this year, and that is the penchant of American voters to perpetuate a government divided between the parties. In 1984, for example, voters in 191 congressional districts went for President Reagan, but also elected a Democrat to Congress. That is split-ticket voting at record levels. In short, millions of Reagan voters like Democrats running the House.

This may well be the trump card for the Democrats this year. Louis Harris, an independent poll-taker, observes that his surveys in recent years show that the public is wary of both parties and is perpetuating the political stalemates, wherein the Republicans dominate the White House and the Democrats hold power in Congress.

"People don't want any one party to be dominant," says Harris. "We've asked people: Would you rather have divided government or one party in control? And they will say, 60 to 35 percent, they prefer divided government. They just don't want one party of scoundrels in there. It's born of the cynicism toward politicians. We first got that under Ford in '75-'76. The more Congress stands up to the president, the more they like it. People believe in checks and balances. The funny thing is if the Democrats regain control of the Senate in '86, it could hurt whoever will be the Democratic presidential nominee in '88 because people would not like the House, Senate, and White House all in [the] control of one party."

ROUNDTABLE DISCUSSION

"Congress: Will There Be Realignment?"

PANELISTS: Paul Duke, *moderator*
Hedrick Smith
Haynes Johnson
Charles McDowell
Jack Nelson

DUKE: If Americans really do prefer a divided government these days, doesn't this suggest a preference for moderation as well?
SMITH: There's good reason for believing that. Certainly, that's what Speaker O'Neill and a lot of the Democrats are claiming.
In covering Senate and House races in 1984, I repeatedly heard Democrats in touchy states and tough districts saying quite explicitly to voters, "You need to put me and my party back in charge in Congress to keep a check on President Reagan and the Republicans. You don't want it all going one way." And many of these people who made that argument were reelected.
JOHNSON: And it's not just the Democrats who are acting that way. The Republicans, when given a chance to vote on their new leaders in the Senate last year, went to the center, not to the right, despite Reagan's big win. In fact, they rejected the more conserva-

tive choices, which means many Republican lawmakers view the issues differently from Mr. Reagan.

NELSON: I'm sorry, but I don't think people are consciously voting for a divided government.

McDOWELL: I'll dissent from your dissent and suggest that we're beginning to get evidence that people are increasingly conscious of it, certainly in the Reagan era.

DUKE: Wasn't it James Madison who said that all men having power ought to be mistrusted? Basically, the public is saying that they mistrust both parties and hence don't want either to have too much power.

SMITH: That message certainly came through in the last three presidential elections when the winning candidates ran strongly against the puzzle palaces on the Potomac.

DUKE: The irony is that in 1984 Reagan won by an even bigger margin than in 1980 and the Republicans didn't do as well in other races.

JOHNSON: But I don't think that's an irony. Many people made a conscious judgment that after four years of the Reagan presidency they did not want to give him more power to achieve his program in Congress. So, they put in place people to check him. We're still a country operating mainly in the center of the political road.

DUKE: But that doesn't explain why the Republicans have done so poorly in the congressional contests in recent years, even when we've had Democratic presidents.

SMITH: The Republicans claim they don't get the proportion of seats they deserve from the percentage of the popular vote they get. Bob Teeter, one of the most respected pollsters for the Republicans, says that Republicans would have to get something like 54 or 55 percent of the popular vote in races for Congress in order to get an even split in the House the way the districts are drawn.

So, there's the political bias that's built in from gerrymandering in states controlled by the Democrats. There's also an institutional bias that's built in from incumbency.

What we've seen again and again is that up to 90 percent of all incumbents get reelected. They've got the weight of their patronage, their publicity and the projects they've gotten, the hospitals and the highways, etc.

So the challenger simply has a harder time of it these days. And since there are more Democratic incumbents than Republican incumbents, the Democrats obviously benefit. Furthermore the Democrats have been clever at disassociating themselves from their national party when it suited them; in the South for example, on the civil rights issue for many years. In 1984 many Democrats ran away from Walter Mondale after he came out for increasing taxes, campaigning on their own records.

DUKE: On Capitol Hill, the Democrats also have resorted to a more pragmatic and flexible brand of politics, with many advocating a me-too brand of Reaganism.

SMITH: It tells you something when you have a whole new group of moderate Democrats on the rise in the House, talking about managing things better. It's not quite clear whether they've found the issues to project a new Democratic vision to the country, but they have conceded a point to Reagan.

McDOWELL: They're emphasizing fiscal responsibility more than the Democrats ever have in the past.

SMITH: Like Bill Gray, the chairman of the House Budget Committee from North Philadelphia, who kept saying again and again that as a representative of the Democratic leadership he was going to get more than 50 billion dollars in deficit cuts last year—that he wasn't going to let the Republicans nail the Democrats as the party of tax and spend.

JOHNSON: And in fact, what the Democrats have done is to show that they can match the Republicans in fiscal austerity. They have not proposed any new programs for several years and actually voted for less budget money than Reagan asked in 1985.

SMITH: The Democrats have been adjusting, not only to the impact of Reaganism but to what they're hearing from their constituents back home. Namely, stop throwing any more money at programs.

DUKE: In a way, the Democrats are victims of their own successes. If you go back to the early sixties when they were advocating federal aid to education, new housing programs, consumer protection—well, they got all those things. So, their cupboard is bare these days. A more basic question now is why have Congress and the president found it so hard to work together in solving the deficit?

SMITH: Good question. What we have had is a political system that is not only stalemated by divided authority, the House in the control of the Democrats and the Senate and the White House in the control of the Republicans, but there has been a stalemate growing out of political behavior in which the name of the game has been blaming the other side for not acting.

The Democrats jumped all over Reagan when he made the premature move in 1981 proposing some changes in Social Security benefits, and at every opportunity, they beat the Republicans over the head for being the ones who were going to change the Social Security system. Then the Democrats got nailed by the Republicans as the party that wanted to increase taxes to solve the deficit problem. The paradox is that almost everybody agrees both steps are needed, but all last year each side was unwilling to give up the hammerlock it had on the other.

DUKE: The attitude many people have is—cut the budget, but let's cut it in *your* district, not in my district.

SMITH: "Don't cut you, don't cut me, cut the guy behind the tree." That's what Senator Russell Long said.

NELSON: David Gergen* told me he heard that the title of David Stockman's book, which should be coming out about the same time this book comes out, is going to be *Reaganomics: The Failure of the Reagan Presidency*. When I mentioned this to Jim Baker he said he'd heard a different title: *Reaganomics: Politics Over Economics.*

It's not as catchy a title, but it means the same thing. It has been politics over economics because the White House has not been willing to bite the bullet since they've backed away from any Social Security changes and don't want to cut back on defense spending.

SMITH: What an incredible irony, because for government to work you've got to be able to mobilize a coalition. Such a coalition on the deficit has to be bipartisan. And to get cooperation, there has to be leadership.

So, what we're saying is the man who has gotten so much credit for restoring the presidency, for being the strongest leader we've had since Lyndon Johnson and maybe even since Franklin Delano Roosevelt, has failed as a leader when it's come to the second phase of his own revolution.

NELSON: Exactly.

McDOWELL: Right on.

DUKE: Nineteen eighty-five was hardly a good year for Reagan in Congress. He took a battering on many things and completely lost the initiative on the deficit.

---

*Gergen was the White House communications director from 1981 to 1984. He was named managing editor of *U.S. News and World Report* in September 1985.

SMITH: The Democrats played it smartly. They licked their wounds from the '84 election, lay in wait, let the Republican Senate take on the White House on defense spending and various other issues, and then in the fall of 1985 made their big moves, on trade, on the deficit, on South Africa, and finally began to rework the Reagan tax-reform program so that it had a distinctly Democratic flavor. The bill that passed the House made the Democrats the populists instead of Ronald Reagan.

McDOWELL: The most significant thing in the second term is the Republican rebellion against the White House.

SMITH: To me, what's interesting as we talk about this is the dichotomy between what you might call inside Washington politics and outside politics. Here's Reagan, terrifically popular in the country, and he's had trouble working the old magic because he is not providing leadership that his own party wants to follow, let alone the opposition.

DUKE: There's much bad blood these days between Capitol Hill and the White House, a feeling that the White House is insensitive to the prerogatives and the powers of the Congress. Jim Wright, the Democratic leader in the House, says we have a regal presidency wherein the people downtown want the legislative branch to bow to divine will.

There's also a feeling on the Hill that the administration is trying to achieve some of its objectives by indirection when it can't by direct authority. For example, the failure to enforce civil rights laws or other congressional edicts.

But in some areas, Congress has thwarted the administration's purposes and designs. Civil rights is a notable example.

The administration tried to amend and water down

the 1965 Voting Rights Act, only to arouse the anger of many Republican Senators and Representatives who felt it was bad business to be reopening old disputes long settled. The interesting thing is that Congress not only refused to weaken the law but actually wound up strengthening it in some respects. It repudiated a basic Reagan goal.

SMITH: Look at the battle over the nomination of William Bradford Reynolds to be associate attorney general. It was Mac Mathias, Republican of Maryland, and Arlen Specter, Republican of Pennsylvania, who joined the Democrats to cast the deciding votes to block it, for precisely that reason—they don't want to roll back the civil rights clock.

We have a big division within the administration over where to go with affirmative action guidelines. You've got Attorney General Meese and a couple of others trying to roll back vigorously, and you've got plenty of people on the other side, particularly Labor Secretary Bill Block, who are strongly opposed.

McDOWELL: That prompts me to say that the most interesting thing going on in Congress now is the way Republicans have stopped Reagan's revolution. They've drawn the line on cutting social programs to the bone and reversing the New Deal.

SMITH: I disagree on the issue of the deficit. Bob Dole and Pete Domenici and Warren Rudman and Slade Gorton and many other Republican Senators set out in 1985 to do what they thought Reagan wanted.

They tried to cut the budget even more than the White House, but the president deserted them.

The person who walked out on the Reagan revolution, if you will, was Ronald Reagan. The Republicans from the Senate went to him and said we will give you a massive 350-billion-dollar deficit-reduction program over three years if you will include about a hundred billion dollars of tax increases. He wouldn't go along because of the tax increase.

McDOWELL: Republican votes were not there for severe cuts in social programs, such as food stamps and welfare aid, that the president wanted.

SMITH: That's not true in the Senate. They originally approved a budget fifty to forty-nine in early 1985 that eliminated seventeen programs. They were willing to bite the bullet. In other words, to go farther than their president. Likewise, it was Senate Republicans who engineered the Gramm–Rudman plan, which would impose a much more austere budget if ever implemented.

DUKE: Isn't the real point that the president and the Senate Republicans differ on priorities? The Republicans voted for severe domestic cuts in the hope of persuading Reagan to accept major cuts in defense as well.

SMITH: No question about that part. But it was more than that. They approached the deficit problem as three legs to a stool. They said, If you're going to do something about the deficit, you're going to have to cut the big domestic programs, and that means putting some bite on things, like Social Security. You're going to have to cut defense or at least the growth of defense, and you're going to have to raise taxes. Reagan wanted to do it all with just the first leg of the stool.

NELSON: The Senate Republicans also thought they had a deal with the White House until Reagan yanked the rug right out from under them.

SMITH: See, that's my point. Which is why it's wrong to say that they weren't going along with the Reagan revolution. They actually proposed to carry the revolution further and the problem was the president wouldn't pay the price for doing that.

DUKE: But on tax reform the lawmakers have been *less* revolutionary than the president.

NELSON: There are a number of reasons. Number one, as we've said before, he didn't come in with any mandate for his second term. There was the big shakeup at the White House with Don Regan replacing Jim Baker as chief of staff, bringing in about fifteen or twenty people with him from the Treasury Department, and Baker going to Treasury and taking fifteen or twenty people from the White House. The change didn't go smoothly and Regan irked many Republicans on the Hill. In addition the president had a lot of other issues on his plate and therefore was often distracted from tax reform.

On top of everything, the American people are far more disturbed about the deficit. They don't give a damn about tax reform, and all the polls show that.

JOHNSON: The politics of '86 is all about who is going to be seen as doing something to cut the deficit because everybody is afraid of the economic fallout in the future. They're afraid of a recession, and that means jobs lost, and that means you can lose your seat in Congress in the next election.

SMITH: The economy is coming back as an issue. There's uncertainty whether business is going to turn down in '86 or '87 or '88, but there's a feeling that it will and that's why the deficit is a bigger issue. People are afraid the bottom is going to drop out if we don't get our financial house in order. They don't really want to be bothered with tax reform unless it can be shown clearly to be to the advantage of the overwhelming majority of people.

DUKE: In 1981 the presidential message turned on voters because it was basically a good news message. The president emphasized tax cuts and revitalizing the economy. Everybody wanted to see his taxes cut, obviously.

Now, when the president talks about tax reform, that's a good news/bad news message. Good news for some people whose taxes would be reduced and bad news for other people whose taxes would be raised. Consequently, the president has not been able to rally the country behind this issue as he did in 1981 for cutting taxes—which benefited everybody.

NELSON: But, Paul, Reagan has tried to make it sound like it's good news, and he's gone out and said it's good news.

DUKE: But people don't believe him, Jack. That's the thing.

DUKE: Anyway, the tax reform thicket is a reminder that Capitol Hill often more accurately reflects the public mood on major issues than does the White House. The classic case is what happened in the early 1970s when Congress began turning against the Vietnam War and ultimately forced American withdrawal from that quagmire.

JOHNSON: On a broader level, though, we should point out that Congress institutionally is having trouble dealing with the issues effectively. Is there anybody here at the table who has not talked to a member privately in the House or the Senate who doesn't complain about the lack of will to act in a unified way. The members don't have the discipline. They're splintered. The young Republicans differ from the old ones. Same with the Democrats: Civility has given way to contempt and disarray.

McDOWELL: There's a breakdown, and they all talk about it privately. What you say reflects something Rick was saying about a failure to coalesce, failure to compromise. Well, we cannot avoid an old theme, that political parties of the old style were the institution in which compromise and coalition were patched together. As the members become less accountable to parties because they find their financial support and their public support elsewhere, as parties lose their old function as the home of mediation, conciliation, and compromise, all our political institutions begin to change.

Congress can't function as well. President and Congress diverge instead of merge. We still sit and talk about parties as if they are what they were, and they contribute in their own chaotic way to the disarray in Congress and an increasing divergence between the presidential parties and the congressional parties.

NELSON: Plus that, you've got so many divisions, within Congress itself—all the regional divisions and all the special-interest caucuses—the Frost Belt, the Sun Belt, the Black Caucus, the Steel Caucus, the Hispanic Caucus, the Women's Caucus, and many others.

JOHNSON: Sure, it's fragmented.

NELSON: And you don't have any strong leadership to pull anything together.

DUKE: One reason is the great wave of reform over the past fifteen years. The congressional rules have been liberalized in many ways, and individual members have more power today than they once did. As a consequence, power is more diffuse. People talk about the weak leadership of Tip O'Neill, but if he had come along in Sam Rayburn's days, he would have had greater power to wield because the Speaker had more authority then. In reality, we have too much democracy in Congress today.

SMITH: They called the 1974 reforms in Congress the Magna Carta of the subcommittees, meaning that they created so many subcommittees that the members all got a chunk of power with staffs that permit them to operate independently of the powerful chairmen, the people who used to be the feudal barons that made the deals.

I remember talking once with Mo Udall, the veteran congressman from Arizona, after this had happened, and he said, "There are so many new members in the House and so many subcommittees, that when I'm in the well of the House and can't remember somebody's name, I greet them by saying, 'Good morning, Mr. Chairman.'" He said, "Chances are I'm talking to a subcommittee chairman because about one-third of the members are chairmen of subcommittees."

McDOWELL: A relentless move to individualism reflected in what we've said about campaigning, in what we've said about the presidency, and in what we've said about money and political action committees. Everything we've talked about around this table keeps going back to the theme of a move away from organization to individualism, and it's "Mr. Chairman" to 140 people.

JOHNSON: I agree. Exactly.

SMITH: No question about it.

DUKE: There's a real power gap in Congress these days at many levels. As one example, Danny Rostenkowski doesn't pack the power of Wilbur Mills, who was head of the House Ways and Means Committee twenty years ago; Bob Packwood doesn't wield the power of Russell Long when he was head of the Senate Finance Committee.

SMITH: Danny Rostenkowski had to do a lot of bargaining just to pull together the two-thirds Democratic majority on the Ways and Means Committee in writing tax reform legislation. He had to bargain with the oil interests, with the three members of the New York delegation on keeping the deduction for state and local taxes, with the people who represented the banking industry.

There's only one institution in the past that's been able to give cohesion in the face of this kind of special interest attack, and that's been the party, and the party has been weakened. I think the attitude toward political parties among people who watch the system operate in Washington is different from the attitude of the general public. The public looks down on parties, but there are more and more people close to government, whether journalists or academicians or practicing politicians, who think that we need to revive the parties somehow, or we'll never have the glue that holds the system together.

JOHNSON: Some of the younger members have treated O'Neill contemptuously. In their private meetings they hoot at him and ridicule him. He just doesn't have the kind of authority, as Paul said, that Mr. Sam had. He can't order people to vote. He doesn't have the power to control committees. It's gone.

NELSON: But isn't it true that Tip O'Neill himself has not shown leadership? I mean, it's not entirely the system or the institution's fault here. He has just not been a strong leader.

DUKE: I disagree totally.

SMITH: I don't agree with that, either.

DUKE: I think of all the people that I've covered and dealt with on Capitol Hill over the years, Tip O'Neill, under the right circumstances, could have been a truly great leader.

NELSON: There are sure a lot of Democrats in the House who don't agree with that.

DUKE: I know. But it's those Democrats who've made it impossible for Tip O'Neill to lead.

NELSON: But nevertheless, Paul, if he can't command the allegiance of his own Democrats, he's not showing much leadership in my opinion.

JOHNSON: If you look ahead, though, O'Neill will be soon gone. And no matter who takes his job as the leader of House Democrats, he's going to have a hard time pulling the Democrats together.

NELSON: Oh, I agree with that.

DUKE: In the old days, Sam Rayburn, Charlie Halleck, the Republican leader in the House, and Howard Smith, the conservative leader who was chairman of the House Rules Committee, would go into a back room and cut a deal, and that's how a bill would emerge. You can't do that these days because democracy is running rampant in the House. [Laughter.]

JOHNSON: Down with democracy [laughing].

SMITH: If the system was working well, you'd say democracy was flourishing. [Laughter.]

DUKE: The turmoil precipitated by realignment also is having an effect on the way Congress operates.

SMITH: It contributes to the political confusion we're talking about. If you lose the hegemony of one party and its capacity to move government in one direction or another, and you see the rise of another party but not to the point where it controls all the major institutions of government, then you have this kind of stalemate because the partisanship intensifies.

NELSON: Despite this, the Republicans have been able to join with Southern Democrats to form an effective conservative coalition to prevail in many legislative battles. And at times actually to control the House. That's how Reagan got so much his first term—by having the support of Republicans and southern "boll weevils" in the House.

DUKE: So, we have to say that party labels don't always mean as much as they seem to mean.

McDOWELL: When we talk about the Republican Party and the Democratic Party, we're almost using obsolescent terms if we don't differentiate between the presidential party and the congressional party.

There is the Democratic presidential party which has lost four out of the last five elections, and the Democratic congressional party which has held the House since 1954. The Republican congressional party has had mostly tough times over the past thirty years but the Republican presidential party has had great success. The Democrats have carried one western state in the presidential contests since Barry Goldwater. The Republicans own the West. We are watching, meanwhile, a comeback of Democratic candidates for governor and Congress in the West.

DUKE: The 1985 elections certainly produced fresh evidence that the two-party system is alive and flourishing in this country.

McDOWELL: They also confirmed the continuing lack of interest in parties and party image.

Here were two states—Virginia and New Jersey—that went strongly for Ronald Reagan in both 1980 and 1984, and yet moved in opposite directions this time. Virginia went strongly Democratic, electing a white man, a black man, and a white woman from its statewide ticket, while in New Jersey, a Republican governor, Thomas Kean, was reelected handsomely with 60 percent of the black vote and 60 percent of the labor vote.

The politics of moderation clearly beat the politics of extremism.

DUKE: There was a move toward the center. Is that what you're saying?

McDOWELL: Clearly a move toward the center. When a Republican governor gets a large black and labor vote, when a Democratic ticket in a very conservative state wins statewide with a black and a woman for the first time in any state in America, you have not just the politics of the center, but you seem to have the center growing in both directions.

JOHNSON: And the message for both parties was that if you go too far, the voters are going to reject you. The ideological approach to politics is not popular with most Americans.

McDOWELL: Virginia tells us a lot about personality and character in politics. Governor Charles Robb, a moderate Democrat, is the most popular political figure in Virginia. Ronald Reagan is the second most popular. The lesson is that people are not hung up on ideology.

DUKE: Did the elections tell us that there's no great conservative tide in this country?

JOHNSON: No, I don't think you can go that far. But the results did suggest the country wants stability and sanity, and that's in the center.

DUKE: There's growing ferment among young blacks as among young whites. The young blacks don't appear automatically wedded to the Democratic Party as their fathers were. They want candidates who offer more than the old-style leadership, just paying lip service to all the old liberal themes.

JOHNSON: There's a split in the black vote. It's astonishing that a Republican candidate for governor in a traditionally Democratic state, New Jersey, rolled up 60 percent of the black vote. That's got to tell you something, that younger blacks, like younger whites, are identifying more with Reagan in what he represents, and that is, success.

McDOWELL: As black people are integrated into the society, they begin to respond like the rest of the society.

DUKE: How crucial are the 1986 elections to the Republicans?

SMITH: Very crucial. If the Democrats recapture the Senate and increase their House strength by ten or fifteen seats, it would be a terrific psychological blow to the Republican hopes for realignment over the long term.

This would not be out of keeping, by the way, with the pattern of past elections. When a president has occupied the White House for six years, his party tends to lose heavily in the sixth year. So, if you're trying to build momentum for the future, it's pretty hard if you get knocked back to a pretty low base in 1986.

DUKE: The Republicans just can't seem to overcome the Democratic monopoly of Congress. It is incredible that none of us has known a Republican House of Representatives since we've been covering national political issues.

SMITH: This is why Frank Fahrenkopf, the Republican national chairman, is putting so much stress on trying to capture the state legislatures. If the Republicans control most of the fifty legislatures after the 1990 census, they'll be in a strong position to redraw congressional districts. In a way that could greatly diminish Democratic power in Congress.

When Fahrenkopf talks about a Republican majority in Congress, and by the way, I'm skeptical that he'll make it, but when he talks about it, he is realistic enough to say that 1992 would be the year, not '86 or '88 or '90. Actually, they are making some striking gains at the local level in some places. They've done well in Texas and North Carolina, for example.

NELSON: Remember the last time that they talked about political realignment in the South and how the Republicans were going to take over? That was after 1964 when Barry Goldwater carried five states in the South. Five state officials in Georgia switched to the Republican party, but in the next election every one got thrown out of office, and there never was much political realignment in the South after that. I'm not sure it is taking hold, although if they are electing sheriffs and courthouse officials that is real progress.

DUKE: It goes much beyond that. The Republicans have made remarkable headway in breaking the Democratic domination of congressional elections in the South. They've got the two senators from Virginia, the two senators from North Carolina, and other senators from Alabama, Georgia, Mississippi, Florida, Texas, and South Carolina. The Virginia congressional delegation has turned completely around from being overwhelmingly Democratic twenty years ago to being overwhelmingly Republican today. There's been big change.

McDOWELL: The old ways are dying. In many places the socially respectable people are now Republicans. Democratic candidates across the South often don't carry a majority of the white vote these days. Race figures in a lot of this. Certainly in my state of Virginia, the Republican Party is pretty enlightened about racial issues. But the fact remains that people who are opposed to some of the civil rights laws are gravitating toward the Republican Party.

NELSON: You would agree that the Republican Party in power in Washington today welcomes all of these Southern white segregationists into the party?

McDOWELL: They have welcomed them.

NELSON: Yeah, right. Courted them, too.

McDOWELL: Yes.

DUKE: To me, one of the more puzzling things has been that amidst all the change we still don't have many women and black members of Congress.

JOHNSON: Many more women are running for public office at the state and local level. So inevitably, they are going to be running in congressional and senatorial races in a few years. Blacks are something else. They are 16 percent of the population in this country, but there is still a lot of disturbing racial polarization. You can see it in the Congress, you can see it when you travel the country. I heard stuff I hadn't heard for twenty years down South in the 1984 campaign. I mean, more open hostility from whites, as if they were stepping back into the past.

McDOWELL: There's a pretty good case to be made that black membership in Congress is held down by gerrymandering throughout the country.

JOHNSON: That was Jesse Jackson's point. But there is something else worth noting, and that is the effect of the stepped-up black activity. In 1984 they registered masses of black voters in North Carolina who had never voted before. But the whites also registered many new voters—and many more in total numbers than blacks did—as a reaction to the blacks. And the fact is, when you go back to the population figures, blacks in no way are close to a majority in most places, so regardless of gerrymandering it's tough for them to make progress.

McDOWELL: The other side of the coin, the Jesse Jackson side, is, well, the way you solve it is to create black districts. But that's a sad solution.

JOHNSON: That digs you deeper into the situation.

DUKE: One final question: Has Congress served the country well during the Reagan period?

McDOWELL: Anyone who believed deeply in Reagan and his revolution, and in reversing the New Deal, it seems to me those people would have to judge by now that Congress has not served the country well. It has impeded the revolution.

If you look at it from the point of view of those who were skeptical of Mr. Reagan's revolution, the Congress has served the country classically well by slowing and correcting the president's program.

JOHNSON: I think it was a healthy thing that Ronald Reagan was elected president. It was important for the country to have an alternative, to see if the different proposals could work. By giving him almost a blank check that first year, Congress was a reflection of the mood of the country in a classic democratic—small *d*—sense. It was an affirmation of the popular will to try something. It didn't work as planned.

In the ensuing period what I have been struck with more and more is how many people in the Congress have been the ones who have taken the lead in dealing with our problems, particularly the deficit. The fact is, there's been a consensus in Washington about how to deal with the deficit for at least three years. You have to raise taxes, cut defense, and reduce the social entitlement programs. What is sad is the way the country has blamed Congress for not tackling the problem, when in reality the president's refusal to compromise has been the main difficulty.

NELSON: Congress pretty much did what it had to do in the first year of the Reagan first term simply because the president did win an overwhelming victory, and he did spell out his proposals in the campaign so people knew where he stood. How well his programs may serve the public in the long run is another story. They certainly don't serve all the American people equally.

DUKE: Congress has served the country well in the civil rights and civil liberties area by serving as a bulwark against administration attempts to roll back the clock. But it has not necessarily served the country well in the budget and tax areas because it let the president have his way too often. That is hopefully changing because the lawmakers are now showing more guts in standing up to the White House and in setting national priorities.

SMITH: The country in 1981 wanted a new leader to have a chance with a new program, and Congress went along. Basically the legislators believed that the public had lost its taste for the old ways, for the New Deal, and the Great Society, and they wanted to move in a new direction. In that sense, the Congress represented the country quite well.

Come the '82 recession, the country felt quite differently, and Congress began to put the brakes on. And it's been putting the brakes on ever since. You start asking the public about how they feel about cutting farm subsidies, curbing Social Security benefits, reducing Medicare, and stopping support for the national parks, you now get majorities going the other way.

The public is not ready for the consequences of its own major conclusion, which is do something about the deficit, and I think Congress reflects that very, very well. Certainly, from the standpoint of productive, legislative enterprise and moving the country in one way or another, it hasn't succeeded very well. But in terms of representing the ambivalence that the public feels on controversial issues, the Congress has represented the country well.

Star Wars

Charles W. Corddry

CHARLES CORDDRY, 66, has covered defense and foreign affairs in Washington for forty years—first with United Press, then with the *Baltimore Sun*. As the dean of Defense correspondents, he has reported on the Korean conflict, the Cuban Missile Crisis, the long policy disputes over Vietnam, the struggles to control nuclear weapons and the problems of the North Atlantic Alliance. His reporting has taken him to virtually every corner of the globe, and he has spoken on defense matters at numerous military schools. His work has won several notable awards, and he is a member of the Washington Sigma Delta Chi chapter Hall of Fame. He is the longest-serving member of the *Washington Week* panel, having joined the program shortly after its beginning in February 1967.

It's early in the twenty-first century, and the miracles of science have made nuclear arms impotent and obsolete. Researchers in laboratories have made up for the failure of nuclear age politicians to control instruments of mass destruction. Brand-new forms of defensive weapons—able to dart across the skies at the speed of light—have made a reality of the "vision" the American President articulated as the previous century wound down.

Some derisively, some with great faith, had called Ronald Reagan's vision Star Wars, after a motion picture that had stirred the imaginations of millions. Mr. Reagan hadn't much liked the *Star Wars* analogy; his term was Strategic Defense Initiative. But he had been quite able, just the same, to convey his confidence in missle defenses by declaring, straight out of the movie, that "the 'force' is with us!"

Now, in the twenty-first century, lasers, atomic particle beams, hypervelocity guns and things barely imagined in the late twentieth century have caused nuclear arms to be laid aside, dinosaurs no longer able to terrify or to back up power politics. Directed energy beams—bolts of lightning—can travel 186,000 miles per second; what chance do offensive missiles, plodding along at a mere three miles a second, have against such defenses?

• • •

Is all this an impossible dream?

Yes, says Harold Brown, the nuclear physicist and former defense secretary, "a dream, though not an ignoble one."

Surely, in the 1980s, as many learned scientists and variously motivated politicians—perhaps more—believe it is hokum as believe it is sound.

"Surreal" was the word Mr. Brown used when we discussed the President's proposal two days after his startling speech of March 23, 1983. The implication seemed to be that there wasn't much there, or, if there was, it had a dream's lack of order.

"What if," Mr. Reagan had asked that night, "free people could live secure in the knowledge that their security did not rest on the threat of instant U.S. retaliation to deter a Soviet attack; that we could intercept and destroy missiles before they reached our soil or that of our allies?"

The President's frustration level must have been rising at the time. Congress was resisting his MX missile plans. The Soviet Union's nuclear arsenal was continuing to expand. Many in the scientific community opposed Mr. Reagan's nuclear policies and many advocated a nuclear freeze.

Very well, the President said in effect:

"I call upon the scientific community who gave us nuclear weapons to turn their great talents to the cause of mankind and world peace, to give us the means of rendering these nuclear weapons impotent and obsolete."

What they actually turned their talents to, many of them, was the business of trying to strangle Mr. Reagan's baby in its crib. In two days, Hans Bethe, a Nobel laureate in physics and one of those who gave us nuclear weapons, had decided, "I don't think it can be done." He may not have been the first to call it Star Wars, but he was close. In short order, the Union of Concerned Scientists put out a book, *The Fallacy of Star Wars,* which became a sort of bible for many of Mr. Reagan's detractors.

A reporter is paid to be skeptical and usually finds that skepticism pays. This one's conviction is that we will do well to learn what we can about the pros and cons of Star Wars, to make up our minds to follow its course—for it isn't going away—and to keep our minds wide open as the controversy rages among scientists, politicians and both friendly and adversary governments. (We must not be put off by the near certainty that computer age teenagers and subteens—old friends of ET—will probably find Star Wars far less baffling than we do.)

I recall the chilly early spring evening when the inevitable anonymous "senior administration official" briefed reporters at the White House on the gradual but potentially drastic shift in strategy that Mr. Reagan was about to herald in that night's speech. Most listeners, it is fair to say, were tuned to the conventional wisdom that the only defense against a thermonuclear attack was to be able to absorb the attack and then incinerate the attacker. That was "assured destruction," as Defense Secretary Robert S. McNamara had named it in the 1960s.* It was deterrence by threat of retaliation; it would maintain the balance of terror.

Now the President was about to propose what could become the most—really, the first—fundamental change in national security strategy since the cold war began in the late 1940s.

---

*Later, as the Soviets pulled at least even, it got to be called Mutual Assured Destruction, so that nuclear-age worriers demanding arms reductions had a nice acronym: MAD. There is some irony that MAD can now draw fire both from the true believers in Star Wars and from its opponents.

I was as surprised as others at the briefing, but maybe a trifle less skeptical than I am paid to be. I had seen Hiroshima, Tokyo and Berlin after they were razed in World War II. So much for strategic defense. On the other hand, technology (the Spitfire, radar), trickery (false radio signals to mislead attackers) and bravery and tactics (never was so much owed by so many to so few) had prevailed in the Battle of Britain.

In the years after, as mass destruction weapons proliferated and became ever more accurate, American military leaders had reason to be increasingly concerned about the bind that deterrence theories put them in. Charged with defending the country, they had to count on rational calculations in the Kremlin about the ability of the United States to retaliate if attacked. In crudest terms, the military high command would have to see the country destroyed before it could destroy the attacker in return. Small wonder that military leaders had pressed the Strategic Defense Initiative on President Reagan a month before he announced it.

As for impossible dreams, it does the SDI doubters no disservice to recall some other reveries that wistful souls have engaged in. Remember those fanciful bicycle repairmen Orville and Wilbur Wright? Remember how compressed and turbulent air would break up an airplane trying to get through the sound barrier? When aerodynamicists and Chuck Yeager proved that wrong, we remobilized our doubts and wondered whether we could stuff enough power in a rocket to escape earth's gravitational pull and send out space probes.

Vannevar Bush, the World War II scientific research director, doubted that missiles could be made accurate enough and nuclear warheads small enough to fly between continents. Defense Secretary Caspar W. Weinberger relishes the assertion of Albert Einstein in 1932: "There is not the slightest indication that [nuclear] energy will ever be obtainable. It would mean that the atom would have to be shattered at will."

The space station Mr. Reagan wants the National Aeronautics and Space Administration to build is a descendant of the Air Force Manned Orbiting Laboratory that Mr. McNamara canceled in the 1960s, and the space shuttle is a grown-up version of the winged space plane canceled in the same period.

Putting men on the moon was not going to be a lead-pipe cinch either, when President John F. Kennedy made it a national goal. But it was achieved, right on schedule.

The *Apollo* moon-flight precedent, incidentally, has probably helped to generate interest on the part of many companies in participating in the SDI. As a West German optics company executive put it to me one evening, *Apollo* did not prove that America needed to have men on the moon—there aren't any there now—but it certainly was a lasting stimulus to scientific and technological advance. The point was that SDI, whatever comes of it as a defensive shield against nuclear attack, is a massive program in high technology and, as such, is a powerful magnet for participation by countries, companies and campuses. We will return to that point later.

Past realization of impossible dreams, it scarcely needs to be said, is not enough to justify confidence in achieving a defense against presently unstoppable missiles spouting thermonuclear warheads. It may be true, as Mr. Weinberger never tires of saying, that SDI "offers more hope to mankind than any other proposal in recent times."

But it is also true that the Star Wars quest has an ingredient that was wholly missing in other visions. No Russians were trying to interfere with *Apollo* landings. In the cases noted above, the opponent was nature, and nature was alternately accommodating and unable to devise countermeasures. The Soviets say they will be rather more disagreeable. They will build more missiles and warheads, if necessary, to try to be able to saturate any U.S. defense. They will devise countermeasures to foil the defense. And they will go on working on their own SDI, which they deny doing in spite of the excellent satellite photographs and other evidence in American intelligence files.

My friend Richard L. Garwin, IBM Fellow at the Thomas J. Watson Research Center and another of those physicists who gave us nuclear weapons, is wholly able to contain his concerns about the menace of a Soviet SDI. He trudges to any forum in behalf of the Concerned Scientists to preach against the Reagan program, arguing that an almost infinitely complex system of space- and ground-based missile detectors, computers, directed energy weapons and command stations can be overcome with much less complex measures. One of his favorite countermeasures is space mines or inert objects (sand, for heaven's sake), which he believes could tear up lasers and the mirrors that would bounce their beams at missile targets.

"It's much easier to break a fine watch than to make a new one," Mr. Garwin says. So he favors research on a modest scale so that the United States will know how to counteract and penetrate a Soviet defense—to break a fine watch—if one is attempted.

Curious, and confused by the certitudes from all sides, I set out on a trip, blessed by the *Baltimore Sun,* to places where electromagnetic guns, high energy laser systems, neutral and charged particle beams, pulse power, magnetic fusion and other such baffling matters were under investigation or experimentation. Could we really put up a defense that would, at first, ensure that anyone would think twice before shooting nuclear weapons at us and, in the end, lead to abandonment of such weapons? The very short answer is that there are hopeful skeptics and there are those who believe that defense could come into the ascendancy, after years of superpower mutual vulnerability.

No one, however, expects that to happen in this century. And most agree that it must be paced with arms control negotiations that bring down the levels of offensive weapons during what would be a very tricky, not to say dangerous, transition period for untrusting superpowers.

Over a Chivas Regal nightcap in his spacious, modern home in Austin, Hans Mark, chancellor of the University of Texas, shared some thoughts he was putting in a book about people in space. Technical people who think a space-based defense cannot be done, he concluded, are wrong. He cited Arthur C. Clarke's first law of prophecy: "When a distinguished scientist says that something is possible, he is almost certainly right. When he states something is impossible, he is very probably wrong."

Hans Mark's credentials entitle him to a respectful hearing. He is a physicist, engineer, former head of the Lawrence Livermore National Laboratory's experimental physics division, former Air Force secretary and former deputy administrator of NASA, where he had much to do with the successful space shuttle and the Reagan Administration's decision to push for a manned space station.

As we pursued the conversation the next day in his office, Mr. Mark reflected on the interplay between policy goals and technological capabilities. Politicians, debating, reaching consensus and voting tax dollars, make new technologies possible. Technology then provides a framework for political action; to wit, nuclear weapons and the balance of terror. Now a new turn is coming with the fantastic progress in microelectronics, sensors and all those other Star Wars possibilities: a new framework that will diminish the importance of nuclear weapons.

"There will come a time in the not-too-distant future,"

he argued, "when the technical pieces will fall into place and when people will wonder why anyone ever doubted the feasibility of space-based missile defense systems."*

While President Reagan's announcement of his defense vision on that March night came as a complete surprise to the nation, I found that it was not so much so to the scientists and engineers in the great national laboratories in Albuquerque, Los Alamos and Livermore, California.

"It is not strange that we are back in the strategic defense debate," Roger Hagengruber, director of systems studies at Albuquerque's Sandia Laboratories, told me. The 1972 antiballistic missile treaty with the Soviet Union barred deployment of missile defenses except for one site on each side; Moscow has one, but Washington decided against one—but it did not ban research. Now, Mr. Hagengruber went on, there were technologies holding promise of reducing the advantages lying with the offense. And the Soviets had moved rapidly, not just with traditional defensive weapons such as ground-based interceptor missiles but with investigation of directed energy weapons as well.

Echoing these premises, Stephen Rockwood, director of defense research programs at the Los Alamos National Laboratory, said: "This lab has always been involved in thinking of ways that one might eventually negate the threat of the ICBM." And it was not only the strongly anti-SDI scientists who had raised the possibilities of Soviet steps to counteract a U.S. defense. "We are playing both sides," Mr. Rockwood said. "Anytime we have developed a capability that we think might be useful, then we immediately test it against one of our own systems and figure out how to make a countermeasure."

---

*Some of the pieces may come from work done at the University of Texas. Under contracts predating the SDI, the university's Center for Electromechanics is working on rail guns—weapons that would use electromagnetic energy rather than chemical energy, and drive a projectile at, say, a speed of sixty miles a second; SDI officials hold high hopes for them.

The United States, then, had never stopped looking for ways to end its vulnerability, and research had gradually been bolstering hopes that once seemed forlorn. What Mr. Reagan did with his SDI was to drag an array of separate programs out of the many competing bureaucracies and order a focused effort.

The idea obviously had long been on Mr. Reagan's mind. He thought there must be a better way than the balance of terror. In a visit to the North American Air Defense Command headquarters, deep in Cheyenne Mountain at Colorado Springs, before the 1980 campaign, Mr. Reagan was told what would happen if the command's satellite detection systems saw a missile headed this way. There would be a few minutes' warning, and that was it. Martin Anderson, a former presidential aide, wrote in the *New York Times* in October 1984 that Mr. Reagan "expressed deep concern that our nuclear missile policy had driven us into a box. We could retaliate massively, but we could do nothing to protect millions of Americans if—for whatever reason— we detected a nuclear missile soaring toward us."

In the middle of his first term, Mr. Reagan's National Security Council was secretly taking a new look at the possibilities of missile defense. Edward Teller, the "father" of the hydrogen bomb, told the President of defense possibilities. The military leadership did as well.

Government being the way it is, though, a year went by after the March 1983 speech before establishment of the Strategic Defense Initiative Organization, with Lieutenant General James A. Abrahamson, the dynamic officer who had directed the space shuttle program for NASA, as its head. It would be the fall of 1984 before Congress approved the organization's first budget—$1.4 billion.

Not much more money would be spent in that first year, fiscal 1985, than would have been spent anyway in the wide-ranging programs previously run by various elements of the Defense Department. These had been under way for years. (It was little noted at the time, but on the same day that Mr. Reagan made his Star Wars speech, a high Defense Department official testified to Congress quite by coincidence that decisions for "on-orbit demonstrations" of lasers might be made by 1988.)

Thereafter, though, the SDI was "spinning up the wheel," as Gerold Yonas, its chief scientist, put it. A six-year $33-billion outlay was projected to learn whether an effective defense seemed feasible and affordable, so that Congress and the President of the time would have the technical foundation for deciding—at the turn of the decade—whether to go ahead with development.

This was the timetable, with all the demonstrations and tests it implied, that stirred the foes of missile defenses in Congress, universities and elsewhere. Instead of a steady year-in, year-out level of effort, hedging against Soviet surprises, the opponents now thought they saw figurative milestones laid out and more than a suggestion of actual systems development with some initial operational date in mind.

Presidents more usually are castigated for letting weapons with big constituencies drive their strategies. This was one of those rare times when a President laid down in advance a policy to guide strategic developments. As Colin S. Gray, a public policy "think tank" proprietor, wrote in a Brookings Institution book on missile defense: "This is one of those historically unusual cases where a government has decided what it would like to accomplish long ahead of technical realization."

That any Star Wars defense is far from technical realization is not in doubt. Congressional restraints on the wished-for research budget may slow the planned pace. Antinuclear forces are mounting heavy resistance, seeing it as sure to provoke Moscow into producing even greater stocks of nuclear arms with which to overwhelm such a defense.

But traveling about the national research establishments and watching the award of contracts to universities, one must conclude that, whatever the uncertainties and the resistance, the program also has a compelling attractiveness. This will draw in better people—so many of the better people, some critics say, that other areas of science will suffer.

If physicists of one university turn thumbs down on Star Wars, those of another sign on for multimillion-dollar research contracts. One consortium of five universities,* for example, has taken on a large research effort on nonnuclear power for driving the space-based machinery of a strategic defense system, and will educate engineers and physicists, the Pentagon says, to meet "the growing manpower demands of the space power industry."

It affects "the character of a program when you feel that the President and members of Congress and the country really want to succeed, and that's really not what's been going on [in missile defense] for the past fifteen years," Richard J. Briggs, a key research director at the Lawrence Livermore Laboratory, told me. "The best people would look for areas where they felt there was a real commitment." Now those areas may be in the SDI. "If in fact the enthusiasm builds up and better people indeed want to look hard at it, I think we may find that some good things may come out of it."

There are research programs—and missile defense seems to have been one in the past—where there is a feeling that not too much progress is wanted, for that would send it "up the political chain to face hard questions of what to do with success," Mr. Briggs observed.

The evidence now is that current political leaders want

---

*Auburn University, the Polytechnic Institute of New York, State University of New York (Buffalo), Texas Tech University, and the University of Texas (Arlington).

their hands forced, so to speak, by Star Wars research success. On that score, Mr. Briggs offered:

"I think that I can predict with fair confidence there are going to be some tough decisions about what to do with the technology that will come along in the next three to five years."

In summary, then, both the United States and the Soviet Union have had long-running research programs on how to defend against nuclear weapons. There is a good deal of conviction in the laboratories that technological progress over recent years makes the Star Wars pursuit worthwhile. There is also enormous disagreement with that viewpoint, as such an expert judgment as Harold Brown's makes evident. There is some belief that defense could be less dangerous than the alternative—a huge new effort to build up our offensive forces. Steady research progress may force ultimate decisions on politicians sooner than they expect. But Star Wars remains a twenty-first century—not a twentieth century—prospect.

Assume that a time does indeed come when research results convince political leaders that Star Wars defenses are feasible and affordable. How, you then may ask, would the system work, and would it be wise to build it?

Caveats are indicated here. The Star Wars directors are far from deciding which of the many bits and pieces of exotic hardware, now in research, might be chosen for a complex defensive system. Consequently, estimates that it would cost $1 trillion, or any other amount, have to be regarded as just that—estimates. There is no debating that it would be enormously expensive, a characteristic that it would share, incidentally, with the great arsenals of offensive nuclear weapons built over the post–World War II years. The real price issue is whether Star Wars would cost less than the design and production of means to defeat it, of new or improved missiles toughened to withstand lasers, for example, and of warheads so numerous that they would overwhelm the defense.

"If we deploy anything," Mr. Yonas says, "the weapons will have to be very lethal, very cost-effective and very survivable . . . I can't do a cost analysis now. I can't even tell you what the component parts [of a defense system] are. That's why we keep saying it's a research program."

In general, though, to return to the question of how it would work, the idea is to cover the earth with layers of electronic nets that would detect, track and fire off weapons—some at the speed of light—to knock out missiles launched at the United States and/or its allies. SDI directors are far from knowing how much of the system would be based in space and how much on the ground. The operation would be managed by computers, yet to be built, that keep tabs on tens of thousands of objects in space. Directors talk of designing small computers that could perform a trillion operations per second.

Would war be declared, then, by computers rather than by political leaders? No, say the SDI managers; there would be "humans in the loop." But much of the system would surely be semi-autonomous. Ground-based commanders would determine, on evidence beamed from space, that a missile attack had roared out of Soviet silos. They would then command space-based automatic battle stations to go into action.

Intercontinental missiles—Star Wars targets—span 5,500 miles in thirty minutes. They need 150 to 300 seconds for the boost phase, when their rocket engines lift them above the atmosphere, giving off a bright flame that registers nicely on infrared detectors waiting in space.

In the post-boost phase, a "bus" riding on top of the missile separates from the spent rocket and releases nuclear warheads and decoys—fake warheads to confuse defenses. Now the attack enters the midcourse phase, a longish period of about twenty minutes when a "threat cloud" of warheads, decoys and junk sails through space six hundred miles above the earth.

Finally, in the terminal phase, the warheads plummet through the atmosphere toward separate targets. This takes about five minutes. The last-ditch defenses go into action.

It is important to bear in mind that what is described here is a "structured attack," an attempt to time the descent of thousands of thermonuclear weapons to predialed targets in order to disarm the country attacked. Anything less would guarantee destruction of the attacker by surviving missiles launched in retaliation. This is the "balance by terror" that keeps the peace through the threat of mutual annihilation.

In asking for something better, President Reagan said: "The human spirit must be capable of rising above dealing with other nations and human beings by threatening their existence." The Union of Concerned Scientists thinks human minds can't perform the technological feat. Declaring "there is not a shred of scientific evidence" that Star Wars will work, the UCS says the "Buck Rogers components" would work together only by "the wildest coincidence of miracles."

Maybe so, but the Star Wars men are scientists and engineers, too, many of them of a new generation that can mix optimism with caution about the technologies and concepts that have marched along in recent years. "Some really new ideas" are coming into play, says Bruce Miller, the thirty-eight-year-old chief of directed energy research at Sandia National Laboratories.

Certainly, the almost frantic opposition from Moscow suggests that the Russians, having themselves long explored some of the more exotic aspects, believe the Buck Rogers components might work together. Here is a plain worry that American technology is again about to leapfrog theirs. Doubts like those of the UCS would persist. But on the wild chance that they might contemplate an attack, wouldn't military planners in Moscow have to make the worst-case judgment—that the defense indeed would work—and thus be deterred?

The possible weapons of Star Wars are what quickly gave Mr. Reagan's Strategic Defense Initiative its nickname, indicating to some that it was nonsense and to others that reality was about to take over from science fiction.

These weapons are space-based lasers (light amplification by stimulated emission of radiation) and atomic particle beams, ground-based lasers that bounce their deadly light beams off mirrors in space and thence to the targets, chemical rockets with their own tiny computers and target seekers, electromagnetic guns that fire "smart" self-guided projectiles or "dumb" ones that need laser beam guidance and, says Mr. Yonas, devices yet to be invented.

The idea behind all these is to deliver bursts of energy over great distances—500 to 1,800 miles—and knock out nuclear weapons before they can do any damage.

If a laser beam can be held on a fragile rocket booster long enough, after reaching it at the speed of light, it will melt the surface. In SDI's first "laser lethality test" in September 1985 at the White Sands Missile Range in New Mexico, a high energy laser beam destroyed a Titan missile booster in a few seconds. One aim of such tests is to see what it would take to "harden" rocket boosters to withstand laser attack. Laser beams will propagate through the atmosphere, so these Star Wars weapons can be based either in space or, for greater security and ease of maintenance, on the ground.

Neutral particle beams—that is, beams of hydrogen atoms stripped of their extra electron—do not stop on the surface as lasers do but can penetrate the nuclear warheads' innards and cause electronic failure or, if powerful enough, structural failure. Since the atmosphere would interfere with the particle beam, the beam accelerator would have to be based in space.

Los Alamos' Mr. Rockwood pondered that necessity. Putting the necessary machinery in space for particle beam weapons would be essentially an engineering job because "there isn't much we don't know about accelerators." It would be a "nice challenge" though. The thing would be up to fifty feet long, at least two loads for the space shuttle to ferry into orbit. "It will take a fairly dedicated effort." Mr. Rockwood is not given to overstatement.

For all the talk of beam weapons and the rapid progress in technology, however, the most advanced weapon now available is the self-guided chemical fuel rocket. It possesses its own little computer, thrusters to keep it on course and a device to seek out the target. In June 1984 the Army dispatched one of these homing interceptors straight into the dummy warhead of an intercontinental missile above the atmosphere over the Pacific. (The Army said the infrared sensor in the projectile was so sensitive that it could sniff out heat equal to a human body's from a distance of a thousand miles.) Weapons like this could intercept attacking missiles and might also be placed in space battle stations for self-defense.

The chemical rocket has a problem, however; it lumbers along at barely three miles a second. It might be a bit of a chore for it to deal with a target moving almost as fast. So Star Wars managers have rekindled enthusiasm for the electromagnetic slingshot—the hypervelocity gun that might be a gap filler between beam weapons, which do not yet have the power to kill missiles, and chemical rockets. It could combine speed and killing power. This weapon is sometimes called a rail gun because its projectile is fired off by an electric arc propelled along two rails. The projectile can be a "smart rock" or a "dumb" one. A reasonable hope for the rail gun, say its partisans, is that it can be developed to hurl a 1- to 10-gram projectile at sixty miles per second, which would be like a hurricane driving a straw through a tree.

Thus far, we have been speaking of nonnuclear weapons—the kinds that the Administration constantly says will make nuclear weapons obsolete. There is, however, a strong exception to this nonnuclear theology, a sort of third-generation nuclear weapon (the first two generations being fission and fusion bombs) that is being vigorously pursued by the Energy Department and particularly by the Lawrence Livermore National Laboratory.

This is the nuclear-pumped X-ray laser, essentially a hydrogen bomb explosion in space with fractions of the immense energy converted into directed beams to destroy missile boosters and warheads. The weapon would be "popped up" from the ground on top of a rocket on warning of an attack and would self-destruct after releasing its X rays in a millionth of a second.

The argument can be made that the third-generation nuclear weapon is plainly defensive and is quite different from its offensive atomic fission and thermonuclear antecedents. It is nuclear, nevertheless, and causes some friction inside the SDI organization. The main backers of the X-ray laser are Edward Teller, the "father" of the hydrogen bomb, and his protégés at Livermore.

James A. Ionson, the young physicist who in Washington heads SDI's most far-out investigations, says the nuclear-pumped laser weapon "kind of defeats the whole purpose" of the Star Wars quest and, in any case, is not the best way to go about the task.

He looks for more efficient ways to produce X-ray beams with special kinds of lasers, making the Teller concepts "antique."

President Reagan has seemingly had it both ways. In his

speech in May 1985 to the European Parliament in Strasbourg, France, the President spoke of technology that "may soon make possible, for the first time, the ability to use nonnuclear systems to defeat ballistic missiles."

At the end of the same month, he issued a national security directive that included a call for continued exploration of "the promising concepts which use nuclear energy to power devices which could destroy ballistic missiles at great distances."

Defense authorities press forward with nuclear X-ray work not only to see whether the devices have defense promise here but to learn how effective they might be if developed for the Soviet arsenal.

In this connection, the SDI organization has awarded contracts to numerous universities for research on protection of space-based electronic systems against electromagnetic waves, atomic particle beams and other "man-made influences on the earth's space environment."

The toughest missile-interception task that the SDI directors have set themselves and the most rewarding if they bring it off—whatever weapons they may finally decide on—is to catch attacking rockets in the boost phase. Researchers in the labs point out that there is an "incredibly" short time to do this, five minutes at most. ("Incredibly" is one of their favorite words, for the difficult nature of the defense job they have been given and for the great technological strides that may result.) If a speed-of-light weapon flashes across 1,800 miles and zaps a missile booster, it destroys ten warheads, the number on top of a single missile. If a single space battle station shoots down fifty missiles, the leverage for the defense is 500 to 1. If!

Remember that the "threat cloud" sails along for maybe twenty minutes. Star Wars lab people believe this is where there can be a huge payoff. Particle beams could tell the real warheads from the decoys and space junk; this is called discrimination. The beams would go through the light decoys and these could be ignored. But when they strike the warheads, the objects with mass, they would give off radiation that would inform sensors these were the targets to attack. Mr. Rockwood likens this to Superman's X-ray vision.

Weapons like the homing interceptor demonstrated by the Army would probably be used for last-ditch terminal defenses.

Star Wars rests on the microelectronics revolution, making possible the harnessing of computer power to weapons, sensors and communications systems. This, says SDI's systems director John L. Gardner, means solutions for problems "you couldn't have touched ten years ago."

Head spinning, I dropped in to see one Cory Coll, a major figure in defense research at Livermore and one of Star Wars' hopeful skeptics. He had a knack for bringing one down to earth. Sure, all the pieces could be developed separately in maybe twenty years. Whether they could be assembled in space battle stations and ground facilities and made to work, well, that was a different question. Mr. Coll, feeling like someone told to turn the Wright brothers' "flyer" into a 747 overnight, put it this way:

"If I walked into a room and looked at all these [Star Wars] pieces, I'd feel like I'd walked into a room full of automobile parts; boy, they're the best parts that money can buy. There they are, just sitting out there, and I say, Gee, that looks pretty impressive. But I don't have a clue when I put all that stuff together, am I gonna get a Mercedes or an Edsel?"

Managing a space battle between missiles and Star Wars ray guns, he noted, would be pretty much up to the fantastic computers yet to be produced. Warning satellites 22,300 miles out in space would give notice that a massive attack had started. They would tell ground commanders—and computers. The computers would count and start tracking the targets and assign weapons to go after them. They must be able to tell which were hit and which must be reattacked. Through each stage, from boost to terminal, data must be relayed.

Computers are, say, like a bunch of people who know how to add and subtract, but need instructions to solve complex problems. Do one thing if this happens, another thing if that happens. Expect different problems from one day to the next. Instructions have to be written.

Mr. Coll reckoned maybe ten million lines of instructions might have to be written for the Star Wars computers—anyway, more than ever done before.

"It's hard to imagine a half-dozen people understanding enough of the program to be able to understand the whole thing and make sure that there aren't some quirks or errors introduced in just the computer software," Mr. Coll judged.

Star Wars apart, computers are becoming so capable that writing the instructions is a challenging new problem. SDI directors, more optimistic than Mr. Coll, expect to make a major contribution to automated software production—computers writing instructions for computers—and spin off benefits in many other areas where handling complex problems in "real time" is of the essence; air traffic control is an obvious one.

To digress further, the certainty of revolutions in technology is reason enough for a conviction that the Strategic Defense Initiative will not be turned off. Concern about being left behind is bringing foreign companies to the SDI door to line up with domestic companies and campuses for shares of the action.

"Almost everything you can think of has some bearing on SDI, except maybe the biology of cacti," says Jim Ionson.

Whether or not it ever renders nuclear weapons obsolete, as Mr. Reagan fondly expects, it is coming on as the vastest research and engineering enterprise there ever was. It will produce forward leaps in military and commercial technology that will boggle the mind.

Free electron lasers that can be tuned to tell the difference between a real warhead and a fake hurtling through space can as well be tuned for bloodless, nontraumatic surgery. They can diagnose the complex structure of the human organism, just as they can probe a "threat cloud."

The need for great bursts of power in space battle stations is leading to development of new materials for capacitors, devices to store electrical energy, that will have many times the power previously available and can as well run industrial and medical lasers and keep automobiles—electric cars—running for weeks. An experimental refrigerator, just three inches on a side, can cool infrared sensing chips for detecting enemy rockets—or for astrophysicists' star searches and satellite surveillance of weather patterns.

Mr. Ionson expects to participate in a computer revolution, with photons (packets of light) replacing electrons as the information carriers. Before he's finished, he says, he expects to "fit into a coffee cup the equivalent of a Cray supercomputer." The list could go on and on.

President Reagan, as dedicated as he is to change, has nowhere else stimulated a longer-lasting or farther-reaching debate than he has with his proposal for a "splendid defense" to replace the "balance of terror."

The controversy, though, centers chiefly on how fast to proceed with research and toward what ends, rather than on whether to strangle the SDI outright: Toward steady inquiries like those over the years since the 1972 Anti-Ballistic Missile (ABM) Treaty was signed? Toward more diligent efforts to guard against technological surprises from the Soviet Union's large program? Or, and this is the real center of contention, toward some planned date for deciding to deploy a full-scale Star Wars system on the earth and in orbit about the earth?

Representative Les Aspin, the Wisconsin Democrat who

chairs the House Armed Services Committee, has very large doubts about the feasibility of a Star Wars defense. But he speaks for many when he says, "It is too appealing a prospect to dismiss without examination." Research should go on, within the boundaries of the ABM Treaty.

Suppose, then, that a decade of multibillion-dollar examination demonstrates that a defense against offensive nuclear weapons would work; that is, foredoom an attack. General Abrahamson, the SDI director, would be right in describing as "hogwash" claims that the system would be fragile and would lead to unprecedented destruction. He would be right in asking, as he does, who could hope to time the arrival of thousands of warheads on predetermined targets in a structured attack when there was no idea which ones or how many would penetrate the multilayered defense.

Suppose all that. The question remains: Would it be wise policy to deploy a Star Wars defense?

Many are rushing to judgment in both directions—Mr. Weinberger, for example, is a self-announced "true believer"; the UCS says it's "foolhardy."

While the real answers may lie years (decades?) in the future, domestic and international political controversy heats up now. That is as it should be. In virtually countless ways, Star Wars is a threat to the status quo and in all those ways it must be debated.

In its vision of a "splendid defense," thoroughly reliable, it fundamentally challenges the strategic doctrine that has governed since World War II, that is, deterrence of war by threat of nuclear retaliation. The new concept, as Mr. Reagan tries to popularize it, would be to kill weapons instead of people. Perfected, it would make militarily unsound the idea of a preemptive nuclear strike. What is seen here as defensive in intent, however, could be seen by the other superpower as aggressive, as, indeed, Russian leader Mikhail

Gorbachev told the President at their Geneva Conference in November 1985. In this view, Star Wars would be regarded as an American scheme to be able to launch such a first strike and then sweep away the puny Soviet counterattack with space-based man-made lightning bolts. This could make for a dangerous period while the strategic defense was being deployed and the Russians were rushing ahead with weapons to attack it, and with their own defense, of course.

The "splendid defense" is intended to protect allies as well as Americans, as is repeatedly argued here. But Europeans—not consulted in advance and always jittery about U.S. defense departures—imagine some sort of American astrodome and a return to isolation under it, while they end up providing a battlefield for the superpowers. French President François Mitterand has bluntly rejected U.S. Star Wars and tried with indifferent luck to establish a European technology effort called Eureka. Britain has decided to participate in the research. West Germany is divided and rightly concerned for its Eastern relations, but is likely to come along, too. All over Europe, where technology lags, companies want to know, however, how to get into the SDI enterprise. And one can cynically look for European antinuclear forces—the "peace" forces that tried to keep out American intermediate-range missiles—to protest a Star Wars switch to "provocative" nonnuclear defenses.

The status quo in arms control is exemplified, to many, by the 1972 Anti-Ballistic Missile Treaty, which greatly restricts what can be done about ballistic missile defenses. Star Wars research so far is within treaty tolerances, and the Administration keeps saying it will observe the treaty. There is no evident way, however, that Star Wars itself could be realized within the pact as it now stands. The congressional Office of Technology Assessment observed in a report last year that proposed technology experiments raised compliance questions and that the sense of urgency behind SDI raised political questions about the U.S. commitment to the treaty. There was a fundamental issue, it also said, of whether the treaty "continues to be compatible with our national interest." Washington and Moscow recognized in framing the treaty, however, that changes could come. They agreed to review it at five-year intervals and they also agreed to discuss limitations on future technological developments beyond those contemplated when they signed the agreement.

American military backing for Star Wars is solid today. But, as we have said, the SDI is a high-cost undertaking. Someday, perhaps soon, it could bring distortions in the defense budget that would worry the leaders of more conventional air, land and sea formations, with their immediate needs. This would be another threat to a status quo and one that comes in a time of much slower rising military budgets than the forces had grown used to in Mr. Reagan's first term.

In debating Star Wars, we are all of necessity caught up in a time problem. We argue the politics and technology in today's context, but we are arguing about something that will happen—if it happens—in a far different time that many of the present protagonists will not see, in the twenty-first century.

Hear Gerold Yonas on the point:

"People who pursue beyond the state-of-the-art technology have to be by nature optimistic people. You don't go on exploring new territory if you're continually convinced that you're going to fall into quicksand. If somebody goes into this kind of venture with a fundamentally negative attitude, or the feeling that the twenty-first century is going to be like the twentieth century—that we've reached the plateau in knowledge, all of man's knowledge has come to the highest level it's coming to, all of the frontiers have been pushed back—that kind of a person is not going to play much of a role in this kind of program."

Who is? "People who have a feeling that there's a continuity, a continuous evolution of knowledge, and the past was just one step leading to a future, and see a flow of history, and are working in their own little project to believe there's a solution."

Laurence Martin, while professor of war studies at the University of London, had a pungent and still-relevant observation on all this when he wrote in the summer of 1969:

> The notion that the safety of the world must rest forever on mutual vulnerability is, after all, the product of no more than two decades of thought, and there is some intellectual arrogance in assuming that such a brief period of reflection has produced answers that must henceforth go unquestioned.

As for Star Wars itself, it remains to offer a reflection, as twentieth-century people mull over its wisdom. It is simply this: Wherever there is something important to nations (or whatever we have in the twenty-first century), they will defend their interest in it. There are very important assets in space now—satellites of many kinds, manned shuttles flying somewhat routinely, the beginnings of small production enterprises, the tracks that missiles would fly. More than 200 humans have been there and Hans Mark is "willing to bet" that 50,000 will have been there by 2011, just twenty-five years hence.

Explorers and settlers have historically had cops to look after them. Space is not likely to be different.

ROUNDTABLE DISCUSSION

"Star Wars"

PANELISTS: Paul Duke, *moderator*
Charles Corddry
Georgie Anne Geyer
Haynes Johnson
Charles McDowell
Jack Nelson
Hedrick Smith

DUKE: Could Star Wars be one of those major turning points in history such as the arrival of gunpowder or the airplane or the atomic bomb?

CORDDRY: What I am suggesting is that we may be headed into a period where defense might be in the ascendancy and the importance of nuclear weapons might diminish. I'm talking about the twenty-first century. Scientists by that time may be able to bail out the politicians who have not done so well on getting rid of nuclear weapons.

JOHNSON: What intrigues me is the possibility of a fail-safe system to negate the horrors of nuclear war. That's certainly worth pursuing.

At the same time, isn't it true that throughout human history every time there's been a great new advance supposedly to safeguard human beings against the threat of war, someone always comes along and pierces it? The upshot is that the level of danger is constantly being raised.

CORDDRY: It's awful hard to fault you on that,

Haynes. It could be pointed out that for all the years since World War II we've had a stable situation, at least as far as World War III might be concerned, because of the existence of the atomic bomb and then the thermonuclear bomb. I think that the evolution of military defenses and offenses is not going to be stopped.

So, looking way into the next century, I can imagine Star Wars. In other words, if you can shoot down missiles with beams, you can shoot down spaceships with beams. I would remind you wherever man has gone, wherever explorers have gone and established new frontiers, they've been accompanied by their defense forces who have managed to get in a fight.

JOHNSON: And therefore something that starts out as a peace-saving device could wind up as the most dangerous of all ventures.

McDOWELL: Does anyone here really think we can hold back the advance of technology?

DUKE: But Haynes is making a more fundamental point, that we're fooling ourselves if we believe this grand new design for our defense offers real security. History teaches the point. Back in medieval days they had castles which they thought were impregnable. Then gunpowder was invented to blow down the castle walls. We had ships that were considered difficult to knock out, and then submarines came along to sink the ships. The French had their Maginot Line in World War II which was supposed to be impenetrable until the Nazi blitzkrieg tore it to shreds.

So the question is, where is there a secure defense in anything?

McDOWELL: I'm only trying to make the point that the advance of technology is inexorable. That it's best not just to throw up our hands and resist Star Wars. We're probably going to have to accept it.

SMITH: I am convinced that technology is not inexorable. There are choices that we can make. We made a choice fifteen years ago when we reached our first set of arms agreements with the Soviets. We had a choice then as to whether we were going to go along with the technology. We made a political choice about whether we were going to put multiple warheads on top of individual missiles.

I remember sitting in a hotel in Moscow, listening to Henry Kissinger in 1972 give a briefing on the arms agreements that Richard Nixon and Leonid Brezhnev were about to sign the next day, and he argued that the sophistication of American missiles with their multiple warheads was going to provide great protection and counterbalance the large, huge single-warhead Soviet missiles that so threatened us.

We made a decision to go ahead with that technology because we thought it would buy safety. And ten years later, the Soviets had the same multiple warheads mounted on those huge missiles, and they're now frightening the hell out of us. At that time, though, we could have reached an agreement with the Soviets not to have those warheads. We could have stopped that technology, but we made a political decision not to do so.

GEYER: But the political decision has always been to go ahead, and I think that's the way it should be. Perhaps the scientists and the military geniuses will fight it out in the skies and the people on earth will be left to kill one another with axes and handguns and all those other wonderful things that we use today to kill one another.

CORDDRY: We also made a choice at that Moscow conference, Rick, not to have ballistic missile defenses. The benefit that we got out of that was to save a lot of money that we would have spent on defenses that didn't work. In the meantime, though, both sides have continued to develop defenses that now are revolutionary compared with those banned in the 1972 ABM Treaty. I simply don't think that nations are going to make treaties that say, in effect, you can't use your brains.

From the American point of view, the Soviets now have an enormous arsenal. The 1972 agreements did not prevent them from building more missiles.

Now you're coming to a point where you must choose whether to expand the American offensive arsenal or to attempt to devalue the Soviet arsenal by building some kind of tough missile defense.

If you build a ballistic defense system, the argument runs, the Soviets will try to saturate it. But the Soviets have a defense of their own, and they've got a heavy investment in it, and if they attempt to race us on offensive weapons again, they run the risk that we will respond, and that will devalue their defense.

So my point is that we've got some immediate problems, and the answers aren't clear. They're not all on one side or the other.

The onward march of technology is not something that's going to be stopped, not by agreements of superpowers talking in Geneva or elsewhere, because both have enormous far-flung laboratories. You can't stop Star Wars research because the same research applies to short-range tactical weapons, to medical matters, to commercial enterprises—there's nothing that Star Wars doesn't encompass in the end.

SMITH: We're talking about a rivalry between superpowers who are getting ever more sophisticated weapons. I'm not talking about whether this system can work or whether the Soviets are going to counter it, but every time we thought that atomic bombs or hydrogen bombs or MIRV warheads or whatever were going to take us to that point where we're secure, it hasn't worked.

A more important question is whether there's a way in which we can use the research that is already under way as a bargaining chip, even though that's not what Reagan wants to do, to try to get the kind of restraints that will provide a greater degree of safety than we have today.

JOHNSON: We keep advancing weaponry to safeguard ourselves, and devote more time to that than to disbanding the weaponry that created the tensions.

NELSON: That's the point—that Star Wars will make for more destabilization by transferring the military rivalry into space. Defense Secretary Weinberger even acknowledges that it could be destabilizing if you give one side a shield that the other could not penetrate, and hence that side could launch a war behind it.

CORDDRY: Mr. Weinberger would not entertain that view if we had the shield. But he thinks it'd be horrible if the Soviet Union had the shield and we didn't.

McDOWELL: The Star Wars concept may seem awful and destabilizing but I'm persuaded we're going to go into space with this sophisticated stuff.

GEYER: Of course we are. All of this is bringing out the President's idealistic side. When he talks about Star Wars, he talks about ending warfare, about ending nuclear threats. I'd like to know whether Nancy is behind this.

DUKE: Isn't there a nostalgic side to this? Doesn't it fit Reagan's politics? The politics of a man who wants to see America as Mr. Big in the world again and wants to return to a simpler time when we all felt secure?

GEYER: That's what I'm trying to get at.

DUKE: But isn't that illusory?

JOHNSON: Reagan does seem to give an impression that he ardently believes that there is a formula by which you can safeguard humanity. I am reminded that Winston Churchill believed that the tank would end war.

McDOWELL: It may be illusory, as some of you think, but the balance of terror has to be the maddest notion that mankind has ever devised. So it may be a good thing if we can develop a weapon to control weapons.

SMITH: Of course, that's the dream—to control weapons.

The real question is whether the process of getting there sets loose political and technological dynamics which are even more disruptive than what we face today.

We're talking about technology, but the real issue is politics.

DUKE: The late Senator Henry Jackson, who used to be the foremost Democratic defense expert on Capitol Hill, was fond of saying that the one thing you had to guard against was making the Russians feel cornered. Isn't it entirely possible that the Russians will feel that the United States is trying to gain a strategic advantage over them, and hence they might be encouraged at some point to make a preventive strike against the United States?

CORDDRY: There's the rub. If Star Wars works, it could indeed put nuclear weapons out of business. Or at least they would have greatly diminished value.

But the question is how you get there. It requires Russian and American cooperation all the way. The day will come, let's say, when both countries decide they do indeed know how to mount a ballistic missile defense. Do they dare agree that, therefore, they will reduce their offensive missile arsenals by 30 percent a year while making the transition to the new defense system?

This would be the dangerous period. This is the period that the Union of Concerned Scientists and many other critics worry about because neither country would trust the other to throw out its missiles. I don't know who you'd get to police that.

NELSON: If, for example, the Soviets developed such a shield first, we would be concerned that they would launch a first strike. So they've got to have the same concern about us.

CORDDRY: I'm sure they see us as Romans with a shield and sword, and the Romans never won anything just using their shields. But somehow we have to persuade them that that's wrong, and that's why I say it's dangerous.

Now, let's bear in mind that Mr. Reagan's not going to decide this thing because he'll be gone, and I don't know whether Mr. Gorbachev will either, although he may if he's around for a good long time.

DUKE: Rick, having been a Moscow correspondent for several years, what do you think the Russians' real feeling is about Star Wars?

SMITH: Well, one of the most important things to know about the Russians is they have the biggest Avis complex in the world. Whatever it is they're saying publicly, deep down they're convinced they're number two, and this is historic. They felt that way when they were fighting the Swedes in the seventeenth century. They felt that way when they were fighting Napoleon. Many of them will tell you in private conversation that they can't really believe they beat the Germans because the Germans had a higher culture and greater technology and were more modern. And there's no question from my experience living there that they regarded us as number one.

So they have an insecurity and an inferiority complex which often drives them to excesses along with their ambition for world power. Their arms buildup that dates back over twenty years comes from the humiliation they suffered at the time of Cuba when they had to pull their missiles out, and they felt inferior to us. They couldn't stand up to us, and they said, "Never again, we're going to build up to the point where the Americans can't push us around again."

So I think what happens when we come along with something like Star Wars is all those deep cultural anxieties and insecurities are activated. They're scared stiff even though they may talk boldly in public about what they're going to do.

GEYER: They're scared for another reason as well. I had talks with several high-level Russians recently—the political editor of *Izvestia*, people from the Soviet embassy—and the thing that they stressed is the cost to them. They are terrified because they don't have the money to put into a counter-Star Wars program. They want to deal with economic problems at home.

SMITH: Gorbachev is a high tech leader of the new generation. He wants to move that society in the direction of high technology. He has even begun to bring back some of the military leaders who were inclined to move in that direction.

The Soviet leadership historically has looked for reasons to rally their people to a cause, whether it's to fight a Nazi invasion or to oppose foreign embargoes, and to make sacrifices. The bugaboo of Star Wars used by Soviet propagandists, not at the world at large but at home and with Soviet bureaucrats over the allocation of resources, is a marvelous tool for Gorbachev to mobilize his own society to do what he wants to do otherwise.

So Star Wars is a vehicle for modernization of the Soviet economy as well as their military technology.

JOHNSON: From the American standpoint, then, Star Wars may be counterproductive in the sense that it could make the Russians stronger, not weaker.

DUKE: That would be a great paradox.

GEYER: But I see it differently. Gorbachev won't be able to do it. He can't afford it.

SMITH: I don't believe that. When the Soviets have to make sacrifices for security purposes, they do it, and they squeeze the belts of their people in ways that the Americans just simply wouldn't tolerate or wouldn't believe. They've done it again and again.

DUKE: In a broader political frame, we've been thinking that perhaps Gorbachev is a man that we could do business with, that maybe East-West relations would improve under this man. How will Star Wars affect the overall world struggle? The argument advanced by Gorbachev and the Soviets at the Geneva Summit Meeting was that Star Wars is a sham, a U.S. smokescreen to develop additional offensive missiles.

CORDDRY: The Russians can't really be so stupid as to believe that. The idea that we would build more missiles behind this facade—I mean, there's no way the Russians would not know about it if we did.

GEYER: The President keeps saying we'll share Star Wars technology. Is that for real?

CORDDRY: I assume that he means it, but as Robert McNamara says, if the U.S. won't let Japan have the Apple II computer, it's certainly not going to let the Soviet Union have Star Wars. [Laughter.]

NELSON: The President often refers to this as his dream, and that's what I think it is. It's a dream—to make it available to the entire world for the elimination of all nuclear offensive missiles.

GEYER: To Muammar Qaddafi?

NELSON: The whole world.

GEYER: To the Ayatollah Khomeini? To Pol Pot? To Idi Amin?

CORDDRY: It's just absurd.

GEYER: What we might be seeing in Ronald Reagan, the man who tries to come across as a hardliner, as a cynic about human nature, is the American idealist who thinks there really is a technological answer to mankind's problems.

DUKE: That may be, but many scientists contend that Star Wars can never be made to work. These critics say you can't devise a trustworthy computer system to run such an enormous defense system.

CORDDRY: One short answer would be to tell that to AT&T and then go look at their system. But the fact of the matter is, yes, of course, it's exaggerated, as all these great issues are in order to sell them, and I think the further fact is that every point raised against SDI is accepted by the people running the program, with the answer that we should at least try to find out if it's workable. We may want to do this because the Russians are sure working on a system of their own. It's a technology race.

DUKE: Even if we do put it up, Charlie, even if the scientists do ultimately deliver, then the question becomes: Can we trust it? Can we trust such an unbelievably complex system to really work during an emergency?

CORDDRY: Those are good points because you're never going to test it in its entirety but once.

NELSON: [Chuckling] And it won't be a test.

CORDDRY: But the counter-question is: Can the Soviet Union assume that it doesn't work? They simply cannot make that assumption, because if they're already scared of it, what are they going to be when they find it there? Again, the declared policy is to negotiate the deployment, not to put it up unilaterally. You have to keep that in mind.

McDOWELL: When will the national choice be made?

CORDDRY: The choice is being made right now, and it's being done in the following manner:

The Congress is putting up a sum of money each year, less than asked for but I suspect enough. The Strategic Defense Initiative Organization is involving industry as fast as it can, it is involving the campuses as fast as it can and it is involving the Europeans and the Japanese if it can. Those are powerful forces.

And on the day that the national choice that you speak of ought to come up and be a big deal, it already will have been made.

McDOWELL: That's a discouraging answer.

JOHNSON: How does the military see all this? I have heard Maxwell Taylor, the former chairman of the Joint Chiefs of Staff and a great Army general, say we never sufficiently debate *real* security issues. And there's such a thing as spending so much money you might weaken the country's defenses by weakening its economy and therefore its real security.

CORDDRY: The Strategic Defense Initiative has the highest priority, and the military services have been told that, and they saluted and marched forward.

Once the big military spending spree comes to an end and the defense budget levels off, Star Wars will begin eating up a larger share of the Pentagon funds and then you will get your infighting from the armed services.

JOHNSON: There are many things pressing for federal dollars. Take the AIDS epidemic, and the enormous outlays in research funds that may be needed to conquer that disease.

If you're spending more money for a large new defense project, there may be less for other worthwhile things. Doesn't there have to be a mix of the nation's health, wealth and security?

CORDDRY: The Star Wars budget is projected at $33 billion over six years, and this just to find out whether we know how to do it. I think Congress won't vote this much money, and there's no reason it should, for heaven's sake. That's a very steep climb.

NELSON: Didn't James Schlesinger, the former defense secretary under Gerald Ford, testify that if you finally did develop it that the cost would be anywhere from a half a trillion to a trillion dollars?

CORDDRY: Right. The first trillion-dollar weapons system.

JOHNSON: There seems to be an American need to believe that there's a technological answer to human life, that the big car is best or the big space shuttle or some other big thing you put in your ear that blasts your head off—that these things will make us happier human beings. [Laughter.]

No, I'm serious. We are wrapped up in this belief that somehow the answer to all tough problems is technology.

DUKE: There's another defense issue here. It involves the raging argument in this country about whether we are building too many nuclear weapons and ignoring our conventional forces.

Are we creating new problems for ourselves by putting too many of our defense eggs in the Star Wars basket?

CORDDRY: This may seem a silly answer, Paul. It's going to depend on how many defense eggs there are. The Europeans, for example, worry that Star Wars would regenerate isolation in this country. Nobody thinks Star Wars is going to do away with war, and that there wouldn't have to be money for conventional defense. The question is, how much? The short answer is yes, the Strategic Defense Initiative will, in my judgment, distort the defense budget at some time in some way.

GEYER: Couldn't the argument be made that it will allow more conventional warfare by giving a false sense of security to certain types of military thinkers?

CORDDRY: Sure, Gee Gee, but that's what the A-bomb did. We've had more wars since peace broke out than ever in human history.

McDOWELL: I sit here, and my colleagues have made a pessimist of me. As if anyone cared, if I had to cast a vote on getting into Star Wars or not, I would vote against getting into it irretrievably. I would be tempted to get into it to see what it is. But I would assume the technology goes on anyway.

CORDDRY: Let me give you some hope. It is conceivable that the two sides can learn enough about this, through research, to scare each other into some kind of arms control which would get rid of, for example, those deadly MIRVs.

McDOWELL: I talked to a man today who said Gorbachev, by the life expectancy charts, would deal with four to five American presidents. You're now suggesting that somewhere down the line, number three or four, that this new technology would drive President Blank and Gorbachev to a real accommodation.

CORDDRY: It's conceivable.

SMITH: What worries me is the focus on the technology and not the interrelationship between the two cultures and the two countries, and whether we may be moving too rapidly down a path that promotes the dynamics of distrust. If there's anything that comes through in this discussion, it is the unpredictability of it all, even though the concept itself is aimed at achieving total safety. Even if you can get there, it's the time from now until then that's dangerous.

JOHNSON: I'll be the romantic, and I hope a realist, too. I refuse to believe that human beings can't master their own fate. I take the Faulknerian view that somehow man will prevail.

DUKE: But it really would mean a radical break with past history.

JOHNSON: We never have been able to stop wars, and we've never been able to stop the advances of new materials that kill human beings, and yet, in the end this may be the ultimate choice.

GEYER: Let me inject another note of optimism. Despite all the bellicosity since World War II, the two superpowers have not used their nuclear weapons.

DUKE: It's only been forty years.

CORDDRY: That's a lot longer than it was between the two world wars.

DUKE: But there are a lot of years to go, we hope.

CORDDRY: And that's what makes Star Wars interesting as a new concept for peace.

DUKE: Winston Churchill once said that the Stone Age might well return on the gleaming wings of science, so isn't it a perilous course that we're embarked upon with Star Wars?

GEYER: Many parts of the world that I cover are returning to the Stone Age to some extent. But that has nothing whatsoever to do with development of advanced weaponry. In fact, these weapons may be protecting the developed societies from the breakdown occurring in the Third World.

SMITH: If we and the Soviets can reach some kind of an agreement for limited and controlled Star Wars research and then scale down our offensive weapons, that would be a genuine step toward peace. If we can't, the world will remain a dangerous place.

DUKE: I feel a strange ambivalence of optimism and pessimism. Optimism that it does offer us a new opportunity, and pessimism because the whole history of man is that we don't usually seize the opportunity for peace.

CORDDRY: I'm not as worried as several of you seem to be. I think that probably in the end enough common sense will get into the act that the Soviet Union and the United States will work out some kind of mix of offensive weapons and defensive weapons. But I must also say that I have been around long enough to know that an awful lot of these outcomes don't come out.

Television Politics

The Medium Is the Revolution

Charles McDowell

CHARLES MCDOWELL, 59, of the Richmond *Times-Dispatch,* has been a reporter and columnist with the Virginia paper since 1949. In 1965 he shifted his base from Virginia to Washington. He has covered every national political convention since 1952. At the 1984 conventions he was a commentator for National Public Radio. Author of three books and numerous magazine articles, he is also the recipient of the 1984 award from the Miller Center of Public Affairs at the University of Virginia for "an enduring contribution to the understanding of the American presidency." In addition to his *Washington Week* reporting, McDowell has participated in many other PBS programs, serving as a commentator for *The Lawmakers* and as anchorperson of the award-winning *Summer of Judgment* retrospective on Watergate. He has been a *Washington Week* regular since 1977.

In the summer of 1952 television dawned on American politics. The occasion was the Republican National Convention at Chicago and, yes, there was one of those outrageous camera towers blocking the front of the hall, and the floodlights cutting through the traditional layers of cigar smoke seemed suddenly to be exposing a mystic rite. But the true dawning was the glow of 18 million little screens on which politicians walked and talked and looked the citizens in the eye in their living rooms all over the United States.

Television had made a pass at the conventions in 1948, but only about 400,000 squinty sets were in use then. The coverage was a limited curiosity, not a national experience. By 1952 television was ready to become a force. There would have been great television interest in the convention as a folk festival, but the Republicans were offering more, a classic confrontation: the popular hero from World War II, General Dwight D. Eisenhower, taking on Senator Robert A. Taft of Ohio, who was not called Mr. Republican for nothing. An austere and respected conservative, Taft had the support of the party bosses and nominal control of the convention machinery. He figured to hold off Eisenhower by using his insider's power in the ruthless custom of these things. The first stage of Taft's nomination for President would take place in the convention's credentials committee, where his supporters expected to use their narrow majority to reject the Eisenhower side's challenge of fifteen Taft delegates from Louisiana. There was a case to be made that the delegates had been chosen unfairly in Louisiana, but Taft needed them and intended to keep them.

I was in Chicago for my first national convention. When I showed up for the credentials committee hearings in the Gold Room of the Congress Hotel, no seats were available for junior reporters from the provinces. An official explained that television had to be accommodated in the press space. Alas, it was the beginning of that, too. A kindly security guard let me slip into the serving kitchen adjoining the Gold Room, and from there I covered the credentials contest for a couple of days. The huge tiled kitchen, with its racks of glasses, stainless steel sinks and signs saying "Keep It Clean," became the caucus room for the members of the committee. While witnesses testified and the committee argued before the television cameras in the Gold Room, the leaders of the Taft and Eisenhower factions came to the kitchen to talk tactics. I was taken for a hotel functionary of some sort and overheard a lot from both sides. By the morning of the second day, the Taft managers were talking about conceding the Louisiana delegates to Eisenhower.

What was happening was that people back home, following the debate on television, were telephoning and telegraphing their delegates to say that Taft's case was coming through as weak. Republicans of consequence were saying that a steamroller approach would look bad on television and hurt Taft more than yielding the delegates. I particularly remember a Minnesota member of the committee, technically a backer of the dark horse, Harold Stassen, bringing Taft partisans from the Gold Room to the kitchen to persuade them of their public relations problem. He rested an elbow on a dishwashing machine as he talked. He was earnest and deep-chested and had a big, hollow voice, and there was no trouble in hearing him tell the Taft people that they could ruin their candidate if they insisted on arrogantly running over Eisenhower in this little controversy. The Minnesota delegate was Warren Burger, who was headed for a career in the federal judiciary.

Taft's manager on the committee, Congressman Clarence Brown of Ohio, recommended to the candidate that he concede Louisiana as a public relations gesture. He was talking to Taft headquarters by telephone from the kitchen. The candidate, as Brown later confirmed, was instinctively against conceding Louisiana but told Brown to do what he thought best. Into the kitchen he fetched Congressman John Hesselton of Massachusetts, manager of the Eisenhower faction, and said, "John, you fellows keep your shirts on in this Louisiana thing, and I think we'll vote with you."

"Whatever you want to do, Clarence," Hesselton said without changing expression. He was standing by a sink and a rack of glasses. When Brown had moved away, Hesselton allowed himself just the least flourish as he had a drink of water from a champagne glass. (I remember thinking television might be in the Gold Room but it wasn't getting the good stuff. It was a newspaper reporter's thought. From Eisenhower to Ronald Reagan, we have clung to our fancy that television tends to get the superficial action.)

The concession would be on television in the Gold Room. Up to now in the debate, the Taft spokesmen had tended to be the crusty elders of the party. The Eisenhower spokesmen were somehow younger, trimmer, clearer of eye. To make their motion to seat Eisenhower's Louisiana delegation, to claim acquaintance with fairness, the Taft side passed over the elders and chose a young, clean-cut, well-spoken committee member from Virginia, Eugene Worrell. Two days into the era of television politics, and everyone was beginning to catch on.

Worrell's talk of fairness only encouraged the Eisenhower supporters to press their case elsewhere. They insisted on similar concessions in contests involving a potentially decisive batch of delegates from Texas and other states. The Taft side became adamant and held the line in the committee. The Eisenhower managers announced they would appeal the decision and went before the cameras to explain their case again and to lecture on sportsmanship. The document of appeal was called the "Fair Play Amendment," and in retrospect that name will do for me as the first great artifact of the television era in politics.

So the crucial battle was fought amid the turbulence and drama on the floor of a national political convention, all on television. It became a morality play. Here was a national hero standing above politics and demanding simple justice from the cynical bosses of what had always been a closed process. By the rules of the Republican Party and the customs of American politics, the merits of the proposition were at least doubtful, but there was no doubt about the public perception of the struggle. The telephone calls and telegrams poured into Chicago; the feedback was pro-Eisenhower.

The convention ended with the "I Like Ike" signs dancing in the almost blinding light. And there was the general on the platform with his arms thrown up in a V for victory and his smile beaming out to all those little screens. We could write like poets on the press stand or broadcast it faithfully on the radio, we could explain and analyze the event in the context of the great issues of the day, but now politics was acquiring a new reality and its medium was television. The Eisenhower persona—and the notion of rising above party politics—was at the center of the ensuing campaign against Adlai Stevenson. The Eisenhower movement attracted millions of former Democrats and brought about the first great realignment in American politics since Franklin D. Roosevelt. (One of Ronald Reagan's advisers calls it "the television realignment.") Eisenhower might have been nominated and elected without television, but anyone who thought about it knew that politics would never be the same again in a country where people in their living rooms would watch their politicians at work. Thirty years later, the *Economist* of London was still trying to help us get used to it: "Today's are the first politicians since the Athenian statesman Pericles, in the fifth century B.C., to be seen by all their electors."

The people see the picture—moving, instantaneous, compelling—and that is a remarkable thing. But it is much more, of course: It is a personal experience, and the reaction is intuitive and emotional as well as logical. The politicians, for their part, are dealing directly with people, one on one, tens of millions at a time. In this circumstance, the personal qualities of politicians matter very much. Television becomes a medium of personal trust—or mistrust, or yawns. In the time of Ronald Reagan, we have seen personal trust for a President at the core of an Administration's viability. In the second term, when the public opinion polls and Republican congressional leaders boggled at parts of the President's program, his somehow separate status with a national majority allowed him to hedge here, to stand pat there, and even to fail with minimal blame for himself. Over the long haul in politics, I would say, television's inherent function as a medium of personal trust is far more significant than all the passing sensations that often dominate discussions of the subject—whether history will be changed by an ignorant answer at a televised press conference, whether an election rode on the brilliant one-liner that a media consultant devised for a debate, whether Dan Rather smirked at the misfortune of a conservative.

Television has affected American politics beyond involving everyone in events and in the personalities of leading politicians. It has been the catalyst of profound organic change in the political system itself. It has rendered hallowed political institutions obsolescent. This has created problems that we have coped with feebly, partly because the velocity of change has been so dizzying since television became an adjunct of the system.

Theodore H. White, the senior chronicler of politics, says, "Television in modern politics has been as revolutionary as the development of printing in the time of Gutenberg." Tom Shales, the hip television critic of the *Washington Post,* says, "Television turns everything into television." Consider some trends since 1952:

• Since television eliminated the middleman in politics, or anyway gave the politician direct access to the voter, the parties have lost much of their coherence and influence. The notion of compromise and consensus in politics is notably weaker.

• Television has undermined the importance of presidential nominating conventions (while paying almost fanatical attention to them) and has promoted the shift of their function to a crazily distorted series of primaries and caucuses. Neither party's convention has required a second ballot since 1952.

• Television, selling time for political advertising, has enhanced the power of money in politics beyond prior imagining. The cost of campaigns—national, state and local—has risen astronomically as the television age has advanced. Reliance on special interests and single-issue zealots to finance campaigns has increased to the point of a clear and present danger and a disgrace.

• As television grants to candidates an increasing independence of party identification, financing and program, a kind of populist fervor has been rising in the land. The message seems to be that politics itself is sinful; antipolitics is virtue, and the way to get elected and get things done is to campaign on television against politics.

One way to trace the relentless rise of television as a factor for change in American politics is through the Presidents who used television most successfully. The ones who suggest themselves to me are, besides Eisenhower, John F. Kennedy, Jimmy Carter (are those hoots I hear?) and Ronald Reagan. All of them used the medium to beat the system in one way or another, but they hardly provide a stereotype of a successful television image. Eisenhower on television was a modest hero and sturdy father figure who bumbled his lines. Kennedy was eloquent, youthful, charismatic. Carter was plain, a moralizer, and positively dull. There are times when Reagan reminds me of all the others. Maybe he is the stereotype. In any case, he was more than a Hollywood cowboy when, talking amiably to cameras, he was able to alter the tone and mission of the federal government more drastically than any President since Franklin Roosevelt. Reagan, by the way, was by my lights the second antipolitician elected President; Carter was the first. Richard Nixon, distinctly a politician, got elected twice, partly because he was fortunate in circumstances and opponents. It would be hard to contend that television was a boon to him. It was instrumental in removing him from office in 1974 after the country had witnessed at the congressional hearings what kind of public servants put on Watergate. At the other end of Nixon's national career, his famous "Checkers speech" on television saved him as the vice presidential candidate on the Eisenhower ticket in 1952. He invoked his humble dog, Checkers, to demonstrate his own humility while refuting charges that he had improperly accepted donations to a private expense fund as a senator. Messages of support did come in, and Eisenhower, wincing, kept him. But it was a fatuous speech that marked Nixon for the rest of his political life. When he was first a candidate for President in 1960, he was haunted by his Checkers image. And he ran afoul of the cameras in television's first presidential campaign debates. But this man kept coming back and sometimes was able to rally the country, reminding us that there is much we do not understand about the convoluted relationship of television, personality and politics. And reminding us that Richard Nixon never lets us off easy.

John Kennedy, going for the Democratic nomination in 1960, hardly could have been a candidate without television. But besides being personable, he was running in a political landscape that had undergone tremendous change since television came on the scene in 1952. The nominating process was evolving into a whole new game. In the selection of national convention delegates, primaries were replacing the old state conventions and back-room appointments. The process was opening up. Presidential candidates were not soliciting party leaders' support as much as before; they were campaigning more among the people. Television liked it: local color, crowds, hands to shake, competition out where you could see it, and, in the end, real people's votes to count and announce and color on the map. There were only sixteen primaries in 1960, as a matter of fact, but we sensed watching television that somehow they had eclipsed the old system. Kennedy, campaigning in Wisconsin or West Virginia, was being seen and heard in all the states. An individual primary on television was a national event, and a sequence of strong showings in several primaries could become a national bandwagon. When the Democrats gathered for their convention in Los Angeles, Kennedy had already done what had to be done. His first-ballot nomination was dramatic but a formality. In the first decade of television politics, a young, Catholic, back-bench senator, and not one who had shown extraordinary promise in Congress, had knocked over Hubert Humphrey and Democratic elders in the primaries, then controlled the convention easily against Lyndon B. Johnson, the fabled inside operator and acknowledged leader of his party in Washington.

Kennedy's successful campaign against Richard Nixon is remembered mainly for their four debates on television. More than 100 million adults watched. The issues, which both candidates discussed skillfully, are not much remembered. At the time, people who heard the debates on radio were fairly evenly divided as to who won. On television, although Vice President Nixon had experience on his side and represented a reassuring continuity with the popular Eisenhower Administration, he had problems. One was Kennedy. Not only was the upstart young senator more engaging, more relaxed and cooler than Nixon, but he came through as more mature and thoughtful than the Kennedy many people expected. He turned out not to be a boy, somebody said. They were there to be compared, and Jack Kennedy could more than hold his own with the man on the stage with him, the Vice President of the United States.

Another problem Nixon had in the first debate was pallor, five o'clock shadow and perspiration on his face. Too much may have been made of cosmetic considerations in the debates. Too much may still be made of performance values generally in political television. Twenty-five years after Kennedy beat Nixon in an extremely close election, media experts still have difficulty assessing the relative effects of performance and substance on the public perception of a politician. Of course substance matters. But it matters in a world where the standard of performance matters far more than ever before. We are not talking about the ability to make a powerful oration that moves the partisans in a vast hall. The crucial ability in the new era is to be heard and felt as an authentic person in a living room, one on one. The person, the performance and the message merge. Much of what is said tends not to be received as literal information but as part of a general impression of the politicians. Television has not changed human nature. It has changed politics. For television, as the new medium of politics, is good at personality and not very good at abstractions (issues). It pulls the viewer past literal information into intuitive responses. It invites, almost demands, judgments on personal trust.

Tony Schwartz, the political consultant and disciple of Marshall McLuhan, says in his book *Media: The Second God:* "Radio, and then television, drew our attention away from issues and caused us to focus on the more personal qualities of the candidate, his ability to speak, and his style of presentation." Voters watching candidates, Schwartz says, "look for what they consider to be good character: qualities such as conviction, compassion, steadiness, the willingness to work hard. That is why we have so large a party-crossover vote. This emphasis on people and feeling is the product of an instant-communication environment."

Of course the good vibes received from a Kennedy or a Reagan do not convert droves of committed Republicans or Democrats. But 20 percent or more of the electorate has little or no commitment to party and has varying, often ambiguous, views of issues. These are the people who decide most elections. Long before television or Tony Schwartz came along, many of these people were making a point of being concerned primarily with the personal qualities of candidates for public office. Wary of politics in general, they voted for "the best man." Television gave them access to the personal evidence they wanted. And increased their numbers, according to Edward J. Rollins, director of the 1984 Reagan campaign. While some of his brothers talked about a realignment of the parties, Rollins insisted that the major political phenomenon of his time was a "dealignment" attributable to television. In any case, nearly everyone agrees that all voters are influenced to some degree by a candidate's style, although our impressions are filtered through political prejudice, self-interest and, most would insist, conscious analysis. But those primal vibes from television obviously influence the whole process of decision.

Isn't print journalism supposed to be in there somewhere, calling the voters' attention to the issues and away from personality, blowing the whistle on hokum, countering the hype and fizz of much of what passes for a political campaign these days? Yes, and the print press can seem gray and boring as it stakes out the important issues and summons television to the serious agenda. The press has a problem, too—really the citizenry's problem—when political rhetoric tends to be timed, tailored, capsulized and sloganized, and perforce trivialized, with the evening news on television in mind. Newspapers, magazines and even television perform marvels of serious journalism, but the herky-jerky quick summaries are the common currency on the tube. The big news, of course, imposes itself on everybody; economic trouble, a war scare or a scandal can change the whole context of politics. But day by day in routine coverage, the print press is drawn into the same lore of personality and performance that all those millions watching television are interested in. A combative exchange, a line misspoken, a sweaty brow—they become news if only because so many people are watching. The press watches television and vice versa. A provocative sound bite from a campaign is validated for the television producers when the press writes about it, and it gets another round for reaction on the evening news, which makes it fodder for the weekend talk shows, which brings it back into the Monday morning papers as something the syndicated heavyweights may want to write a column about, and on it goes.

For all its blurry problems with issues generally, television on occasion conveys a truly important issue to the consciousness of the country, and with awesome effect. That has happened when television was able to show the essence of the issue and not just politicians and commentators talking about it. The Vietnam War, of course, is the classic example. When television gave the war reality night after night for

American families at home, public opinion began to sour and assorted politicians were put at peril. At the same time, reporters in both print and television were becoming more aggressive in contrasting the government's claims and reassurances to other versions of reality. President Lyndon Johnson, one of the most accomplished politicians of the old school, decided in failure and frustration not to run for a second term in 1968.

In the early days of television, in 1954, the broadcast of thirty-six days of the Army-McCarthy hearings in the Senate effectively brought an end to a dismal reign of bullying demagoguery by Senator Joseph R. McCarthy. He had been discovering "communists" in and out of government, slandering good people and intimidating both the Congress and the Eisenhower Administration. The press had done a poor job of documenting his depredations, and he had a national following of dim patriots. But he went too far in harassing the Army, of all things, and Congress investigated. When television focused on the senator week after week—and on a pixie Boston lawyer named Joseph Welch, who could make civil liberties understandable as well as exposing hypocrisy and thuggery—the McCarthy monster collapsed. He was censured by the Senate and became merely a haunting embarrassment.

There have been other instances of television crystallizing an issue for the country. In covering the civil rights movement, television explored the historical background, the constitutional arguments and the muffled themes of moderation in the South, but television's transforming power was simply in its pictures of events. The immediacy and the emotional content of those pictures were felt throughout a society. The images defined the crisis in the starkest terms: There were the peaceful black protesters, the preachers of nonviolence, the marchers singing hymns, the children walking solemn and brave to school, and then there were the white hecklers and haters, the swaggering sheriffs, the Klan and the neo-Nazis, the violence. The impact of the scenes was cumulative. The Reverend Martin Luther King's eloquent call to conscience went out from the Lincoln Memorial to tens of millions of television sets, where it was received amid the echoing images of the police dogs of Birmingham.

Watergate was another overarching controversy in which television was a medium not only of information but of the issue's resolution. In its own time, Watergate was an event closed to cameras. It was uncovered by newspaper reporters and explored relentlessly in print as the third-rate burglary expanded into a constitutional scandal following President Richard Nixon's reelection in 1972. The television coverage had a secondhand quality; it could not seem to engage the issue on its own terms. But when television put Senator Sam Ervin and the Nixon staff conspirators on the screen for weeks at a time in 1973, and put the House impeachment inquiry on the screen in 1974, public opinion was mobilized to support the removal of the President from office and, when he resigned, was conditioned to take it for granted.

Disillusionment with Watergate set the stage for Jimmy Carter, a presidential candidate who personified moralism and skepticism about politics. And he was as fascinating a television phenomenon as any we had seen before 1976. Here was an obscure former governor of Georgia, distinctly from the boondocks, not a commanding presence personally, not a leader of any established movement, an outsider to the traditional political fraternity—and he came from nowhere in the presidential polls to win the Iowa caucuses and the New Hampshire primary. He went on to defeat a clutch of veteran liberal Democratic candidates for the nomination; then he defeated the incumbent Republican President, Gerald

Ford. Carter was different from stereotypical politicians, and he boldly and ingeniously exploited television to emphasize the difference.

Carter understood how television had revolutionized the nominating system. He was willing to concentrate a couple of years of effort on the earliest tests, Iowa and New Hampshire, betting that a good showing would be a sensational payoff because expectations for his candidacy were so low. He was right and he became a national figure within a couple of weeks. Carter believed the delegate-selection process was subject to a sequential effect, state by state, down the chain. He believed in momentum. With a front-runner's access to television and the conferred charisma of a miracle worker in Iowa and New Hampshire, he offered the country a vision that was essentially antipolitical. He knew people had long been skeptical and resentful of the whole pack of politicians and their big talk, big government, red tape, inside deals and slickery. Well, he personified opposition to all that. The very look and manner of the man set him apart from the others. He was slight, almost shy. He had a high voice and a drawl. He was a farmer and small-business man, trained as an engineer. For him problems had logical solutions. A plain, practical man without a politician's bombast and wheeler-dealer ways might impose some common sense and efficiency on Washington. He would stand up for morality, too, and was not too sophisticated to keep saying so. He was a religious man, a Sunday school teacher in a fundamentalist church, and he called attention to his religion often. But he was not a hypocrite; he lived his commitment.

The crucial issue that blended into the image of Jimmy Carter was civil rights. It authenticated him as a southerner who could be President. In his long-shot bid for the nomination, his record in Georgia on behalf of civil rights brought him the support of southern black leaders, some of them nationally known associates of Martin Luther King. With black leaders seen around him from the beginning of the campaign—and going as his missionaries to the North and West—Carter overcame the suspicions that many liberals had of a white southerner and a relative conservative in the Democratic field. In the primaries of 1976, as well as 1980, Carter ran strongly in predominantly black precincts, North and South, against famous liberals of his party.

Carter's defeat for a second term had a major television component, of course, and it consisted of far more than Ronald Reagan, the Great Communicator. President Carter's fortunes had faltered at home and abroad. The worst was the Iran hostage crisis, which obsessed television and the country for more than a year. In a regular ritual of humiliation, television counted off the days that the American hostages had been held by terrorists in a pitifully backward country while the United States engaged in futile diplomacy, empty threats and, finally, failed military rescue. Meanwhile, the terrorists demonstrated a keen sense of American television. By allowing crews from the West to televise images of the hostages and to interview their captors, Iran gained leverage over a superpower. As in the case of the TWA hostage crisis in Lebanon five years later in the Reagan Administration, the American public's very personal concern for the safety of their fellow citizens soon dominated the policy options of the American government. In the incident in Lebanon, the hostages on television—sometimes under threat of death as they spoke to us—tended to become our national authorities on the nature of the terrorists, their point of view, their demands, and the best American approach to the problem. Indeed television became a medium of diplomacy. A representative of the terrorists was drawn out on possible settlement terms by network anchors and morning-show hosts. The same kind of thing occurred in interviews with a member of the government of Israel, which held prisoners the terrorists in Lebanon wanted freed. Officials in the State Department confessed that in some of the crucial moments of the crisis they were watching television, trying to keep up. If that seems unsettling, that is because it is.

Jimmy Carter's hostage crisis was not resolved quickly, as Reagan's was. For Carter the preoccupying misery stretched out month after month and into a second year. What that did to Carter was to make him the living image of the country's humiliation, pain and loss of confidence. And we had to watch that image on television. Understandably, there was not much inclination to reelect it.

Ronald Reagan came to office running against the hapless Carter but also against Washington and politicians generally, thus ironically doing what Carter had done. He was a Republican and a conservative, but he presented himself more as a citizen-reformer who would save us from politics. In saving us, he would reduce the cost, the size and the meddlesome power of the federal government at home, strengthen it militarily in the world and restore patriotism, religious values, adventurous free enterprise and confidence. All this came to be called a conservative revolution. But for many voters assessing Reagan in 1980 the big test was not whether he should have a mandate for his revolution. The test was whether he seemed safe enough to justify voting the incumbent out. He passed easily, although he was older and more ideological than many who voted for him would have wished. Reagan looked undeniably vigorous; the visible evidence minimized the age issue. As for the extremely conservative views he expressed, his temperate, amiable personality took the edge off. It was true, as the old Hollywood story had it, that Ronald Reagan just naturally fitted the role of Best Friend.

He had the qualities of a best friend on television, all right, and this level, likable man soon had the personal trust of much of the population. That Reagan had been an actor most of his life has been cited—beyond all previously known limits of redundancy—as the explanation for his success in communicating on television. In my minority opinion, acting background is an all-too-convenient, point-missing rationale for Reagan's effectiveness on camera and microphone. Oh, experience might help him read lines and not squint into the lights and not trip over cables. But what makes Ronald Reagan effective on television is that he is authentic. He knows who he is; he is himself. He is comfortable with that, and he knows not to act. This confident, consistent sense of self makes the compelling presence on television.* Reagan seems especially effective because the television performance level of so many other politicians of the day is so low. They tend to strike attitudes. They project, or hold themselves in. They work at television and remember what the media consultant told them about posture and gesture and pace. They try to be natural while getting the effect they want. They act.

If Reagan himself is consistent and fairly uncomplicated, his presidency has been full of paradoxes. He is remote but somehow very much in charge. He has left an almost unprecedented proportion of his job to staff, and yet he has to be ranked with the assertive, strong Presidents. He is an ideologue who frustrates the Republican pragmatists in the Senate, and he is a pragmatist who disillusions the Republican right wing. He takes unyielding public positions on principle, and then allows them to be compromised—without apology, sometimes without conceding they were compromised. He holds relatively few news conferences,

---

*I note that a political scientist at the University of California at Berkeley picks up the argument that Reagan "knows who he is"—and carries it right back to Hollywood. Professor Michael Rogin says: "Ronald Reagan found out who he was by whom he played on film. Responding to typecasting that either attracted him or repelled him, making active efforts to obtain certain roles and to escape from others, Reagan merged his on-screen and off-screen identities."

preferring set pieces to the risk of error in give-and-take, but he seems the most accessible President in the world as he walks from his helicopter on the White House grounds giving good-natured, noncommittal answers to the bumptious, shouted questions from Sam Donaldson of ABC—a ritual both Donaldson and the White House find useful for their own purposes. Reagan is the natural man, just being himself, and yet his staff spends more time than any in memory moving him around to appealing and symbolic settings, keeping him visible, contriving events to play to his credit and obscure his failings, and always promoting and briefing him for television appearances as if he were a forgetful old, well, actor.

The paradoxes all are accommodated in the positive perception of Ronald Reagan. It is not that the people are fooled; many seem to be quite aware of both sides of each paradox. In crowds of Reagan supporters, reporters constantly encounter fans who will talk about his flaws. Public opinion polls keep showing large blocs of voters who disagree with Reagan on this or that issue, or a whole swath of issues, but give him high ratings as President, anyway. Mary McGrory, the liberal columnist, has written in some despair: "Reagan has a lock on the affections of the American people. They are almost blindly fond of him. He is not exactly a father figure—he is rather too jaunty and nonchalant for that. He is more a jolly, reassuring uncle who comes to call amid much laughter and many stories. Never mind his views—wrong, but strong, they are generally considered, and they add to the fondness."

Christopher Matthews, who is on the staff of the Speaker of the House, says Reagan is "the nation's host." But Matthews has more for us than a wisecrack. He says Reagan has redefined the presidency: "He is not *in* government but some place, previously uncharted, *between* us and government." If we take that seriously, and we should, it carries us well beyond personality in explaining Reagan's success. His approach to the function of being President seems to be to reassure people that he has not given himself over to Washington. He shares the public prejudice about government and politics, and he keeps his distance. He would rather talk to the people.

Henry Fairlie, a journalist with a British parliamentary background, made this observation on politics in America in the time of Reagan:

> The American presidency is being transformed into a radically popular institution—more and more dependent on, and at the same time able to exploit, a direct and uninterrupted relationship with the people. . . . For some years now almost every important development in the American political system has been encouraging the direct relationship between the President and the people. These include the weakness of the parties and disarray of the party system; the dissipation of power in the House and Senate; the reliance on direct mail and media consultants in election campaigns; and of course the new prominence of the media, dominated by television.

That assessment is not far out of line with the views of many American academics, politicians and political reporters, although I would insist that television is not just one of the developments but the driving force behind all the others. In any case, much of the contemporary furor about television is not about its pervasive effects on political institutions and perceptions but about efforts to exploit it, indeed to manipulate it day by day.

Politicians and consultants lavish creative energy and money on commercials to make points already market-tested by pollsters. In buying their own airtime—the record shows Republicans can afford it more often than Democrats—

candidates get at the viewers without intervening questioners or editors. For the "free media" they contrive short, provocative statements that will intrigue producers and resist editing. Former Governor Jerry Brown of California is said to have been able to talk in twenty-second sound bites, stringing them together, each with a beginning, middle and end. For debates an important part of the strategy is coming up with one-liners catchy enough that they will become enduring images in a campaign—Walter Mondale to Gary Hart: "Where's the beef?" Spontaneity is rehearsed until it's right. The political fraternity studies the personal quirks and presumed political biases of correspondents, morning-show hosts, the news anchors. Conservatives take a liberal bias in the networks for granted; it is part of their ideology and has some public following. Liberals gripe less about philosophical bias; they complain about assorted slights and failures of judgment in the coverage of themselves. The professionalism of network journalists is often admirable, but they are coping with burdensome logistics, ridiculous little time slots and the need to shoot for the gist of a story on a visual medium whose impact is monstrous. So television news executives rarely get through a day without having to consider criticism of inconsistencies, sensationalism, superficiality and perhaps plain irresponsibility in the snapshots they take of politics. When the networks really monkey with the minds of the electorate, as in broadcasting "exit polls" and "projections" while people are still voting, everyone from righteous print journalists to congressional committees comes down on them.

So television is subject to pressure and control from both outside and inside. Assignment editors, reporters, cameramen, producers, network managements and the Federal Communications Commission are forever making decisions that influence what is shown of politics. Politicians are forever devising strategies, ploys and gimmicks to gain advantage on the tube. Much of the apprehension about television politics arises from all this manipulation, and there is a notion that the effect is vast. This is exaggerated. For one thing, the television audience often knows when it is being used. It has lived with television and has some sense of illusion; what the audience will accept on a game show or a melodrama it will not necessarily treat the same way in true-life public affairs. True, politics is trivialized when it is played for television. But that is only a part of the larger reality: Politics has been transformed by the very existence of television. Yes, the medium is the message. The medium itself has changed the way people connect to politicians and the way the political system works. As Reuven Frank, the former president of NBC News, has said, "The truly serious criticisms of television can be reduced ultimately to the proposition that it shouldn't have been invented in the first place."

It *was* invented, and in 1952 at the national conventions it became a part of the presidential nominating process. There has not been a contest that went past the first ballot at a convention since 1952, when the Republicans chose Eisenhower in a flurry of vote switches at the end of the first roll call, and the Democrats chose Adlai Stevenson on the third ballot. The nominees have been designated before the conventions in a burgeoning series of televised primaries and caucuses. These contests in the states are open, competitive affairs for ordinary voters, not closed convocations of wrangling, deal-making factions and bosses. The old, closed process could not survive under television's eye. Of course, the eye did not really pick up the positive meaning of the old conventions: All that wheeling and dealing was a national political party negotiating among its constituencies, balancing its interests, compromising its differences. Such conventions were uniquely American, and political scientists here and abroad gave them a lot of the credit for the stability of two-party government, for avoiding extreme swings to the right and left.*

The primaries are the nominating system now. In 1952 there were twelve primaries and they bound only a small fraction of the national convention delegates. By 1980 there were thirty primaries and they elected more than 75 percent of the delegates. A slight reduction in the number of primaries in 1984 only increased the number of state caucuses, which usually were merely another format for popular voting to pledge the delegates to a candidate. The field was winnowed quickly in the first few contests, for they were crucial to a winning image and campaign contributions. Over the years it evolved that the first caucus, in Iowa, in the winter before the late-summer national convention, would establish the contenders in rough order. Then the first primary, amid the frosty scenery and commercialism of New Hampshire, would narrow the race to two serious possibilities, or maybe one—such was the national impact of the televised battle for less than one-half of 1 percent of the convention delegates. The primary schedule ran on, from February into June, offering the candidate almost endless opportuni-

---

*What is the evolving purpose of the conventions now? Surely more than being a kind of electoral college to certify the results of the primaries and caucuses. Surely more than voting *aye* on the nominee's draft of a platform and choice for vice president. Besides those pro forma functions, recent conventions have settled for being reconciliation rallies to kick off the presidential campaign. But how long will the networks be willing to give away a week of prime time for that sort of enterprise? At the 1984 Democratic convention, even the rally was a charade because everyone in the hall knew Walter Mondale could not beat Ronald Reagan. Aha! That became the unstated point of the convention, and prime time was devoted to showcasing likely Democratic candidates in 1988. Governor Mario Cuomo of New York was the big hit both as a television performer and as a prescriber for the party's future. Is the evolving role of the convention to present the candidates and themes not of the campaign at hand but of the next one after that? Campaigns start earlier all the time, they say. I would not be surprised—no, I would be very slightly surprised—if the new convention-four-years-in-advance someday offers as a climax a straw ballot with suspense, deals and dark-horse victories just like the old days.

ties to make an impression, not only on primary voters but on the 80 percent of the national electorate that would wait to express its opinion in November. As for the ritual convention, most of the delegates would already be pledged, morally if not legally. The candidates, not the constituencies of the party, controlled the delegates elected in their names by the voters in the primaries and caucuses. The presidential nominee in such circumstances was less a product of a party process than an independent operator with his own political base and organization, his own obligations and agenda. When I think I overstate, I reread Professor David B. Truman of Columbia University, who said the primary system "tends to destroy accountability. It does so because it disintegrates and ultimately eliminates the political party as an organization which the voter once could hold accountable for the performance of a government. The single-issue groups, political action committees, faceless image makers, and professional media manipulators that occupy the resulting vacuum cannot be held accountable for the results that they produce. They are basically irresponsible and ultimately subversive of the common good."

Most observers would agree, anyway, that political parties have undergone a drastic decline in the age of television. In local and state politics as well as at the national level, the party program can be a burden to a candidate appealing to voters essentially as an individual. Politicians are less dependent on the party as an organization that develops leaders at its lower levels and promotes them through the ranks. Now the sharp ones can promote themselves. In the matter of campaign finance, where television advertising is a wildly escalating cost, the parties' role is far less important than it once was. Television candidates increasingly rely on contributions directly to themselves from individuals and from that booming new source of money, political action committees. These PACs represent special interests—insurance companies, defense contractors, all kind of corporations, labor unions, trade associations, a mind-boggling assortment of ideological groups—and often a PAC's concern is so narrow that it comes down to a single issue. The distinctive thing about most PACs is the sheer specificity of what they want in return for their contributions; they don't trouble the officeholder for accountability on any issues but theirs.

Ten years ago there were six hundred PACs. In 1984 there were four thousand of them raising and distributing campaign money. Presidential elections, which are federally financed, are somewhat insulated from this influence, but Congress is up to its knees in PAC money. Senate and House candidates, especially incumbents on key legislative committees, frequently get more financial help from PACs than from their parties. For the last election PACs raised $288 million. The total receipts of the Republican Party were $300 million; the Democratic Party, $97 million. The PACs delivered a much higher proportion of their receipts directly to individual candidates than the parties did. That was because each party spent so much to sustain itself as an organization and to promote itself and its entire team of candidates as representing a coherent political philosophy. Meanwhile, as the PACs grew, a candidate could pay less attention to parties and coherent political philosophy and rely more on his own conglomerate of assorted special interests.

If strong parties really matter in the American system, if accountability is a good thing, if compromise is the essence of a viable politics, then some of the trends since the dawn of television are troublesome at best. Maybe the political system will adapt without severe damage; it has adapted to new conditions before, though not to a universal, instantaneous communications technology that keeps throwing off secondary effects that nobody expected. Those secondary effects are organic changes in the system—the erosion of old institutions, including the conventions and the political parties themselves, the rise of the distorted sequence of primaries, the quantum leap in the cost of campaigning and the emergence of the mighty swarm of disparate new special interest lobbies to finance the new politics.

Meanwhile, the primary effect of television—to focus the attention of huge audiences on the visible personal qualities of politicians—will presumably endure. And there will be those compelling presences on the little screen reassuring us that they are not politicians at all but something more independent and righteous. I, for one, lament the passing of politicians who are frankly politicians. For it is still the politicians who balance competing interests, negotiate coalitions, see a wisp of glory in the notion of consensus and make our kind of government work. We are a diverse people. We are a collection of factions, minorities and ideologies. More than television is needed to hold us together. What holds us together, as from the beginning, is the practice of politics under a Constitution drawn by politicians.

ROUNDTABLE DISCUSSION

"Television Politics"

<u>PANELISTS:</u> Paul Duke, *moderator*
Charles McDowell
Haynes Johnson
Hedrick Smith
Charles Corddry
Jack Nelson

DUKE: The political system obviously has been affected by television in many basic ways. How is the system now adapting to this powerful force?

McDOWELL: Well, first I start with a couple of assumptions. It seems to me that the basic impact of television on politics has been *organic.* It's changed the system as much as it's changed events and, as a part of that, it's changed the way people connect to politicians.

If you think of this in organic terms—what has television done to the system, to how politics works—then the question of adapting is not about how to control television's treatment of a given incident or how a politician can say something on television that affects events. We're talking about a fundamentally changed political system. So what can we do besides view with alarm and say "This ain't the way it used to be" and decry it?

A pretty good example would be our national recognition that the primary system is out of hand; that it is warped, loaded with power at the front end, controlled to a degree by those individual states which hold primaries at given times for everything from political reasons to commercial purposes. And so there are educational institutions, party subcommittees, all kinds of people trying to find some way to make sense out of the primary system. There is the effort to try one more time to get primaries regionalized so there are, say, four primary days instead of thirty—to put some order into this system.

PACs—political action committees—and the way they influence politics is really an outgrowth of the decline of the parties and the rise of assorted individual politicians, each relying increasingly for money on hundreds of special interest groups rather than from a coherent political party. If undue power is passing to special interests, doesn't that increase the case for some sort of federal financing of elections?

In 1984 the Democrats made a special effort to reload some politicians into the convention process, to try to reinvigorate the convention. Everybody seems to concede by now that during the television era the conventions have decayed, becoming an increasingly powerless confirmation of the popular electoral process in the primaries. Allowing the states to add members of Congress to their delegations is an effort to put some negotiations back into the conventions.

There are a lot of other changes, but these examples show some adaptive process taking place.

SMITH: Charley, one of the striking things about both your essay and your comments is the assumption that the decline of political parties is a bad thing. This seems to be a spreading assumption among the politicians themselves, the people who are in government and the press that covers them.

This Washington perception may not be shared by

the country as a whole, which tends to look on political parties as bad. People proudly announce, "I'm an independent."

And what you're suggesting here is that if we want our political system to work better, we've got to put more potency back in the political parties so we have cohesive alignments, cohesive coalitions and clearer choices for people to get behind rather than individual candidates who look glamorous and come across well on television, which is a medium that directly connects the voter to the individual candidate, but not to a party or a group which can put a program in. And it seems to me to that degree the country and the Washington political community are out of whack.

McDOWELL: What you say does summarize my general notion about it. I can't disinvent television. We have to adapt, so I have suggested as objectively as possible that yes, 150 or 200 years of history tells us that the political parties have been the site of the effort to balanced interests, compromise, and organize a government around two fairly clear alternatives.

SMITH: Well, if parties are that important, then one of the first reforms would have to deal with political money. Isn't the way to gradually revive them to channel the money to candidates through parties, not just by raising funds but even through subsidies that give national political leadership some leverage with all those independent candidates out there? You don't hear many talking about that at the moment.

McDOWELL: You sure don't.

JOHNSON: Personality is now the engine that drives American politics, at least national politics as distinct from state and local politics. The fact is, the parties let television run the process. And the biggest change, aside from the camera, has been the political industry that now has supplanted the old party brokers, the people who used to make the decisions. The smoke-filled-room cliché of Warren G. Harding doesn't take place at all in the way it used to.

It is now a question of how best to get your candidate—whether it's the President or someone seeking to be President—before the camera in the most favorable light. And I must say that when we talk about the primaries and all the money it takes to run, those of us who cover politics find that *everyone* decries it and says it's out of hand. Yet the primaries expand and proliferate.

The fact is that if the parties themselves really wanted to change this system, they could write the rules to do so. They *do* write the rules. It suggests to me that somewhere there is a consensus among party leaders that they like the present system, that they like television and its ability to make them be seen and reach out.

DUKE: That leads to another question, Haynes, and that is, does it make us more susceptible to charlatans and to a brand of hucksterism that wasn't readily apparent before.

JOHNSON: Yes, and what we're seeing more frequently in the age of Ronald Reagan is his consummate skill of using the public media to be heard and seen. I'm not saying he's a huckster or a charlatan or what have you, and I do think the public is a rather shrewd judge of character. I think Charley's correct—that character somehow comes through. Americans have supported Mr. Reagan despite what they understand may be specific weaknesses in policies because they see something else in him. I don't think we've been taken over by the charlatans yet.

NELSON: If you look at Ronald Reagan, what you see is what you get. Jimmy Carter's big problem was that he tried to be somebody else. Jimmy Carter tried to be the caring, compassionate person. At the same time, he was also a very tough politician. He tried to act like he wasn't a politician, but he was very much a political animal, and I think that came through to a lot of people. They saw this person on television who tried to constantly be looking out for their welfare and who lectured them and sermonized. Somebody told him that he'd better look out because the press is writing that you wear your religion on your sleeves. He said, "That's all right, it'll get me votes."

McDOWELL: Carter said that, Jack?

NELSON: That's right, he did say that during the '76 campaign. But I think that television exposure does give people a good idea of the politician's character. So I think we shouldn't be so concerned about a charlatan coming in and mesmerizing the American public, because he'll be found out.

DUKE: How would Richard Nixon figure into this analysis, then?

NELSON: Nixon?

DUKE: Yes. If you consider that television exposes the character of somebody . . .

NELSON: Nixon went on television and denied what had happened in Watergate, and I think it came across clearly on the screen that he was lying. In the end that, as much as anything else, is what drove him from office.

McDOWELL: It seems to me that we could safely say that the print media exposed the situation and laid it out on the table for everybody. Television then helped us reach a national judgment.

DUKE: But he did have the reputation for being "Tricky Dick" long before Watergate, and somehow he managed to win two elections.

McDOWELL: Look at the alternatives to Nixon the

two times he won. In a time of national distress and urgency, the opposing candidates offered large negatives of their own to the American people. It doesn't mean they sanctified Richard Nixon by electing him President. It means they chose him over somebody that worried them more.

CORDDRY: Charley, you give a great deal of importance and consequence to television, and all our colleagues around the table are doing the same thing, but I wonder whether, without denigrating anything you've said, it wouldn't pay to look a little bit at history. FDR was able to collect a few votes, too. He was able to put together an utterly improbable coalition of New Dealers and southern Democrats without any assistance from television. Maybe we shouldn't use the term "charlatans." Maybe we should use the term "actors who have appeal to people who might be for them" and then set FDR off against Ronald Reagan and see where you come out.

All I'm suggesting is a little perspective here as we try to see how television has changed our lives. We're dealing with a self-correcting process, and I expect the pendulum will swing. I don't know where it'll go. But I don't think the political parties have collapsed for all time. Have they?

McDOWELL: I don't think so.

SMITH: I wonder the same thing, too. I wonder whether to some degree Reagan's mastery of television and the effect of personality politics will look different if the economy goes down in 1986 and 1987, and if that happens, whether being the anti-Washington outsider who's got a real way with television will be an attractive way to go in the 1988 presidential campaign. I think any politician from now on has got to be able to handle television. But just being a terrific television performer may not be as great an advantage three or four years from now as it appears today.

McDOWELL: I think that's wisdom. Television is not, has not been and will not be the be-all, end-all of politics. It is just where voters get their principal impression of politicians. They still have to look at their own politics, their own notion of whether they're doing well economically, their own notion of foreign affairs. We haven't abandoned being good citizens. We're simply using the impressions from a new medium.

To Charlie's point, Roosevelt rose during the radio era in politics. Before that, there was only print. When we talk about personality politics, there is considerable danger that we assume personality means *everything*, and I don't think it does at all. I think it has simply become a larger factor than before, just as radio added a dimension.

When we say Reagan has rare skill on television, I wonder if that is really as balanced as it ought to be. Isn't the really important part of Ronald Reagan's success on television that he doesn't seem to be using it at all? Should we assume that he's doing something terribly conscious and crafty on television, or should we assume that he's the right man giving the impression of the right politics at the right time and that he's a reassuring presence for people? Also, people's notions of the presidency are changing; they don't see anything very odd about being for Reagan and for a Democratic congressman.

NELSON: I think Reagan is losing some of his television magic. Look at all the difficulty he's had in selling tax reform to the public. And one other thing, Charley: You're right that he's more than an actor, but being an actor doesn't hurt. I can tell you that. When he says, for example, that the Soviet Union is an evil empire, he doesn't say it with a glint in his eye, right? He just says it, and so he doesn't look like an extremist. He doesn't look like a zealot. Now we all know, frankly, Mr. Reagan is a zealot. He's zealous in his causes; he believes in them strongly. When he talks, he doesn't bare his fangs like Nixon used to when he talked about the press. So when Reagan denounces the press, the public doesn't think that he's being extreme at all. They just think he's being good old Ronald Reagan.

JOHNSON: There's a much more serious criticism of television than the mastery or lack of mastery of the performer who happens to be President, and that's the way the President uses the medium to dominate the agenda of the country. Everything is focused from the White House in a way that it wasn't before.

SMITH: You touched on a point that I wanted to raise, Haynes, and that is the degree to which, apart from the performance of the individual in the White House—or for that matter the Senate majority leader or the Speaker of the House, because they've both become television personalities to some degree or another—television and the news media set the national agenda. Iran is one clear case in point. Jimmy Carter may have made a brilliant move in the short run and a disastrous strategic error in the long run to focus his presidency so heavily on Iran. But even if he had wanted to walk away from it, a Walter Cronkite on CBS saying "This is day 122; this is day 123" means that at least at some point television begins to set a political agenda and becomes a power center apart from the President and not just a medium through which he communicates to the masses.

McDOWELL: The very existence of television keeps changing things. Look at the example of the TWA hostage crisis. Not only did television keep that before us, but what we saw began to influence how we responded to the crisis. That influenced the resolution of it. What people saw in their living rooms on television ended up changing the announced Reagan policy of how we would deal with the hostage crisis. As people saw the hostages, came to know the hostages, the national will shifted—predictably—to protect the hostages. The notion of retaliation, endangering the hostages, became unthinkable because real people were involved. I'm not saying whether that's good or bad. I'm saying it changed the whole approach of an administration to a crisis.

NELSON: There's little question that television helps set the agenda when the White House, for example, offers deals to the networks on a basis such as: *We will let you have an interview if you have anchor so-and-so sitting in on the interview,* or *Are you going to take the anchors with you when we go to the summit meeting?* That sort of thing. So it's obvious that television has a powerful influence on the presidential agenda.

DUKE: In the Iranian crisis the thing that I remember so clearly is Jimmy Carter, who thought he had some very good news about the release of the hostages, saved that to go on the *Today* show in the morning, and it blew up in his face.

CORDDRY: I do think governments run whether TV cameras are on or not. I may be in a minority here. I suggest to you—

DUKE: And did before the cameras ever came.

CORDDRY: —that if the Carter effort to rescue the hostages had succeeded, what a different outcome there would have been in that case. If the Reagan Administration had known how to retaliate against the TWA hijackers as they did with the Palestinians from the *Achille Lauro,* what a difference you might have seen. I think whether they retaliate or don't retaliate has more to do with lack of intelligence on how to retaliate than television. I do think governments continue to run whether the cameras are on or not.

SMITH: Even so, one of the things I heard from one of the very top people in the White House in the TWA hostage crisis was that because they were getting such rapid information via television interviews of the hostages in Beirut, they knew a bit more about their location, they knew a bit more about their safety and they also knew something about the state of mind of Arab Shiite leader Nabih Berri. One of the reasons they decided to go with the very tough tactic of announcing a potential embargo of Lebanon and to put more pressure on Berri was because they'd seen exactly how he was performing in public, and they got that report much faster by TV than they would have the old-fashioned diplomatic way. Television helped them fashion a response. In other words, politicians are not always helpless victims of television's influence over events when the public thinks they're helpless victims.

NELSON: Well, that's right. ABC-TV, for example, had set up at this motel on a rooftop overlooking the hostage site and had constant communications with the site which the government didn't have. ABC had a command post in New York, and the command post in New York had contact with the command post at the State Department, and they were continually feeding the government information about it.

JOHNSON: Television's power extends in so many ways. The networks do set an agenda, not by a conspiratorial act of all sitting in a room and deciding what's right or bad for America, but by choosing to amass the cameras around a few places, Washington primarily, and the White House most specifically. Congress often gets ignored and a lot of other things as well.

NELSON: The interesting thing is there does seem to be a trend a little bit away from Washington coverage now, and I wonder if that's because we're in the second

Reagan term. With Reagan's legislative agenda stalled, perhaps television is beginning not to look at Washington quite so closely as it has in the past.

JOHNSON: Probably so, but the symbiosis is still a pervasive fact of life. I don't think the public understands the way it works, that the White House tells the networks whom it will make available for the talk shows, and it will tell the majority leader of the Senate we want you to go on or don't go on, and he'll do it. There's a symbiosis here that exists between the two sides. They are willing participants in setting an agenda.

SMITH: You mentioned the White House getting a lot of coverage at the expense of Congress. I submit that's basically because television needs a story line. It needs to focus on a personality.

JOHNSON: And a central figure, too.

SMITH: The President becomes a political John Wayne strapping on his six-shooters going out to do battle with the other side, whether it's Tip O'Neill or the Russians.

JOHNSON: Exactly.

SMITH: And to follow a defense appropriations bill through a labyrinthine committee process with negotiations and conferences and people popping out of coalitions here and there is complicated and not something that lends itself to the cameras. The actual working of government becomes less and less covered, and what becomes covered more and more is: is he up or is he down, did he win, did he lose, are they for the President, are they against him?

DUKE: A horse race.

SMITH: A horse race.

JOHNSON: And the stereotypical figure is one—I am struck in the Reagan era particularly—where people have locked in impressions of Ronald Reagan: the John

Wayne, all-American figure, number one, dominant; or Tip O'Neill, the corrupt, bloated caricature of the old pol Democrat. Neither one is correct, but they have taken hold in the country.

McDOWELL: One last note on that that's interesting. Y'all were asking earlier whether people in the end see through the bad guy or see just the good part. Take Tip O'Neill's image as the corrupt stereotypical politician. The poll readers explain that, over time, that image has tended to go away, and he's now fairly popular in the country.

DUKE: The vice presidency may still be a lowly office, Charley, but vice presidents have been getting more attention in the press and on television in recent years. Has television given new life to the vice presidency?

McDOWELL: To me, the most remarkable running anecdote in American history would be the vice presidency and the sudden change in it that came with television.

It has risen from a national joke, the subject of every wit that's lived in the last century and a half, to the number two office in the land and the place that logically would produce Presidents. Now, surely, a lot of other factors go into this, but it just happens to have changed.

John Adams said the vice presidency was "the most insignificant office that ever invention of man contrived." Old Thomas Marshall, Woodrow Wilson's vice president, told a very vice presidential joke—he was one. "Once there were two brothers. One ran away to sea and the other became vice president. Neither was ever heard from again."

For 150 years we had nonentities and ticket balancers in that job. The vice presidency has a historian, Irving G. Williams, who is the great historian of the vice presidency. He says, and I quote: "In the composite, the vice president would be a second-rater, pleasant enough, but neither taken seriously nor taking himself seriously, a man sharing the popular belief that election to the office was the surest way to obscurity." That was the vice presidency for 150 years.

In 1960 Richard Nixon, after eight years in the vice presidency under Eisenhower and in the opening decade of television, was nominated for President by the Republican Party. That was the first time a vice president had been nominated for President since Martin Van Buren, 124 years earlier.

Since Nixon, leaving out Spiro Agnew, seven vice presidents have been contenders for the presidency— Nixon, Lyndon Baines Johnson, Hubert Humphrey, Jerry Ford, Nelson Rockefeller, Walter Mondale and now George Bush. Our fathers and grandfathers would find it incomprehensible that that job has become what it has become. I suggest a large factor in it was that the guy's on television all the time.

CORDDRY: Before we spin this great TV web around it, let me suggest to you that there was a very important event which had a lot to do with the increasing prominence of the vice president, and that was the Eisenhower heart attack.

McDOWELL: I think that's a reasonable observation.

NELSON: It's also true that no vice president has ever been elected since Martin Van Buren *directly* from the vice president's office.

JOHNSON: That's the point. The recent vice presidents don't do well running from the vice president's office. They all lose, as a matter of fact. Nixon and Humphrey the most recent examples.

DUKE: Jerry Ford was catapulted by fate into the presidency but then couldn't win on his own.

JOHNSON: Ford, a loser, right.

SMITH: One of the things that struck me as you were talking earlier was the suggestion that maybe regional primaries could bring order to this disorderly process. It seems to me if you do that, you will give television more clout and the vice president—talking about nomination, not election—but the sitting vice president, if he is serving a President who has not left a war or an economic disaster, will have a terrific leg up precisely because of the television exposure. The first *sine qua non* is name recognition and some kind of personal identification on the part of voters with the individual in the office.

DUKE: To shift the topic, are people better informed today? H. L. Mencken once said you should never overestimate the intelligence of the American voter. Do you think they are now better informed through television, that we have a higher quality voter?

SMITH: I don't think so. The election participation figures have not gone up with the television age, even though TV brings the candidates directly into the living room and gives you access to live debates and so forth. I think if people were better informed they'd be participating more.

DUKE: Why is that?

SMITH: Well, television communicates character and personality and a few essentials, but it doesn't lead to an extended discussion of issues and the real political choices that are available. It puts a premium on clever framing, phrasing and personality and not on information.

JOHNSON: By definition it trivializes—fragments and sloganizes, to coin a bad term—the political process.

NELSON: But people have the opportunity to be better informed than they ever were before because, to begin with, newspapers do a much better job than they used to in covering issues and politics generally.

SMITH: Newspapers and magazines are going into issues in much greater depth. There's much, much more information available about the political process and about government.

But I don't see a lot of evidence to suggest that people are using it particularly well.

DUKE: Do we have better political reporters today because of television?

NELSON: Let the record show a long pause here. [Laughter.]

JOHNSON: I don't know how to handle that one because I think *television* has changed. Television is becoming an entertainment medium where news is taken over by entertainment divisions. For instance, ABC's *Good Morning America* is run not by the news division but by the entertainment division.

DUKE: If television is so powerful and reaches so many people, how come it doesn't inspire a greater voter turnout? How come more people aren't flocking to the polls to vote for the candidates they like or against the candidates they dislike when they see them on television?

NELSON: Many people have been turned off by politics, and I think television has a lot to do with that. There's overexposure. You have politicians on TV day in and day out. In addition to the news, you've got all the political TV commercials, and people just get fed up.

JOHNSON: There is a high level of cynicism among people about being packaged and used and sold. Children growing up in American life today understand at age six that Brand X toothpaste does not make you sexy and wiser and healthy, and they grow up with an awareness of the phoniness, of the synthetic nature of it. This double edge translates into politics, too, and they're very wary about what they see.

NELSON: It all goes back to John Kennedy's assassination and one of the most divisive periods in our history; probably the most divisive period since the Civil War. There were the civil rights troubles, the assassination of Martin Luther King and then Bobby Kennedy. Then you had Richard Nixon and Watergate and all the government abuses—of the IRS, the FBI and the CIA and everything. Plus Vietnam. So you had a tremendous turn-off on government.

McDOWELL: What you guys are saying proves that television does exist in a context.

One of the subthemes that I got carried away with was that the television era embodies a distinct antipolitical tone even to successful politics. Successful politicians tend to rise above politics as they state their positions on things.

The notion that's put out to the people is that this is not a politician, certainly not one of those *bad* politicians. This guy rises above politics, which is a theme I don't think we can miss. I attribute the nomination and election of Jimmy Carter to his having capitalized on the antipolitics feeling in the country and his success and sincerity in stating, "I ain't one of them." Well, once television becomes a medium in which we denigrate ordinary politics, that suits the American character and theme anyway. We've always put down politicians.

At the very same time we're having all these successes of trustworthy candidates on television, all of us in the public are really being told that ordinary politicians and politics is a lowly business. The word is out, there's no compulsion to get involved unless there's some exceptional candidate who appeals to people.

JOHNSON: The very strengths that enable people to win—running against the political system, running against the "corrupt" parties, running against the old politics of the past, running against "Washington"—have brought us people who are not skilled at the art of government. Conversely, a skillful legislator may not be effective on television.

NELSON: You could get another Jimmy Carter. As Charley correctly points out, Carter exploited television by running for President as an outsider, but he very much was a politician. He ran for state senator and had it stolen from him and went to court to get the seat back. He ran for governor and lost and he got so upset and distressed that he took a walk in the woods and became a born-again Christian. Then he came back to win the governorship, and went on to become President. This is one very tough politician.

McDOWELL: Whenever I say that Carter was as striking a product of the television age as is Ronald Reagan, people look at me like that poor fellow's just drawling away and doesn't know what he's talking about. But I really believe that.

I also suggest, and perhaps it's gratuitous but it may be important, that this lack of people who really get in and work in the business of balancing interests, arriving at compromises, that old hard work that's so dull on television, the lack of these people threatens the future.

Now, politics won't necessarily die. I think the system will adapt to this, but we're living in a period of change.

JOHNSON: It seems to me, that one adaptation is that you have political consultants who are media consultants, essentially giving advice to candidates on how to win individually. They don't even run under the party labels anymore.

NELSON: I think maybe even more interesting than the fact that these media advisers are meeting with the candidate is that they're meeting with the guy after he's in office and telling him what the people are thinking and helping him with governing.

For example, Richard Wirthlin, the pollster for the White House, meets on a regular basis with Reagan and tells him what people are thinking about tax reform, what they're thinking about the trade imbalance or deficits and so forth, and they've become a very integral part of governing, not just politicking.

McDOWELL: That marvelous Columbia professor David Truman finds what you just mentioned to be the most serious veering away from American tradition that he's seen. Is the media consultant type becoming truly an adviser? And then he makes the fairly obvious point—bless political scientists for making obvious points sometimes—a media adviser has no constituency, he's responsible to nobody. Truman thinks that what makes politics work is accountability, and the system now embraces a tremendous number of unaccountable entities—not just pollsters and media consultants but powerful, faceless, PACs, pulling the candidate this and that way on the issues. The political party, which represents accountability, becomes secondary to a conglomerate of special interests. There's nothing coherent there. There's nothing accountable there. And David Truman says there's nothing responsible there. It's irresponsible.

CORDDRY: But the whole object of all this is presumably to get laws by which the country can operate. Are we getting worse laws because of it?

McDOWELL: What I hear among people who think and talk about this all the time are the obvious dangers of all this, but even they say, well, the product isn't as awful as we thought it would be.

CORDDRY: Well, for example, if the tax bill in '81 was favorable to the rich as it has been alleged, that's got nothing to do with television, has it?

McDOWELL: Well, I think television was the medium through which the American people learned what the tax bill was about.

CORDDRY: But it passed anyway.

McDOWELL: And it passed, I submit, because the American people got the impression there was plenty in it for them—that 60, 65 percent of the people were going to get a tax reduction, and that was carried to the people in a direct way that would not have been possible in the twenties or thirties or forties, and it overpowered the arguments about deficits.

NELSON: And it overpowered the argument that the wealthy came out much better than the middle class, and the poorer came out poorer than anybody.

CORDDRY: Just got obscured, that's right.

DUKE: Despite television's impact, many Americans wanted to give the new President a chance to see whether his radical new program would work. When you went up to the Hill and talked to the members of Congress, a lot of them had reservations about the Reagan program. They voted for it, anyway, because they felt it was the politically popular thing to do.

McDOWELL: I do not accept that the American people endorsed the idea of a clear-cut conservative revolution that would be indeed radical. I think they found a man they trusted, conservative themes they liked, but the conservative program was not specifically voted for as a huge revolution. It was a "let's show support for this man, let's let him give it a try." The mandate never really existed for the specifics.

DUKE: Just let Reagan fill in the blanks.

JOHNSON: Reagan was successful because he promised good times after failure.

DUKE: Isn't one of the reasons that Reagan is popular the fact that he repeatedly sounds an upbeat trumpet? He has used television to hammer home his good-news themes, and yet today we don't know whether it's going to turn out happily or not.

NELSON: And it's our job, Paul, here or anywhere

else, in the newspapers, on *Washington Week in Review* on Friday nights, to try to put that in perspective and tell people that the news is not as good as the White House says. When we do, we get an awful lot of criticism from the public saying you're just anti-Reagan.

CORDDRY: Whether we are in the print medium or in the broadcast medium, we are perceived negatively by the public. And television has enabled people in government, particularly the President, but the vice president as well, to deliver their message directly without any intervening filters—such as news reporting—on the part of the various organs of information. This is what's happening: You take your message straight to the people—as Roosevelt did on the radio.

JOHNSON: And in the age of television—to close the circle on what we're talking about here—especially in Reagan's presidency, it is all stage-managed for the television cameras: all of the rallies, all of the speeches, all of the forums, the balloons and so forth, the message is of good times. As long as the good times basically are there, people are going to say, hey, we don't hear any criticism. But it is a powerful thing only so long as things are going reasonably well.

CORDDRY: So, Haynes, the people have a right to wish that the President would tell us the bad with the good, and I judge that what you're saying is that you don't expect that to happen in the stage-managed television era.

JOHNSON: I don't. And in fact, the point should be made again that the genius of great leadership is that it prepares the country to deal with the future in a way that is realistic but also is manageable and inspires a sense of confidence.

McDOWELL: But that does become increasingly difficult then, doesn't it? Particularly so since—I think Charlie is right on the mark—the essence of being an effective politician these days is to deal directly with the people one on one, and keep it positive and keep it going in your direction. Now, I don't know what adaptive mechanism exists to let Haynes's other side speak up. Do college faculties and famous economists and others have a fair opportunity to have their say too?

CORDDRY: Well, that's a question of access to the airwaves, isn't it?

JOHNSON: The answer is they do, but entirely disproportionate to the television presidency, where you do have a direct link, and no one else has that kind of link. No one in Congress, no one in the country. That simply is fact.

NELSON: All you have to do is to look at the attention, for example, that the press gives to the Democrats' response to the President's radio address every Saturday. The President gets tremendous play by the media, but the Democrat, who may be one of 435 members of the House perhaps, gets little attention.

CORDDRY: Then why don't the Democrats pick somebody more important to deliver the answer?

NELSON: Good point.

CORDDRY: Is it that they don't have any—they can't get together on who it will be?

NELSON: Well, it's hard to build up another media personality to challenge the President.

DUKE: Well, has television given us a better brand of American politics, taken as a whole?

JOHNSON: I think it has not. I think it has created a situation where personality is paramount, where the good news is the one that sells the most, where you trivialize issues, and the skills that make an effective legislator are not nearly so appreciated because they're intricate, and it allows you to run *against* something rather than *for* something. That's really a sweeping generalization, and you can make the case where it's not true, not valid. But I think that the emerging breed of television political leader today is somewhere between the soap salesman and the blow-dried candidate.

NELSON: I agree with Haynes to an extent. On the other hand, I think the American public has the opportunity to be better informed than ever for the simple reason that most publications do a better job, and even on television they can get a better idea of what the issues are and who the candidates are. If they watch more public television, if they watch more documentaries, they can be even better informed.

CORDDRY: I think television obviously has not given us a better brand of politics because we get a lot of superficiality. Maybe we need to return to smoke-filled rooms.

SMITH: I don't think so, either. I think there's a much greater dichotomy between the politics of governing and the politics of campaigning and getting elected, and I think that's harmful for the system. The kinds of things that work, the kinds of politicians who come across well on television and in campaigns, are not necessarily the kinds of politicians who do well in putting together coalitions and in working with the opposition.

The system of politics that we have today is out of kilter. The way you get elected in American politics often has very little to do with the way you operate effectively in governing, and you get people who are effective in governing—like Howard Baker, the former majority leader of the Senate, or maybe even Bob Dole, the current one—and they have a heck of a hard time projecting themselves well to the country over television, even though Dole's got a good sense of humor, a quick wit and is always on television. On the other hand, people who are blow-dried and handsome and paying a lot of attention to campaigning out in the country—like Jack Kemp—are rarely known as the most effective legislative leaders.

DUKE: We've always had charlatans and crooks in politics, and it will ever be thus, and in some ways television has helped to expose them. But it also has helped to create a new type of politician—certainly not universal—who is more interested in image than in substance, more prone to self-interest than to public interest.

NELSON: We ought not to denigrate the blow-dried politicians too much. We all care about appearances. Let's face it. Even when you go on *Week in Review* on Friday nights, they slap a little makeup on you so you don't have circles under your eyes.

JOHNSON: I'll confess I use a blow drier myself on occasion.

NELSON: As a matter of fact, Walter Mondale would have been a helluva lot better off it he had let them slap a little makeup on under his eyes during the presidential debates.

DUKE: Is there an inherent evil in television?

SMITH: I don't think so. It would be like saying "roll back the printing press." I don't think you can do it, once it's here.

McDOWELL: If, as a society, we spend our time decrying, saying how bad television politics is, we might feel better. But as we begin to think about improving government, we'd better take television as a given and work from the fact that our institutions are going to have to live with this revolutionary medium. Frank Reuven of NBC said the essential criticisms come down in the end to *it shouldn't have been invented in the first place.* But it *was* invented. It is here, and it seems to me constructive thought carries us to how do we adapt to it.

DUKE: There was a famous Frenchman named De Tocqueville who said a long time ago, as I remember, that the great thing about the young American nation was its capacity to adapt to change. We always have and we always will.

When The Future Becomes The Past

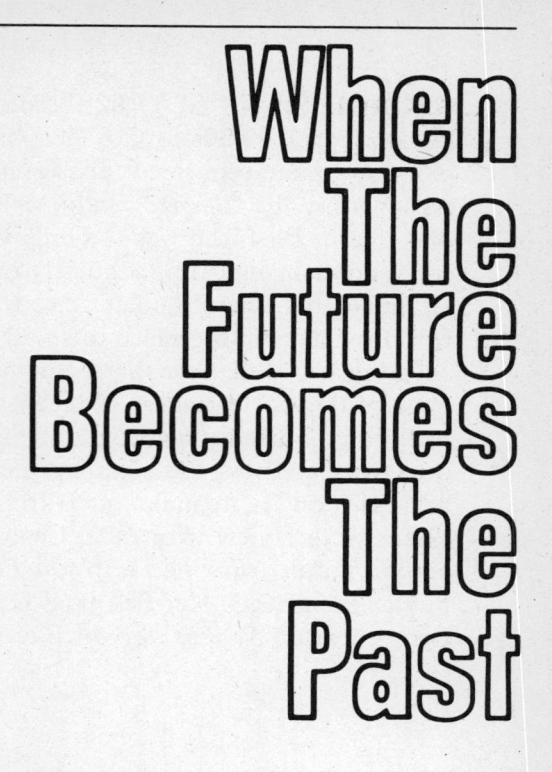

Georgie Anne Geyer

GEORGIE ANNE GEYER, 50, affectionately known to her friends as Gee Gee, has been a pioneer woman reporter in the foreign field. Assigned by the *Chicago Daily News* to Latin America in 1964, she was the only woman correspondent reporting regularly on foreign affairs at that time. She has since traveled the world over, from big place to small place, covering world trouble spots. She has interviewed most of the world leaders of recent times and has had many journalistic scoops. She is a winner of the Overseas Press Club Latin America award for her series on Guatemalan guerrillas and an exclusive interview with Fidel Castro. Her autobiography, *Buying the Night Flight,* was published in 1983. Her firsthand reports have been a feature of *Washington Week* since 1976.

He had entered the room as though he were some great black moth floating in and out of space. During the interview, the Ayatollah Ruhollah Khomeini sat totally and unnaturally still. . . .

It was the cold, snowy December of 1978, and an unsuspecting world was about to begin turning on its axis around the unlikely French village of Neauphle-le-Château, only eighty miles from Paris. The Ayatollah Khomeini of Iran—the type of Old Testament religious autocrat that most Westerners could not believe still existed—had taken up brief but revealing residence in Europe before returning to his own country to overthrow the West's great friend, the Shah of Iran.

That December day, Khomeini, emerging publicly in the West for the first time after fifteen years of exile in the holy Shiite city of Najaf, in Iraq, sat impassively before me on a Persian rug in a small and equally unlikely French summer house.

"Yes," this hoary character was saying of the revolution that had already begun against the Shah by virtually every sector of the population including Khomeini's own fanatical religious followers, "we consider this war as a holy war, and by that we mean for the sake of Islam and for the sake of God and for the liberty of our people. That is why it is a holy war, and it will continue until the abdication of the Shah, the eradication of the monarchy and the end of foreign domination of our affairs and the establishment of an Islamic Republic." Khomeini stared, his eyes never blinking or flickering, at a space between me and his aide, Ibrahim Yazdi, as though he were indeed staring at some vision that we could not fathom.

One had to rub one's eyes to believe that this surreal scene out of the *1,001 Nights* of ancient Baghdad was quite real. (One problem was that I could not even rub my eyes since the Iranians had insisted I wear the black robe, or *chador*, over my blond head!)

As it turned out, Khomeini *was* staring at a very special vision. The odd thing was that his "vision" was *not* forward-looking: It was *not* to educate his people and free them from poverty, pain, hunger and war; it was *not* to modernize his impoverished ancient land.

No. His vision was to transport Iran back to some totally pure and perfect Islamic past that he places historically around the seventh century. This, of course, was the golden age of Islam. To fulfill his vision, Khomeini's perfervid followers were soon to claim that he was the awaited "Hidden Imam" of Shiism—secluded in a cave for more than a thousand years—whose return would presage a new golden age. In fact, it was Khomeini's return to Iran which would set in motion forces of such power, symbolized by hundreds of thousands of black-clad Iranians, fists raised, marching straight into machine guns fired by the Shah's troops. Within months, virtually all visible vestiges of Western influence would be driven from the very Iran that the Shah had set up as "the" inner circle of Westernization in Central Asia.

Living with Khomeinism was difficult enough, but covering it as a journalist was even worse. It presented us with extraordinarily new problems that, in our supposedly rational and pragmatic times, we thought had been left behind in the Middle Ages, and for which there were no guides or guidebooks.

Everything Khomeini told me was, in Western terms, a lie. Everything. The most outrageous examples were statements that a new era of democracy would be ushered in by the new Islamic state, and that women would remain free. But to him, his words may not have been lies in the sense we understand it. Because ancient Persia had been overrun so many times by hostile neighbors and nomadic conquerors, the Persian Shiites had developed as a tenet of their religion the duty to "dissimulate." This meant to lie to the infidel in the service of the faith. For the first time, we journalists were faced with whole groups of people who believed this and who really thought they *were* living in a different time. How do you explain *that* to the readers back in the States?

I had covered many fascinating changes as a foreign correspondent in the sixties and seventies for the Chicago Daily News Foreign Service. But even with this background it took a while to begin to understand this strange new movement in the midst of a supposedly "modern" world. This sort of archaic and retrogressive thing was not supposed to occur anymore. My beat had been the world: Latin America, Europe, Asia, Africa, the Middle East, the Soviet Union and Central Asia. I was trying to study societies at their deeper levels. I assumed, like most Westerners and probably like most Western-educated people from the Third World, that we were "moving ahead," that everybody wanted "progress" and that "modernization" (that was a better word than "Westernization" because it was more neutral, less insulting, to those being "modernized") was the trend of the century. I listened to leaders from Anwar Sadat to Fidel Castro to Prince Sihanouk talk impassionedly about "carrying our peoples forward."

Then one day it came to me with a chilling rush of fear that not everything was moving forward, after all; that some peoples did not *want* to move forward; and finally, that the new movements that were scorning "change" were potentially more dangerous than anything we had seen.

It was not only that Khomeini went on to establish a classic theocratic state with ancient Islamic law, but he also began trying to tear down the societies of countries as near as neighboring Iraq and the fragile and peaceable Gulf states, and as far away as Malaysia and Indonesia. Even as this is being written, the war that has raged since September of 1980 between Iran and Iraq has taken at least 1 million lives.

But the confusion over time was curiously skewing perceptions everywhere in the world. Birgitta Edlund, the talented correspondent for the major Swedish newspaper *Dagens Nyheter,* told me of an incident on the cliffs of Beirut one day during the early fighting in 1974. A young Palestinian fighter who looked dazed but not threatening came over to her and asked, "Are you with the British or the Jews?"

At first puzzled, she said, "I'm Swedish." Then she added, "There are no British and no Jews here."

He repeated the question.

Then she realized what was going on: He had been so brainwashed about the Palestine wars of 1948–49, which had seen most of Palestine incorporated into Israel, that he thought he was fighting in that war!

As I began to cover more and more of the Third World, its conflicts and its movements, I began to see that Khomeinism was not unique at all:

• It was Miami in July 1984. Perry Rifkind, the director of the U.S. Immigration and Naturalization Service there, was talking about the illegal flood of people from other countries entering the United States through Florida. Suddenly, he paused and said, without any particular emphasis: "And then there are the Sikhs. . . ."

Sikhs? Bearded religious Sikhs from the prosperous Punjab in northern India? Sikhs who believe in a religion that is a unique and very ancient mixture of Hinduism and Islam?

"Yes," he went on, obviously puzzled, "they have been coming in for the last two years. We've apprehended hundreds of them. They come through a network that gets them through the British Commonwealth countries and eventually to the Bahamas. From there, it is easy for them to come here illegally by boat."

Then he paused and shook his head. "It is odd," he summed up. "Most of them have been behind the Iron Curtain, some of them for some time. Most of them have a lot of money—five, ten thousand dollars. Some have testified to us that they were told by the Sikh movement to go underground in California, where there is a big Sikh community, and to wait for orders. . . ."

What had happened was that the Sikh independence movement in the Punjab had relocated in the United States and Canada to orchestrate a worldwide assassination campaign. This same group would succeed in assassinating Indian Prime Minister Indira Gandhi, moderate Sikh leaders and many others. And this movement, whose radical leaders want an independent state, dream of that state in spiritually irredentist terms—they dream of returning to a sacred Sikh past.

After radical Sikhs were accused of detonating a bomb that killed 329 persons in an Air India plane disaster off the English coast in June 1985, I began to look into this ominous and untold story. I found that just before the crash thirty-five Indian Sikhs had been apprehended in Houston, trying to slip into the United States with illegal Dutch passports. They were sent back to India.

I found that, yes indeed, most of the radical Sikhs *had* been trained behind the Iron Curtain: in the USSR, Bulgaria, Poland, Yugoslavia and Cuba. I found that the new Prime Minister, Rajiv Gandhi, had discovered this and that it was cooling his warm relations with the Soviets. And I found a pattern not at all unlike those of kindred movements in Iran, Egypt and Turkey.

What led to the Freudian death of Indira Gandhi, "India's mother," and perhaps began to presage the long-prophesied and feared (by Mahatma Gandhi, among many others) disintegration of the Indian subcontinent was actually quite typical of conditions that foster backward-looking movements. First, secularized life-styles had been spreading among the young Sikhs. More and more young men were shaving off their sacred beards and refusing to wear the Sikh turbans.

In trying to salvage their interests in a time of feared changes, the traditional clergy reacted by trying to ignite a new fundamentalism. However, their efforts—and even those of the once-radical Independence Party, the Akali Dal—were soon overshadowed by ultraradical Sikhs led by the ferocious Jarnail Singh Bhindranwale. When he and his men took over the sacred Golden Temple, they transformed it into a sanctuary for murderers and terrorists who thought they would be untouchable within its precincts.

Instead, Indira had her troops scourge them from the temple. The government's efforts to negotiate with the moderate Sikhs had long been broken off, poisoned by the deliberately planned excesses of the radicals. Indira was assassinated. Once again, the acts of fanatics were able to overwhelm and control the acts of moderates and thus destroy the vestiges of the Sikhs' political center.

And the Soviet interest? Ah, there is the mystery. There is no question at all about their having trained the Sikh extremists, in keeping with Moscow's style. It may have been a warning to India not to move its loyalties too far westward. Or it could have been the first step in a Soviet-backed but locally inspired attempt to break up the subcontinent.

• In 1980 a hitherto unknown and unexpected movement burst upon always schizophrenic Peru, a physically glorious country still divided in its soul between the descendants of the great Inca Empire and the descendants of the brutal and greedy Spanish conquistadores who destroyed it. By 1985, this new movement—the Sendero Luminoso (Shining Path)—had brought Peru once again to crisis.

The name "Shining Path" was taken from Lenin's description of communism. As with many such movements it began at a university; in this case, the National University in the remote city of Ayacucho, near the site of the great battle for Latin America's independence fought by Simón Bolívar in 1824. The charismatic Marxist leader of Sendero Luminoso, Professor of Philosophy Abimael Buzman Reynoso, had actually sent some students to Cuba for training as early as 1962, but it wasn't until 1980 that the movement burst upon Peru. Attacks on voting stations, bombings which caused major power blackouts, and eventually massacres of local Indians and government officials precipitated brutal retaliations and more massacres by government forces. The Sendero Luminoso also engaged in such macabre behavior as hanging dogs from the lampposts of Lima and Ayacucho to show their contempt for the revisionist "dog," Chinese leader Deng Xiaoping.

Yet the movement was never more than superficially Marxist. Its passion and momentum spring from the bowels of Peru's Inca past. Its followers believe in the "Hidden Inca" who, like the hidden Imam of Shiism, is believed to have waited for centuries beneath a mountain for the reincarnation of the ancient Inca empire.

According to American diplomat and writer Professor David Scott Palmer, who taught in Ayacucho during the early 1960s:

> Sendero is fighting not for adjustments in the system which will work for the benefit of the grievants at the

periphery but for the total overthrow of the system itself. It is also different in that it is the first full-blown rural rebellion in Peru guided by Communist principles. In its ideology and in its strategy for taking power, it consciously and quite proudly follows the principles and practices of Mao.

However, he adds, "In its plan for Peruvian society after victory is won, it resembles the Indian millenarian movements and most particularly the precepts of primitive and pure Indian communism." The rank and file of Sendero believe that the Hidden Inca will emerge soon to return them to the glories of the Inca Empire destroyed so long ago.

Why should this have descended upon a Peru that had already tried a number of other "paths" that were supposed to lead to increased democracy and prosperity for the masses of poor, especially Indians, on society's fringe? The answer, ironically, seems to be because Peru had tried, but failed. As Professor Palmer has written:

> The major effect of the changes within Peru over the past forty years . . . was to bring into the national system a much larger proportion of the total population. That means that the vast majority of Peruvian citizens are now in a position to make demands on the system—and do so. A government's staying power is thus increasingly dependent on its ability to respond to the concerns of the Peruvian citizenry.

The demand had been created and was there—that devil of the new demand for "progress" and for modernization—but the Peruvian government, like so many other governments, simply could not satisfy it. Yet Peru went through several phases in the attempt: (1) democracy in the early 1960s, (2) a leftist reformist military regime from 1968 on,

(3) democracy again in the late 1970s. None of them could keep up with the demand.

As Palmer outlined, "With the exception of the 1979–1981 period, net economic growth has been negative, wage settlements have fallen behind the cost of living, and inflation rates have increased from a 20%–30% range to 75%–125%. . . . The lower strata of society have clearly lost their incremental gains with the shrinking of the economic pie." One spontaneous answer of the people was the emergence of an "informal economy," another indicator of the failures of nation-states and of ominous problems ahead. Two-thirds of the Lima work force is now employed in the underground economy unlinked to the government or to the national economy.

But remote and beautiful Ayacucho, forgotten for so long, had awakened in those years—or perhaps we should say, half-awakened. In the early sixties, Ayacucho became a kind of model for development policies. The American Peace Corps came there to show what could be done. Europeans came. The Peruvian Peace Corps, Cooperación Popular, came. Cooperatives were formed and roads were built.

Then came the 1968 military coup, and the Americans and most of the Europeans withdrew. Ayacucho was left half-awakened. Into that quicksand of awakened expectation, the Sendero Luminoso stepped, now with no competitors. It remains today the most serious threat to Peruvian society and thus to the Andean countries themselves.

But although the Sendero was started along semi-Marxist tenets (which is natural, since those are virtually the only ones which offer a sure pattern for the total revolutionary takeover of a state), it is important to see that it, too, is basically spiritually irredentist. It is another classic example of "return-to-the-past."

• When Egyptian President Anwar Sadat was killed in 1981, people began looking around for reasons for this bizarre and heinous deed. For he was shot down by some of his own soldiers, the boys he always called "my sons."

To the West, Sadat was the hero, the peacemaker, the inspirer. The world reeled with shock. How could something like this happen? Who *were* these "boys" with the wild eyes and the self-righteously sure vision?

Egypt's Islamic fundamentalist sects—which, it must be noted, were not at all within Egypt's Islamic mainstream—began to form after the intense humiliation Egyptians felt after their defeat in the 1967 war with Israel. But the movement did not stem from the often grotesque poverty of Egypt. Its followers were upward-striving, middle-class students from the villages. Most were the best in their class and were in such difficult scientific disciplines as medicine and engineering. In short, they were precisely the youths with a "future."

Brought to cities like Cairo by the very government they later sought to undo through Sadat's assassination, they soon became shocked by the corruption and lack of piety around them. They found themselves alone and alienated by the strange urban and semi-Western atmosphere. They were easily lured by charismatic fundamentalist leaders who offered them unambiguous security and direction—a "new birth" for themselves and, ultimately, for Egypt, in fact.

Perhaps the final blow came upon graduation when, for all their academic achievement and skills, they found their job prospects severely limited, while inferior classmates with the right connections leaped rapidly up the ladder of success.

It wasn't difficult to incite these youths—torn as they were between idealism and despondency—with *fatwas* (proverbs, or sayings) from Islamic writings that justified violence against the state.

Eventually, they divided into two broad groups: those who withdrew altogether from "corrupt" Egyptian society into completely isolated desert communities—"Repentance and Holy Flight" was one such sect—and those who withdrew "mentally" into fanatically "pure" sects but remained physically within Egyptian society. It was one of the latter groups—"El Jihad" (Holy War)—that assassinated Sadat.

The profile of these outcast Egyptians, drawn up by a brilliant Egyptian sociologist at the American University of Cairo, Professor Saad Ibrahim, is not unique. It closely resembles that of Turkish terrorists (of both the right and left) who also came to the cities from the villages, found "evil" in Istanbul or Ankara and then sought out a new, all-encompassing system of belief—either Marxism (especially in earlier years) or fundamentalist Islam (increasingly in recent years).

"Actually, [the Egyptian cultists] resemble very much the urban guerrilla everywhere," Ali Dessouki, another scholar who has studied these groups, told me. Saad Ibrahim added, "Youth culture is the same everywhere. There is impatience with society, a romantic mission."

• In 1967 I had one of many interviews I was to conduct with Cambodia's able and prescient Prince Norodom Sihanouk while covering Vietnam. At that time, Cambodia was a little paradise on earth: a low-lying, extravagantly green country of (apparently) gentle people and culture.

"I cut off scholarships for Cambodian students going to study in Paris," the pudgy but still somehow princely Prince told me. "I did it several years ago. But . . . it may be too late."

Many years later, when I saw *The Killing Fields*—that stunning film about the Cambodian holocaust under the Khmer Rouge that followed the overthrow of Sihanouk—I remembered that moment. For Sihanouk went on to disclose that those uprooted and deracinated Cambodian students were returning home with a peculiarly demented blend of French Marxism and Cambodian mysticism drawn from earlier empires. Mix it well with psychotic xenophobia and fanatical nationalism, and you have Pol Pot and the Khmer Rouge—*The Killing Fields.*

The Killing Fields is a revealing testament to the dark side of human nature, exposing as it does those utopian dogmas which base their claim to "purity" on their claim to be able to recapture a perfect past. In one extraordinary moment, when the virtually enslaved Cambodians from the cities are struggling for survival in a rural forced labor camp, the ubiquitous and brutal Khmer Rouge commissar intones, "It is year zero. Nothing that was is anymore and nothing that will be is as it was."

Cambodia had been such a blessed land. The majority of this century's Cambodians sprang from the first century A.D. Hunan Kingdom, which was heavily influenced by India. Anthropologists maintain that today's people are an amalgam of races and cultures, including Indian, Chinese and Malay. Cambodia was colonized by the French in 1863, an event that ironically saved the integrity of the little country because it stopped the diligent colonization movement by both Vietnam and Laos into Cambodia.

There is no question that the spillover of the Vietnam War into little neutral Cambodia destabilized the country, leading to the rise of the Khmer Rouge. But the nature of the new regime was due to the deadly mixture of supertheoretical French Marxism (whose danger Sihanouk understood all too well) and the old Khmer mysticism. Pol Pot, the cruel Khmer Rouge leader mainly responsible for the deaths of perhaps 3 million Cambodians, encompassed both as he sat in Paris a quarter century before the holocaust and wrote his dissertation on how he would "purify" his society.

The "purification" took the form of physically liquidating everything bearing a trace of the modern world or of Westernism—at least everything but modern weapons. The cities were emptied of people as millions were uprooted and forced on death marches to the countryside where they were to labor as the simple peasants of antiquity. Anyone suspected of being educated was killed. Owning a pair of eyeglasses was tantamount to a death sentence. They even killed most of the doctors. This was to be their perfect, rural, classless society.

But, as with Peru's Sendero Luminoso, the Khmer Rouge was only superficially Marxist. "What Cambodia's leaders seem to be doing is trying to recreate the antiquated Khmer Empire of the fourteenth century, while at the same time augmenting it with relatively modern Marxist thought," Ronald Yates, a *Chicago Tribune* foreign correspondent, wrote in 1978, when people were still not willing to believe what was happening there.

He added, "The fifteenth century prophecy, known as the Puth Tomneay and repeated often by Cambodian peasants these days, ends with a Buddhist monk rallying the oppressed people against their rulers and eventually driving them out of the country."

That is what the demented Khmer Rouge thought they were doing. What they really did was something unique in the annals of history. The United Nations had to create a special name for it: "autogenocide," meaning genocide committed against one's *own* people.

Cambodia did indeed become "year zero."

How had all of this come to pass? How was it really possible in "modern" times that these return-to-the-past movements and impulses were erupting simultaneously all across the globe? Could a nation like the United States deal with them? Were they even important to a modern power like America?

Actually, what was happening was quite understandable when one looked at the whole phenomenon historically.

The post–World War II period saw the dismantling of the great colonial empires of the European powers. But often—although it was not so obvious at the time—the former empires were reorganized into new "nation-states" that were cohesive and modern in name only. In truth, these new countries would soon come to be seen as quite simply artificial for peoples who still identified mostly with their old ethnic groups, religions, tribes, clans, even villages.

The first generation of postcolonial leaders in the Third World—the "Bung" Sukarnos of Indonesia, the Gamal Nassers of Egypt, the Jawaharlal Nehrus of India—were modern nationalists in a Western sense. They simply assumed that Western-type progress would follow, as night the day, after independence.

Only that was not what happened.

However educated or sophisticated their leaders, the masses lacked the training and the value systems associated with technologically and industrially advanced societies. The communities they lived in were too often organized around traditional political and social patterns inimical to the development of "advanced" societies. (One example: Modern farming methods often met with ideological resistance from conservative peasants afraid to risk even minimal livelihoods on newfangled ideas. Tractors could not be introduced to communities whose myriad farm plots were constantly shrinking to accommodate ever-extending families. And too often there would be no one in permanent residence capable of maintaining the technology of modern farming.)

Finally, all too often "modernism" was introduced too rapidly, only partially and very unevenly—just enough to disrupt traditional cultural patterns, to threaten the customary political and religious elites and to create enormous discrepancies between modernizing (usually urban) and traditional (usually rural) sectors. In effect, two separate, discordant societies would be left to glare at each other across a cultural gulf of a thousand years.

It was not at all unnatural that, in their confusion, disappointment and frustration over "modernization," there would be a desperate search for a panacea. At first, as often as not, it was Marxism—thought to be an alternate path to progress. But increasingly, progress itself was seen as a false god, and the search turned to a romanticized, harmonious past. If only things could be just as they used to be. . . .

One of the best analysts I have found of this trend is Sherif Latfy, an Egyptian developmentalist who is the leading adviser to the Sultan of Oman, a small Middle East country which is developing with unusual wisdom and foresight. "The 'thing' will always be there," Latfy told me one day, sitting in his simple office in the picturesque old capital of Muscat. The 'thing' was the imbalance that came, inexorably, when countries put themselves into this kind of pressure cooker of social change.

"If it were not 'Islam,' it would be called something else," he went on. "It is simply something that comes with modern life. The frustration becomes bigger in the developing countries. You find people are frustrated with change—or without it. The more development you do, the more frustrated people become. Hundreds of years ago, no one knew what development was or what life in the U.S. was. The more development, the more impossible life becomes.

"What do you do? There is no economic solution to it. I can't say, in many cases, what the world should have done, but no matter what you do, there often is no fixed answer. How to go through the transitional period? No one really knows." Then he leaned back in his chair in his office and ruminated over the violent Islamic fundamentalists who had killed Egyptian President Sadat. "Look at those men," he said. "They were the people brought to school by the government—so naturally they are going to blame the government for everything."

The other man who has best interpreted the impact on the individual soul in countries faced by the impossible challenge (or is it really a threat?) of modernization—a modernization usually identified with the United States—was Dr. Heinz Kohut of Chicago, the late psychoanalyst often called the successor to Sigmund Freud. Speaking of fundamentalist trends in Moslem and Arab countries, and Iran in particular, Kohut told me:

"The specifics of that tension arise from the attempt to change a national/cultural/religious 'self' into something that seems not to be it. People in various Islamic countries, for instance, were clearly repressed and backward. They were clearly living a demeaning kind of existence leading to low self-esteem.

"Then came the Shah in Iran, Ataturk in Turkey, Nasser in Egypt. In order to make their people more capable of self-respect, the message is 'Modernize!' But if the changes made are made abruptly, within one or two generations, that threatens the continuity of the ethnic self. It is much like the individual self. We were once children—then adolescents—then mature adults. When a person feels discontinuous, that is a terribly painful feeling. You do not hang together. People will do almost anything to avoid that.

"What happens when it is not within the capacity of people to change is that they want to overthrow those who forced them to move. Change is experienced as an agent of someone else. Discontinuity arouses tremendous anxiety. So when someone comes along like Khomeini with something of a 'new world,' there is a sense of tremendous healing. They will do anything for it, so long as the sense of continuity is reestablished.

"Then there is a degree of sadism that is mobilized—give them [the foreign agents of change] a dose of that medicine that they inflict on others. They feel shamed by us, so they need to shame us. And they know that they can have tremendous power over us, because they are at that stage of development where their goals are compatible with dying. Ours are not. We can't say we'll do the same to you.

"We are at a totally different stage of selfhood in dealing with them."

No wonder, then, that the United States—"the" quintessentially modern, rational and progressive country and the world's very model for "progress"—should constantly be caught unawares by these movements. For they were—and are and will be—of extraordinary, if as yet unrecognized, importance to America and to Americans.

Consider the history:

While recent American administrations have had their attention constantly riveted on conventional and nuclear warfare and relations between constituted states (Europe, the Soviet Union, Japan, etc.), almost every single disaster and serious challenge in foreign policy since World War II has come from Third World turmoil. One need only to name Cuba, Vietnam, Cambodia, Iran, Lebanon, Libya, El Salvador, Nicaragua, Grenada, and now Peru, Bolivia, the Philippines, Chile. . . .

Jimmy Carter's chances for reelection were probably doomed by the Iranian hostage crisis, masterminded by the Ayatollah Khomeini. Ronald Reagan's greatest defeat was at the hands of the Lebanese Shiites—another group largely motivated by return-to-the-past sentiments, and an offshoot of Khomeinism. The Iran-Iraq war, another offshoot of the attempted spread of Khomeinism, threatened the oil supply of the whole Western world. Terrorism out of these movements became the scourge of our times. Peace in the Middle East—something that is crucial to the West—is now paralyzed by both return-to-the-past Arabs *and* the emergence of similar groups within Israel, such as the Gush Emunim, which also dreams of returning to a utopian religious Jewish past and is thus claiming the right to lands held two thousand years ago.

Even in the United States one could make the argument that the fundamentalist impulse—which was certainly showing itself in everything from the desire for school prayer, to the bitter abortion fight, to a return to basics in general—was vociferously present. It is even noticeable in the mood of nostalgia that characterizes the Reagan Administration.

Although the emanations of this retrogression have been all around us, our leaders simply have not been able to grasp what is happening, much less develop any counterstrategy. This, I am convinced, is because American leaders have continued to view the world in our own traditional and conventional terms—largely of inevitable progress.

Perhaps because she is an unorthodox thinker, Jeane Kirkpatrick was one of the few who began to see and address these new themes. In an interview in her New York office on December 19, 1984, while she was still ambassador to the United Nations, she expressed concern about a lack of foresight in U.S. policy. "Most of our planning is only marginally relevant to what is really taking place," she said. When I asked her why, she went on: "Thinking about both political and military problems, there is always a powerful tendency to be governed by what was. It is the Maginot Line Complex. The Power of Conventional Thinking. The conventional management of conventional realities tends to obscure the past. In the present, the baggage of conventional thinking about the continuum of events from the Vietnams to the world wars, I think, tends to obscure realities of the unconventional challenges with which we find ourselves faced."

What, then, if America did not, still, come to understand the unconventional and the irregular?

"Either we have to, or we fail," she answered simply.

A high American official, who cannot be named, also expressed to me the intelligence community's dawning concern with the unconventional and the irregular.

"We . . . share your concern regarding the threat posed by demographic shifts, illegal migration, the risk of irregular warfare and the revolutions of the 'return-to-the-past' and are actively seeking to improve our expertise in these areas," he told me. "For example, we now have two analytic groups devoted solely to studying the root causes of political instability and insurgency in the Third World.

"Perhaps the greatest challenge before us now is to explore how these new social forces are likely to bring about dramatic change in the current political and social order. You mentioned that one hundred or more political, social, religious and ethnic groups are organized militarily and threaten fifty-two sovereign states. Which of these groups are most likely to launch the next revolution? More important, how exactly would they go about it?"

He was referring to some figures on irregular warfare that I had dug out that are closely related to the return-to-the-past movements. For instance, by 1986—at a time when America's political and military leaders were obsessed by the dangers of nuclear war and were still busily building up enormous conventional military machines under a huge defense budget—it was already clear that our military machine was ill suited to deal with the reality of conflict in this "other" world. The American tragedy in Lebanon hammered home the point. Some key figures:

By 1986 there were more than forty wars raging across the globe. They involved forty-five different nations or, to be more exact, "entities" of various forms. Of the eighty wars that began after 1945, only twenty-eight took the traditional form of fighting between the regular armed forces of two or more states. Almost half were civil wars, insurgencies or guerrilla contests, with the remaining six being riots and coups d'état. United Nations Secretary General Javier Perez de Cuellar called the syndrome abroad in the world the "new anarchy" and he characterized it as "armed force, both overt and covert, used and increasingly justified as a legitimate means of obtaining national objectives."

While these changes in the world were enormously complicated, they were not impossible either to predict or to deal with. There were and are, for instance, warning signs, such as: the formation of dual societies (spiritual/secular) within one "nation;" the development of secondary economies totally untied to the society itself; leaders who embrace the West and modernization so much that they lose contact with their own people; changes that come too fast or too slowly; a deep and unredeemed sense of humiliation, change that starts and then is abandoned; a vacuum of present-day values, overdevelopment of cities instead of a balanced development between city and countryside; real or perceived corruption in a country's leadership and the exclusion of traditional religious leaders from positions of power.

For the United States, there are some foreign policy and human lessons that we would do well to heed, for these impassioned and retrogressive movements are going to keep bursting out in a world in which change, development and the desire for and fear of "progress" have become, for the first time in humankind's history, the business of everyone.

First, we must realize that the East-West conflict is not the only conflict and perhaps not even, in immediate and real terms, the greatest threat. We must realize, too, that, while nuclear war is an unspeakable *potential* horror, the *real* millions who are dying are dying mostly at the hands of these return-to-the-past movements. We must try to understand both the enormous attraction of "Americanism" (which I define as "what everybody in the world could be if . . .") and the bitterness against it in some places. Finally, we have to acknowledge that the United States, while still the greatest power in the world, can no longer attempt to solve or even involve itself in every one of these complicated conflicts—we should simply stay away from many until they right themselves. One might call the desirable new policy "selective activism" or even "middlin' meddlin'."

When one really thinks about it, it is all rather stunning. Who would ever have dreamed that, alongside the most sweeping progressive time of change mankind has ever known, there would march this shadow of the past-as-alternative? Who can say what people next will try to find its future in its past?

ROUNDTABLE DISCUSSION

"When the Future Becomes the Past"

<u>PANELISTS:</u> Paul Duke, *moderator*
Georgie Anne Geyer
Charles Corddry
Charles McDowell
Jack Nelson
Hedrick Smith

GEYER: We all assumed in the sixties and early seventies that revolutions in the world were going to carry us toward "progressive" regimes, toward more education for people, toward more freedom, whether it was Castro or the Central American guerrillas. We came out of the postcolonial period with the first generation of charismatic leaders—the Nehrus, the Nassers—and that was their agenda.

Basically, the agenda has not been implemented in most parts of the world. What I began to see with Khomeini was that the response to the modern course in Iran—on the part of some calculating, cunning and dishonest leaders—was to start looking backward and to preach that "things are *not* working because we abandoned our true faith, our true gods." So they said Iran had to return to the past—maybe centuries ago. In the case of Khomeini, it was a thousand years ago.

I began to realize that this was not something *sui generis* at all with Khomeini, but the more I've studied it, the more I realized much of this was a natural thing because modernization is hard to achieve. Progress as we think of it in the West is hard for most of the peoples of the world and impossible for many. So you have this political discontinuity.

My only premise here is simply to say, look, this is happening, it's happening in different places, in different ways, and we'd better seek ways to deal with development and modernization in ways that are less threatening to people.

McDOWELL: It's hard for me to have a sense of all this unless I can get some idea of why those leaders who were going to educate their people, to bring their people along, were suddenly endangered or overwhelmed.

You suggest some of the reasons, but let me say that the sheer velocity of modern change was utterly bewildering and frustrating for the traditional idea of "move the people ahead, teach them to get along with the automobile, the electric motor and the pump and the schoolhouse." And here came the nuclear age, the television age—just the velocity of change was so fierce that it discredited traditional advance, and this bewilderment led people back to icons and old religions.

DUKE: Are you saying, Charley, that they got too much too fast?

McDOWELL: I guess I'm saying, while Third World peoples were trying to begin to catch up in a traditional way, what they were catching up to went like a rocket and mocked them and humiliated them and bewildered them. What they were catching up to changed so radically that it made gradual progressive change seem futile and bewildering.

GEYER: That is it, Charley. You must remember that most societies in the world—a majority of them before World War II—were traditional societies, tribes, clans, etc. They had no image of "progress." That came in afterwards with the educated classes who are mostly educated in the West.

SMITH: You also had a vacuum of values. That is, the assault which came from the modern world came from a set of values which embrace nationalism, Western ideas of individualism, and which assaulted traditional cultures, and if they were bowled over because they could no longer cope institutionally and economically, then what values would these traditional-minded people turn to?

When they then began to find that the modernization process didn't work very quickly, they said "to hell with it" and backed up, went the other way, not only in terms of social organization but just in terms of belief systems. It's just that we could not thrust ourselves that harshly upon them without their reacting.

You did get some cultures like those of Egypt and India, like some of those in Latin America which were capable of grafting on and absorbing enough of the modern world so that real trends developed. You have communist revolutions, you have countercommunist revolutions going on now. You have democracy coming back in Argentina and Brazil. So you have much transition. But at least one of the reactions was the one you're talking about, which is the recoil from the modern world.

The question now is: Does the phenomenon you're talking about, based around Shiite Islam in the Middle East, in Iran, spreading through Lebanon, butting up in the Persian Gulf, pushing into part of Syria, part of Iraq—does that pose a new geopolitical challenge to us that we don't know how to cope with, and for how long? What kind of challenge is it to the power and interests of the West in that terribly rich and strategically important part of the world?

GEYER: It's a terrible challenge. We lost Iran. After

all, the Shah was supposedly our man guarding the Gulf, and then revolution came. Those of us who covered Iran knew that it was the mullahs and not the far Left that was the Shah's greatest danger, and that's why he was toppled. The Shah also did things that fomented a revolution. He cut off all of the fundamentalists in their theological schools from any upward mobility in Iran. They couldn't go into the regular universities, they couldn't get municipal jobs, they couldn't get government jobs. Also, the Shah and his entourage, his followers lived so well—there was the element of corruption.

But Iran didn't boil over—so long as the economic boom was going. It was when the boom collapsed in Tehran, when these young kids from the villages lost their jobs and began roaming the streets. It was then that they went back to the mullahs. It was not before that. It was not while they had jobs, not while everything was going okay.

Now there is Lebanon breaking up into Shiite fundamentalist fanaticism. It's a threat to the U.S. but also to the Soviet Union, which is scared to death of its own Central Asian Islamic population exploding.

So, naturally, the danger from these movements goes in a lot of different directions. They go up to the Arab leaders like King Hussein of Jordan, who moved out of his big palace on the mountainside to a little tiny palace next to his office so he wouldn't appear to the fundamentalists to be living too high.

NELSON: But, Gee Gee, you've had these wars and conflicts and some forms of Moslem fanaticism for years and years. So while the Shiite movement may be somewhat different today, is it that much different?

GEYER: It's bigger.

NELSON: It's different because you have the Western intrusion.

GEYER: And because they want to destroy the Western-imposed borders. Khomeini wanted to break down the Iraqi border. The idea of spreading this Islamic anarchism far and wide is new.

NELSON: But the grudge against the West is not new.

GEYER: No, that's not new.

DUKE: The interesting irony here is that these countries may want to turn the clock back, but they have no hesitancy about using all the modern means of warfare in pursuing their goals, blowing up the American embassy and the marine barracks in Beirut with great loss of life. They also are masters of modern communication. Khomeini's revolution was basically fomented by videocassette, which is rather unique. He was sitting off in France. He sent cassettes to Iran which were spread throughout the countryside, and that's how he got his message across.

CORDDRY: It seems to me that all this talk about recoil is really talk about aftershock. The recoil came with the breakup of the colonial empires, and while this does not obviously apply to Persia, it applies to much of Africa. Having tried to exist as colonies and not having liked it, many of these countries thought they did not want to turn to a republican or democratic form of government, so they turned to something they regarded as socialism, which of course turned out to be dictatorship. And they fared poorly.

I don't know whether this causes them to want to return to the past. I don't even know whether I agree with your thesis that they *are* returning to the past. But what I would like to ask, Gee Gee, is this: During much of the period you are talking about, Robert McNamara was the president of the World Bank, and members of that august institution tell me he did a tremendous job for the Third World. Apparently, they resented it. Your argument logically would come to that.

Where are we now? Are we really threatened with this great wave washing over us? Must we continue to try to develop the Third World in order to avert this catastrophe that may or may not be coming? What I'm asking you is whether there is a threat to the developed world or whether the developed world should go in and develop the undeveloped world. I'm not sure where you come out.

GEYER: The one thing I can say with assurance is that everything is cultural. We don't like to talk about cultural relativism, but as a matter of fact, some cultures—and it doesn't mean they're inferior or superior—have values that are propitious, that are amenable to development and change. Some of the countries along the rim of the Pacific, for example.

If you don't have a work ethic, if you don't have a mixed economy, if you don't have reasonably uncorrupt governments, you're not going to develop, and I think this is what we're dealing with today in terms of analysis.

SMITH: I defend Gee Gee's thesis in this way, and that is that we have been given the picture and have become accustomed as a culture to thinking of whatever goes on in the Third World rather simplistically as either communist or anticommunist, that it's either something that favors and is fomented by Soviet expansionism or is something that favors the West. Here we have a phenomenon that has its roots in the kinds of frustrations and cultural assault and recoil and aftershock that we've all described and which has not necessarily got a path over the short term which is either pro-Western or pro-Soviet in its strategic implications. It's kind of anti-everything. I think it's important to figure out where our policies go, with at least some notion of what the reality is.

What Gee Gee is describing is not the only reality. Some countries—you mentioned the ones on the rim of the Pacific—are modernizing tremendously and are affiliating with the whole Western trading world.

There are others in Latin America that are going democratic with great difficulty, ones like Argentina and Brazil, and those are important, too. There are, in fact, anticommunist revolutions going on in several places. One is Islamic in Afghanistan. There's Cambodia, Angola, Nicaragua. There are a lot of diverse trends, and it suggests that Americans ought to reduce their level of anxiety about what's going to happen in the next year or two and back off and let these forces of history play out without trying to judge everything and worry about whether we have one more red country or one more blue country on the world map.

It's important to look at the world in just this differentiated way.

CORDDRY: You're not, then, arguing that there is any kind of connecting theology or ideology among the movements that Gee Gee has described.

SMITH: In Shiite Islam, I would say there is.

CORDDRY: All right, but what are the outer limits? The Saudis don't seem to be that much excited. I put this in the form of a question: This great revolution that occurred in Iran not long ago seems to have wound up in a perpetual war with Iraq, which I judge the Saudis no longer seem to be mortally afraid of. Having knocked off a couple of the airplanes that the Persians sent over there, they went back to work.

I just don't know what the outer limits of this are, but they're not global. I don't think I've got to worry about a Shiite revolution coming to Washington, D.C.

GEYER: No, but you have to worry about it if you're going to put people into Lebanon. I was at a meeting a few years ago with some top psychoanalysts in Chicago who deal with these things, and I remember one of them asked, "How do you deal with a Khomeini?" And someone responded that you don't, you can't, and that's a lesson that we should have learned—just to stay out of troubled areas like Lebanon, not to put Marines into a trap—

CORDDRY: Isn't that sort of what I'm arguing?

GEYER: Well, this is hard for Americans to take, though, Charlie. We think everything can be dealt with. We put Marines into Lebanon who were slaughtered unnecessarily. If we had understood the Shiite movement and the dynamics of the situation, we wouldn't have used our military might in such a stupid way because you give the initiative to all the little guys in the shadows who know exactly how to get rid of you.

SMITH: Had we understood this fundamentalist phenomenon as it was emerging ten years ago, we might or might not have been able to nudge the Shah of Iran in a direction, or having seen he was going to fall, we might have been able to work with some conservative mullahs who were not radical the way Khomeini is.

I think you're quite right. We got into Lebanon not because we were trying to deal with Shiite Islam but because we saw some way of getting the Palestine Liberation Organization out of Beirut, and then hopefully some way of getting the Arab-Israeli problem on some road toward a solution. But one of the reasons why the secretary of state miscalculated was that he didn't understand the power of Shiite Islam and some of the other difficulties there.

Whether or not we have hit the end of that line, whether it's going to come down and raise hell in the

Persian Gulf and Bahrain and Kuwait, whether the Saudi monarchy is stable for the next two decades—all these are open questions. It's a phenomenon that can still come and hit us, and the thing to remember is that the Middle Eastern area matters to us because the Western world is getting so darned much of its oil from there. Furthermore, if there's a power vacuum, the Soviets might be able to move down and make trouble. So it matters to us in two ways.

NELSON: One thing that illustrated how little we knew about any of these movements occurred on New Year's Eve in Tehran in 1977—I was there—when Jimmy Carter raised his glass in salute to the Shah and said that he wanted to drink to "this island of stability" in that part of an "unstable" world. Of course it was not long thereafter that the revolution came.

SMITH: Which leaves you worried about Saudi Arabia, doesn't it, just a little bit?

NELSON: That's right. You said a moment ago, Rick, that the United States should step back for a year or two and see how these movements are going and not get too involved. That's really not politically realistic, though, is it?

SMITH: It depends upon what countries you're talking about, and it depends upon what time frame you're talking about. I spent a lot of years like Gee Gee covering foreign policy, living in Southeast Asia, the Middle East, the Soviet Union, and I listened to American leaders talking about how many countries were going communist or moving away from us. I mean, they could give you a list of countries that were all going the wrong way, and fifteen years later, it looks quite different.

Nobody worries about Indonesia today, and yet at one time we were deeply worried it was going communist. Likewise with Egypt. Now it has become one of our staunchest Middle East allies. There was Ghana under

Kwame Nkrumah, but with the sergeants and corporals in charge of that African land we don't worry so much these days.

CORDDRY: The question of the Persian Gulf is not whether the United States is going to suppress Shiite movements, because it's not. The question is whether the U.S. is going to counteract any Soviet move in the region.

GEYER: Can I be a little bit hopeful and just quickly list some of the situations where I think we've done pretty well? I do think there is a dawning realization that this is a different world and not a traditionally structured world that we're dealing with.

First of all, the handling of the Shiites who took the TWA plane passengers. I think the Reagan Administration deserves credit for doing that with quite a bit of aplomb. They worked through Syrian President Assad. We got all the people except one back. Nobody was humiliated, which is an important point in all this. You don't set up your next situation.

Grenada. A different type of situation totally. When I went there after the invasion, the U.S. military had done a most brilliant job of separating political prisoners—people who had taken part in a political massacre—from those who were Communists, but did not take part in the massacre. The American military was sensitized to do a difficult and delicate job.

The U.S. military in El Salvador has worked very, very consciously to see that the responsibility for the war against the rebels rests with the Salvadoran army and the U.S. remains in the background.

Lastly, Oman in the Middle East. Again the U.S. military has stayed in the background, as the Sultan wants, and yet has helped protect this tiny kingdom against fundamentalist unrest.

NELSON: Do you extend that to Nicaragua where

we mined the harbors and have encouraged and aided the Contras movement?

GEYER: No, I don't think I would.

McDOWELL: Those of us with vague notions of how to do good have a sort of conventional idea about the Third World generally, including the phenomenon that you're describing, which was that we have a responsibility to help the underdeveloped countries, that a successful future peace with everybody involves encouraging their agriculture, putting money into helping them dig a well, for example.

We have the United Nations and we have the World Bank, and we have all our own foreign aid plans, and we're putting considerable money into the Third World.

Is this still the basic responsibility of a great nation? Are we supposed to be out in the world digging wells and improving agriculture and helping get a school started? Is that still the best general approach for us?

GEYER: You have raised a really big question, and there is no common wisdom.

What didn't work, for instance, was pouring money into countries like Tanzania, and not controlling what was done. Even the northern Europeans now know that African socialism hasn't worked.

What I see coming is a view that the free world should put money into the countries that are working, like those on the rim of the Pacific.

The development experts are thinking more and more in terms of examples that work. But then you get whole new problems like the exhaustion of resources in parts of the world such as Africa; Ethiopia, for example. Forty percent of the land was arable at the turn of the century, 4 percent is arable today. Of course there's going to be famine. How do we deal with that? We sent a lot of food as a humanitarian gesture. Does it really mean anything in the long run?

And we must face up to the fact we're going to have much of the Third World in our own country—we don't have frontiers anymore. We have massive illegal immigration. We'll have more of these problems that we're talking about right here at home. And we don't know how to deal with the poor we already have.

So I would say the whole question has changed so dramatically in the last ten years, Charley, that we're all shocked and dazed by it.

McDOWELL: One quick observation. You mentioned Tanzania. I had a son that lived there with the Hadza tribe for a year and a half and was most earnest about helping those people. And what he saw was that American aid poured in, full of good intentions, and the Tanzanian government found it difficult to use the assistance in a way that coincided with cultural considerations.

My son Will tells me that after looking at how they were trying to improve agriculture, the most striking thing he discovered was that nobody ever sent a plow. Everybody sent a tractor. But the people really needed a plow, or a buffalo to pull it, or whatever pulls a plow in that place.

SMITH: Apropos of Charley's comment, does the whole notion of a Peace Corps, which we felt so good about in the early sixties, have any relevance to these return-to-the-past revolutions? Can we even in a modest way be helpful, or is even this kind of help resented because it's regarded as Western and intrusive?

GEYER: I did not find it resented in the countries I visited. In fact, the Peace Corps was appreciated because it was doing the dogged, everyday work that a lot of the missionaries did years ago in such areas as education and agricultural training.

Where the danger comes in, such as in the case of the Peruvian Sendero Luminoso movement, was that we poured Peace Corps people into this little town of Ayacucho and then suddenly they all left in '68 when the military took over.

So one of the things we should remember is: Don't half-awaken people. Don't awaken them at all unless you're going to carry it through.

But in general, I've found around the world that the Peace Corps people did a good job.

DUKE: It seems to me we've been missing one of the central points, that in almost every Third World country that we've been talking about, we're dealing with two societies—a modern urban society and a primitive or traditional rural society. And they form literally two different countries. Almost everything that we've been talking about comes back to that fundamental point.

And if we're dealing, in fact, with societies that have one foot in what we'll call the modern age and one foot in the past, where most of the back-to-the-pasters come from in the first place, how do you deal with that? Isn't that really the problem?

GEYER: Absolutely. In the example that I gave of Egypt and the fundamentalists who killed Anwar Sadat, I talked about dual societies as one of the great dangers, and that was what had happened there. Those young people brought from villages to Cairo for education—it should have been an ideal thing. Instead, they became alienated and alone. They saw the "corruption" of the government. They were the brightest kids—that's another thing we shouldn't miss—but they were swept up by the unorthodox Islamic sheiks and taken out into their communities in the desert. Many of them couldn't even talk with people in the cities.

SMITH: When you have a society that is well along the path of modernization and has taken some new roots such as Egypt, which after all was modernizing under the British and had several decades of development, the modernizers are in a stronger position. But this goes back to the point I was trying to make earlier. You just don't look at everything in terms of the global struggle with communism because if you do, you wind up by backing some regimes regardless of internal politics. We may be in that situation right now in the Philippines, where the Marcos government has become so unpopular.

DUKE: Do you think the central problem with our foreign policy is that we look at these issues too much in terms of East-West relations, too much in terms of stopping communism? We sometimes appear to ignore indigenous movements arising out of repression unless they involve an attempt to topple communist-leaning regimes.

SMITH: If you're talking about the Third World, then with few exceptions, that's exactly the point that I'm making.

CORDDRY: Do you have any real conviction that you could do it any other way when you think about the two countries that are now the superpowers and how they are going to determine the fate of the world?

Everything is in East-West, U.S.-Soviet terms.

SMITH: I don't agree with you.

CORDDRY: Gromyko may have been right when he said nothing can be done in the world without the Soviet Union's input. If there's any truth to that, the United States cannot stand aside if it wants to influence events.

SMITH: I don't agree with Gromyko.

CORDDRY: I daresay you don't. Okay, you've got the Soviets stopped in Europe, let's say, and then you go to a North-South relationship, and if it doesn't come out in superpower competition, I miss my guess.

SMITH: I don't think we triumphed over the Soviets in any way in Egypt. Egypt worked out its own destiny, and it gradually worked its way out of being first a British colony, then a pro-Soviet "nonaligned" country, and now a pro-American "nonaligned" country. And I really don't think that we and the Soviets, for all the effort and all the diplomacy and everything that we did, guided that course. I think the Egyptians worked that out themselves. The tendency on our part to react every time we think we see the Soviet hand may often complicate and harm our long-term objectives.

DUKE: But you would concede that the driving force of our foreign policy, certainly since World War II, has been concern about Soviet expansionism. That concern has shaped domestic politics in this country as well. Politicians of both parties have been running against the Soviet Union for a long time, using the old theme "the Russians are coming, we've got to stop the Russians," be it in Vietnam, be it in Nicaragua, be it in El Salvador, or be it in the Philippines. That has been a basic staple of American politics.

SMITH: And if you go back and look at the historical record, there's good reason to question whether this has been wise in terms of our long-term national interest . . . all of this Red baiting.

If you're talking about Turkey and Greece in Europe, you're right on. Cuba is obviously an enormous embarrassment to us. Close to our borders, you've got a real problem, not just politically, but strategically as well. When you get to the Persian Gulf and the Suez Canal, you're in touchy, important areas for us.

But I don't think the same applies to Indonesia and Angola and Afghanistan. Those are places that have proved a great nuisance for the Soviets, just as they've created a great nuisance for us in Nicaragua. All of this is strategic tit for tat, and we might both be better off to pull back from each other.

CORDDRY: Yes, but you've put just about everything on limits for U.S. involvement. You haven't left very much that ought to be within our interest as you think back over the countries you've just called off.

SMITH: I certainly meant all of Africa. I've said almost all of Central and Latin America, with the exception of Cuba and Mexico, and almost all the small countries in Asia.

CORDDRY: Almost all of Central America?

SMITH: Central and South America.

CORDDRY: We should not concern ourselves with Soviet penetration?

SMITH: No, we do not have to see every political turn in those countries as being an indicator of where we stand in the global struggle with the Soviets.

GEYER: Look at Iran. When Khomeini came in, the Communist Party was included in the government for a while. Then all of a sudden, he hanged most of the party leaders. The Soviets were naturally upset. Then, last year, there were Russians kidnaped by the Shiites in Lebanon. Now, that was a first.

SMITH: That makes my point because it suggests that the force of Shiite Islam is neither pro-West nor pro-Soviet. It's anti both.

CORDDRY: You suggest the Persian Gulf is of vital interest to the U.S., and therefore we ought to be involved, but you would leave Africa out of it. Now, you can't do that for strategic reasons because from the Persian Gulf you look down to the Horn of Africa, around the southern tip and up through the South Atlantic. Not to mention economic interests. So you can't have the Soviet Union dominating that. You can't say all Africa is off limits, don't concern yourself with it.

We have to import many of our raw materials. We have an extensive list of raw materials that we've got to get, many from Africa. The Soviet Union is meddling around in Africa, for heaven's sake, not because it's interested in development in Africa but because it's interested in preempting us in a number of ways.

It's pretty hard to think of somewhere that your vital interests aren't concerned.

SMITH: But you're talking about Soviet dominance—

CORDDRY: Or meddling.

SMITH: Okay, meddling. But, Charlie, we took it for granted after Nasser came to power and said go jump in the lake to John Foster Dulles that the Soviets dominated Egypt and therefore had a stranglehold on the Suez Canal. We weren't able to do anything successful about it in terms of our foreign policy, and you could have President after President and senator after senator get up and make speeches and win elections and win votes on that. But in fact, there was no effective policy other than waiting. And we waited and eventually the Egyptians changed.

And the same thing was true in Indonesia, which has 100 million people, an enormously important and large area in which we were going crazy. We ran all kinds of stories about Sukarno going communist.

Eventually, the CIA did get involved with covert assistance that advanced our interests. But the basic thrust for change to another setup came from within.

So what I'm suggesting is there may be a number of situations around the world where waiting is the best policy, but it is not the normal American way of doing things.

CORDDRY: So wait it out and let the people become sick and tired of whatever Soviet influence is being exercised. Throw them out, and now we're back to the beginning of the whole exercise here. Then they start returning to the past.

GEYER: I think what I hear Rick saying, and I agree, is that what the United States needs is selective activism, not to try to meddle or to contain or control everything. But we're going to have to select our activist positions and the countries very carefully from now on. We don't have unlimited resources anymore.

SMITH: Last point on this. I guess what I was trying to do was to take from Gee Gee's idea that there are forces at work here that no one can manage to control, and it is both hubris and mistaken to think that you can.

GEYER: There are some areas where we can use our power to anticipate developments. I would say we should be doing more in the Middle East to facilitate an Israeli-Jordanian-Palestinian peace. I don't think we're going to do it. But if so, you would undercut fundamentalism within the Palestinian community, which is so crucial as the wild card in the deck.

Then there are places where it's just gone so far, like Iran under Khomeini, you just have to stay out. It's a madhouse. You've got to let them work it out, and they will after the passions cool.

NELSON: If you look at the political realities, the Mideast peace process offers nothing for this Administration. They've consigned it to the back burner because they don't see where they come out ahead politically in trying to resolve all those age-old animosities.

Look at the Carter Administration. Carter pulled off the Egyptian-Israeli peace accords, and politically it really didn't do him a bit of good in the United States. As a matter of fact, he lost Jewish votes when he ran for reelection. The Reagan Administration sees the Mideast pit as a no-win issue.

GEYER: I agree. But if we want to avoid what's going to happen five years from now, which is, I think, an Israel surrounded by radicalized Arabs with a large radical Jewish population internally, and the two feeding upon each other, then we should be planning for the future.

McDOWELL: I'm trying to find something to be encouraged about, and I believe that maybe we're learning a little bit, that maybe we can begin to be aware of complexity, and we can begin to see how terribly lethal our intrusion into the remote corners of the world can be. But I don't have a lot of problems with Charlie Corddry's concern for geopolitical things done with one eye on the Soviets all the time. I don't have a lot of trouble meshing that with Rick's hands-off notions. It seems to me that some enlightenment is beginning to dawn.

CORDDRY: If we don't deal with problems today, you will not have any use for a policy that looks forward toward tomorrow. I think that essentially the problems that Gee Gee is raising are real ones, but I don't think that there is a great intellectual or theological connection among the various returns-to-the-past. I don't think you can say, there they are and they are separate from the superpower competition, no matter how wise it might be for either of the superpowers to ignore them. I don't think they will, and I think you have to deal with the world as it is. From the point of view of the U.S., we are economically involved everywhere and needfully so. That being the case, then you are required to be involved politically, and obviously you're required to be involved from a security standpoint.

SMITH: I've not been talking of total noninvolvement. Rather, about reacting with agility and not alarm.

CORDDRY: Wisdom and not foolishness.

DUKE: To me the problems are so enormous and the politics so pervasive that I must confess to pessimism in this nuclear age with man's awesome capacity to destroy what has been created. H. G. Wells once said the story of mankind is a race between catastrophe and education, and every day brings fresh evidence that catastrophe ultimately is going to win.

GEYER: We've got to begin understanding the irrational in the world and how to deal with the conflicts that perplex us. My own thought is that someone should start what I would call an unthinkable think tank—people who think originally about all these things we've been discussing. In other words, new ways to make American power and policy again relevant in a turbulent world.

Index

Abortion issue, 109
Abrahamson, Lieutenant General James A., 203, 216
Achille Lauro, see Middle East terrorists
Adams, John, 273
Adams, Sherman, 97
Affirmative action, 45, 51, 177
Afghanistan, 90, 124, 126, 314, 322
Africa, 312, 318, 323, 324
Agnew, Spiro, 24, 44, 274
AIDS research, 230
Air Force Manned Orbiting Laboratory, 199
Akali Dal, 292
Allen, Frederick Lewis, 40
American Business Conference, 106
American Enterprise Institute, 63, 163
American Political Science Association, 37
American Voter, 38
Angola, 124, 314, 322
Anti-Ballistic Missile Treaty, 215, 217, 223

Apollo program, 199
Argentina, 310, 314
Arms control, see Nuclear arms
Army-McCarthy hearings, 248
Aspin, Les, 153, 215
Assad, Hafez al-, 317
Ataturk, 302

Bahrain, 316
Baker, Howard, 144, 150, 283
Baker, James, 102, 122, 158, 175, 179
Barzini, Luigi, 58
Begin, Menachem, 90
Berri, Nabih, 271
Bethe, Hans, 196
Bhindranwale, Jarnail Singh, 292
Blacks, see Civil rights
Block, Bill, 177
Bolivia, 303
Boorstin, Daniel, 18
Bourne, Pete, 103
Bradley, Bill, 151
Brady, Jim, 134
Brazil, 310, 314

Brezezinski, Zbigniew, 96
Brezhnev, Leonid, 222
Briggs, Richard J., 205, 206
Britain, 217, 321, 322
Brookings Institution, 204
Brown, Clarence, 239
Brown, Harold, 196, 206
Brown, Jerry, 256
Budget deficit, 89, 90, 99–100, 101–02, 103, 104–05, 106–07, 111, 118, 139–42, 143, 144–45, 146–52 *passim*, 155–56, 173–74, 175, 176, 177–78, 179, 190
Bulgaria, 292
Burford, Anne, 131
Burger, Warren, 239
Bush, George, 76, 85, 86, 92, 120, 122, 148, 274
Bush, Jeb, 120
Bush, Vannevar, 198
Burt, Richard, 27
Byrd, Robert, 24

Caldwell, Philip, 24
Cambodia, 124, 297–99, 303, 314
Camp David peace accords, 90, 325
Carson, Johnny, 29
Carter, Jimmy, 44, 103–04
    1976 election, 36, 61, 62, 75, 250–51, 277
    1980 election, 12, 34, 86, 144, 249–51, 303
    as president, 11, 25, 64, 68, 90, 101–02, 103–04, 109, 111, 112, 113–14, 120, 132, 135–36, 157, 166, 252, 316, 325
    use of television by, 243, 249–52, 266, 277, 278
Castro, Fidel, 289, 308
Center for Judicial Studies, 109–10
Central America, 90, 123, 124, 308, 323
Central Intelligence Agency, 93, 324
Chandler, Otis, 62
Cheney, Richard, 100, 149, 160
Chicago Daily News, 11, 20
Chile, 303
China, 90
Churchill, Winston, 225, 233
Civil rights, 14–15, 40–41, 51–52, 53, 54, 79, 135, 173, 176–77, 188–89, 190, 250–51
    television and, 248
Clarke, Arthur C., 201
Coelho, Tony, 153, 154, 155, 166
Cohen, Bill, 149
Coll, Cory, 213–14
Congress, *see* U.S. Congress
Conservatism, 14, 17, 18, 45, 49–50, 58–59, 85, 114, 256
Coolidge, Calvin, 55
Corddry, Charles, 5, 11, 21, 195–220
    biography of, 194
Cronin, Thomas E., 111
Cuba, 91, 227, 292, 293, 303, 322
Cuellar, General Javier Perez de, 305
Cuomo, Mario, 120, 258

Darman, Richard, 158
Deaver, Michael, 112, 128

Defense spending, 13, 18–19, 57, 89, 90, 99, 106, 107, 131–32, 140, 143, 147, 148, 150–51, 156, 178, 190, 203–04, 217–18, 230
  see also Nuclear arms; Star Wars
Democratic Party, 35–38, 47–48, 61, 62, 63–64, 78, 103–104, 110, 139–91 *passim*, 260, 282
  see also Political parties
Deng Xiaoping, 293
Denver Post, 23
Dessouki, Ali, 292
Diefenbaker, John, 18
Dole, Robert, 99, 177, 139–141, 143–44, 148–49, 155, 167, 283
Domenici, Pete, 99–100, 177
Donaldson, Sam, 254
Duke, Paul, 6, 9–30
  biography of, 8
Dulles, John Foster, 324

Economist, 241
Edlund, Birgitta, 290
Edwards, Don, 164
Egypt, 66, 68, 292, 295–97, 300, 310, 316, 320–21, 322, 324, 325
Einstein, Albert, 199
Eisenhower, Dwight D., 52, 71, 97, 109, 125, 142, 164, 168, 274, 275
  use of television by, 237–41, 243, 257
Elections, Congressional, 184–86, 141–43, 147–48, 154–55, 167, 168–70
Elections, presidential, 36–37, 141–42, 244–45, 249, 257–58, 260, 266–67, 274–76
  of 1976, 61, 62, 63, 75–76, 142, 144, 163, 164, 171–72, 249–51, 277
  of 1980, 12–13, 34, 36, 47, 85, 86, 142, 166, 172, 185, 251–52, 303
  of 1984, 34–35, 63, 86, 131–32, 139–40, 141, 142–43, 146–48, 154–55, 164, 165, 166, 169–70, 172, 184–85, 258
"El Jihad" (Holy War), 297
El Salvador, 303, 317
Environmental Protection Agencies, 16, 131
Ervin, Sam, 249
Ethiopia, 124, 318

Fahrenkopf, Frank, 143, 187
Fairlie, Henry, 255
Fallacy of Star Wars, The, 197
Falwell, Jerry, 76
Farm belt and issues, 52, 89, 101, 134, 147, 156, 191
Fitzgerald, F. Scott, 50
Foley, Tom, 151
Ford, Gerald, 11, 20, 61, 110, 144, 231, 249–50, 274–75
Ford Motor Company, 24
Foreign imports, 67, 73, 89, 156–57
  see also Trade deficit
Forge on Democracy (MacNeil), 4
France, 217, 298, 312
Frank, Reuven, 257
Fryklund, Dick, 5
Fundamentalist Christians, 75–77
Fundamentalist movements, 287–327

Gandhi, Indira, 291, 292
Gandhi, Mahatma, 292
Gandhi, Rajiv, 292
Gardner, John L., 213
Garwin, Richard L., 200
Gaylord, Joe, 165, 168
Gephardt, Dick, 151, 153, 156
Gergen, David 175
Geyer, Georgie Anne, 11, 287–307
   biography of, 286
Ghana, 316–17
Giardano, Dr. Joseph, 94
Golden Temple, India, 292
Goldman, Eric, 40
Goldman, Sheldon, 109
Goldwater, Barry, 13, 43, 116, 117,
   184–85, 187
Good Morning America, 276
Gorbachev, Mikhail, 93–94,
   124–27, 226, 227–28, 232
Gorsuch, Anne, 16
Gorton, Slade, 149, 177
Gould, Jack, 23
Gramm, Phil, 150–51, 165
Gramm-Rudman bill, 100,
   150–52, 178
Gray, Bill, 154, 173,
Gray, Colin S., 204
Great Society, 54, 79, 190
Greece, 322
Grenada, 44, 66, 69, 91–92, 303, 317
Gromyko, Andrei, 216–17, 321
Gunn, Hartford, 4
Gush Emunim, 303
Guthman, Ed, 62

Haig, Alexander M., 96
Halleck, Charlie, 183

Hamilton, Alexander, 26
Hamilton, William, 154
Harding, Warren G., 52, 136
Harris, Louis, 169
Hart, Gary, 60, 256
Hawkins, Paula, 169
Heckler, Margaret, 15–17
Hesselton, John, 239
Hollings, Fritz, 150–51
Hoover, Herbert, 55
Humphrey, Hubert, 4, 5, 54, 244,
   274
Hussein, King, 311

Ibrahim, Saad, 297
India, 290–92, 298, 300, 310
Indochina war in 1954, 71
Indonesia, 290, 300, 316, 322, 324
Ionson, James A., 211, 214, 215
Iran, 68, 70, 251, 252, 287–89, 290,
   292, 302, 303, 308–09, 310–11,
   312, 314, 316, 323, 325
Iran, Shah of, 287, 288, 302,
   310–11, 315, 316
Iraq, 290, 303, 310, 312, 314
Isolationism, 72–73
Israel, 290, 303, 315, 325, 326
Italy, 66
Izvestia, 227

Jackson, Henry, 225
Jackson, Jesse, 189
Jefferson, Thomas, 26
John Birch Society, 41
Johnson, Haynes, 12, 33–50
   biography, 32
Johnson, Lyndon, 22, 100, 120,
   135, 163, 244, 248, 274

Jordan, 311, 325
Judiciary, federal, 108–10, 118

Kampelman, Max, 3–8, 9
　as moderator, 5–6
Kean, Thomas, 167, 185
Kelley, Gen. P. X., 152
Kemp, Jack, 145–46, 148, 149, 157, 167, 283
Kennedy, Edward, 61, 77, 114, 151
Kennedy, John F., 12, 26, 40, 70, 114, 123, 135, 136, 199, 277
　use of television by, 243–44
Kennedy, Robert, 41, 44, 70, 277
Kerry, John, 151
Khmer Rouge, 297, 298, 299
Khomeini, Ayatollah Ruhollah, 287–89, 290, 303, 308, 312, 315, 323, 325
Khrushchev, Nikita, 125
Kiker, Douglas, 4
Killing Fields, The, 297–98
King, Martin Luther, Jr., 41, 249, 250, 277
Kirkpatrick, Jeane, 304
Kissinger, Henry, 20, 222
Kohut, Dr. Heinz, 302
Kuwait, 316

Labor, *see* Organized labor
Ladd, Everett Carll, 161–62, 163, 166
Laos, 298
Latfy, Sherif, 301
Lawrence Livermore National Laboratory, 201, 202, 205, 211
Laxalt, Paul, 105, 128, 142–43
Lebanon, 71, 91, 92, 129, 251–52, 270–71, 303, 305, 311, 315, 323
Liberalism, 14, 46, 57, 59–60, 65, 114, 256
Libya, 303
Lippmann, Walter, 14
Lisagor, Peter, 5, 11, 19–22
Long, Russell, 175
Los Alamos, 202, 210
Lott, Trent, 149, 160

McCarter, Bill, 4–5, 6
McCarthy, Eugene, 43–44
McCarthy, Joseph R., 248
McDowell, Charles, 11, 26–27, 29, 30, 237–261
　biography of, 236
McFarlane, Robert C., 96–97, 152
McGovern, George, 44
McGrory, Mary, 254
McLuhan, Marshall, 246
McNamara, Robert S., 197, 199, 228, 312
MacNeil, Neil, 4–5, 21, 22
Magruder, Jeb Stuart, 11
Malaysia, 290
Marcos government, 321
Mark, Hans, 201
Marshall, Thomas, 273
Martin, Laurence, 219
Mathias, Charles, 177
Matthews, Christopher, 151, 254–55
Media: The Second God (McLuhan), 246
Meese, Edwin, III, 106, 107, 112, 116, 177
Mencken, H. L., 275
Mexico, 323

Michel, Bob, 160
Middle East terrorists, 44–45, 66, 68, 70, 95, 251, 269–70, 270–71, 295–98, 317, 320
Military forces, employment of, 44–45, 66, 68–69, 70–71
Miller, Bruce, 208
Mills, Wilbur, 182
Minorities, see Civil rights
Minow, Newton, 3
Mitterand, François, 217
Mondale, Walter, 25, 86, 131, 173, 256, 258, 274, 284
Moore, Henson, 101
Myers, Lisa, 29

Nasser, Gamal Abdel, 302, 308, 324
National Aeronautics and Space Administration, 199
NBC News, 257
Nehru, Jawaharlal, 308
Nelson, Jack, 11, 28–29, 85–115
Nelson, Ronald, 135
Nessen, Ron, 20
New Deal, 17, 35, 54, 56, 67, 108, 162–63, 177, 189
New Frontier, 54
New York Daily News, 23
New York Hearld Tribune, 26
New York Times, 23, 27, 203
New York Times/CBS News Surveys, 37, 164–65
New York Times Magazine, 98
Nicaragua, 72, 90, 92, 124, 143, 147, 303, 314, 317, 322–23
Nies, Toni, 33–35

Nixon, Richard, 11, 20, 38, 44, 79, 90, 110, 142, 143, 166–67, 168, 222, 274
  the media and, 21–22, 41, 120, 243–44, 245, 249, 266–67, 277
  see also Watergate
Nkrumah, Kwame, 316–17
Nofziger, Lyn, 122, 129, 132–33
Norport, Helmut, 37, 48
North American Air Defense Command, 203
Nuclear arms, 90, 147, 156, 196, 202, 231
  arms control, 95, 96, 123, 127–28, 217–18, 222–23, 232
  Star Wars, *see* Star Wars

Obey, Dave, 151
Oman, 301, 317
O'Neill, Tip, 105, 121–22, 123, 149, 150, 153–55, 157, 160, 171, 181, 183, 273
Organization of Eastern Caribbean States, 91
Organized labor, 59, 73
Ornstein, Norman, 100–01, 108
Oswald, Lee Harvey, 40

Packwood, Bob, 121, 182
Palestine Liberation Organization, 315
Palestine wars of 1948–49, 290
Palestinians, 325
Palestinian terrorists, *see* Middle East terrorists
Palmer, David Scott, 293–295
Panetta, Leon, 151
Peace Corps, 319–20

Persian Gulf, 310–11, 316, 317, 322, 323
Peru, 293–95, 299, 303, 319–20
Peruvian Peace Corps (Cooperación Popular), 295
Philippines, 123, 303, 321
Phillips, Kevin, 97–98, 166–67
Pipes, Richard, 126–27
Poindexter, Adm. John M., 96–97
Poland, 292
Political action committees (PACS), 259–60, 263, 279
Political parties, 18, 36–38, 48, 139–91 *passim*, 246, 259–61, 264–65
   changing role of, 47–48, 59–65, 262–63, 264
Pol Pot, 298
Poverty, 52, 53, 54, 56, 79, 134
Presidency, 60
   Reagan's legacy, 86–87, 107–15, 136
   see also Elections, presidential
Public Opinion Research, 165
Public television, 3–4, 6, 9, 10
Puth Tomneay, 299

Rather, Dan, 241
Rayburn, Sam, 181, 183
Reagan, Nancy, 128, 224
Reagan, Ronald, 25, 303, 317, 325
   age issue, 81–86, 94
   competence of, 121–23
   Congress and, *see* U.S. Congress
   foreign policy, *see* individual countries
   handling of the press, 15–16, 104, 132–33, 272
   legacy of the presidency of, 85–136
   1976 election, 61
   1980 election, 12–13, 34, 85–86, 99, 142, 166, 172, 252
   1984 election, 35, 63, 86, 131–32, 139, 141, 142, 146–47, 148, 154–55, 165, 169, 172, 185, 258
   optimism of, 44, 102–03, 106–07
   as paradoxical president, 14–15, 102, 118, 128–29, 253
   personal qualities and popularity of, 47, 49, 67, 102–03, 111, 120–22, 167, 254–55, 283
   prestige of America and, 17, 66–70, 72
   Reagan Revolution, 33–81
   Star Wars and, *see* Star Wars
   "Teflon" presidency, 34, 95, 119–20
   use of television by, 241–43, 251–54, 267–69, 269–70, 272, 281
Regan, Donald, 28, 97, 99, 148, 149, 179
Republican Party, 12, 35–38, 47–48, 61, 64–65, 139–91 *passim*, 260
   Reagan's second term and, 88, 98–101, 118
   see also Political parties
Return-to-the-past movements, 287–327
Reynolds, William Bradford, 177
Reynoso, Abimael Buzman, 293
Rifkind, Perry, 290

Ritt, Leonard, 45, 46
Robb, Charles, 185–86
Robertson, Pat, 76, 77
Rockefeller, Nelson, 64, 274
Rockwood, Stephen, 202, 210
Roe, Randall, 23
Rogin, Michael, 253
Rollins, Ed, 63, 76–77, 146, 246
Roosevelt, Franklin, 13, 14, 67, 108, 109, 132, 162, 168, 243, 267, 268, 281
Roper Center for Public Opinion Research, 162
Rostenkowski, Dan, 157–58, 159, 161, 182
Ruby, Jack, 40
Ruckelshaus, William, 131
Rudman, Warren, 149–50, 151, 177
Ryan, Barbara, 23

Sadat, Anwar, 90, 289, 295–96, 301, 320
Sandia Laboratories, 202, 208
Saturday Night Live, 29
Saudi Arabia, 314, 316
Schlesinger, Arthur, Sr., 57
Schlesinger, James, 231
Schneider, William, 63, 163
School prayer, 45, 65
Schwartz, Tony, 246
Self-confident America, 66–70, 72
Sendero Luminoso (Shining Path), 293–295, 299, 319–20
Shales, Tom, 242
Shiites, 289, 303, 310, 311, 314, 315, 317, 323
Shultz, George P., 95, 97, 216–17

Sihanouk, Prince Norodom, 289, 297, 298
Sikhs, 290–91, 292
Smith, Hedrick, 11, 12, 28, 139–170
Smith, Howard, 183
Social programs, spending on, 13, 54, 55–56, 100, 119, 143, 177, 178, 190, 191
Social Security system, 15, 89, 99, 119, 140, 148, 149, 151, 154, 174, 178, 191
South Africa, 89, 90, 91, 101, 106, 128, 135, 143, 147, 156, 176
South America, 323
South Yemen, 124
Soviet Union, 58, 89, 90, 92, 93, 96, 123, 124, 128, 129, 202, 222–23
 fundamentalist movements and, 291, 292, 311, 316, 317
 Star Wars and 94, 95, 196–97, 199–200, 206, 216–17, 224, 225, 226–30, 232–33
 summit with Gorbachev, 93, 94, 95, 124–127
Speakes, Larry, 104
Specter, Arlen, 177
Star Wars, 19, 93, 94, 95, 124–25, 129, 147, 195–234
Stassen, Harold, 238
Stenholm, Charles W., 104
Stockman, David, 139–40, 175
Stoessel, Walter, 122
Strategic Defense Initiative, *see* Star Wars
Suez Canal, 322, 324
Sukarno, 324

Sullivan, Mark, 40
Supply-side economics, 145
Supreme Court, 108, 109
Symms, Steve, 168–69
Syria, 310

Taft, Robert, 14, 237–39
Tanzania, 318, 319
Tax increases, 99, 128, 140, 148–49, 150–51, 152, 178, 190
Tax reductions, 13, 56–57, 89, 106, 107, 118, 119, 128, 146, 179, 280
Tax reform, 86–87, 89, 100, 118–20, 157–61, 176, 179–80, 268
Taylor, Maxwell, 230
Teeter, Bob, 65, 165, 172
Television and politics, 18, 40, 60, 130, 237–284
Teller, Edward, 203, 211
Third World fundamentalism, 287–327
Thomas, L. E. (Tommy), 85, 86
Tocqueville, Alexis de, 45–46, 284
Trade deficit, 52, 101–02, 106, 143, 147, 156–57, 176
  foreign imports, 66–67, 73, 89–90, 156–57
Trumam, David B., 259, 279
Turkey, 292, 302, 322
TWA hostage crisis, *see* Middle East terrorists

Udall, Morris, 181–82
Unemployment, 52
Union of Concerned Scientists, 196–97, 200, 208, 226

United Nations, 299, 304, 305–06, 318
U.S. Congress, 45, 54, 55–56, 64, 94, 260
  Carter and, 103–04, 110, 113–14
  minority representation in, 188–89
  Office of Technology Assessment, 217–18
  Reagan's legislative programs and, 86, 87, 88, 100, 103, 104–06, 107–08, 112, 113, 118, 121, 131–32, 146–47, 155–162, 174, 176, 184, 189–91, 196, 203, 230, 280
  rift or realignment?, 137–193
  television coverage of, 272
  see also Elections, Congressional
U.S. Department of Health and Human Services, 15–16
U.S. Department of Interior, 16
U.S. Immigration and Naturalization Service, 290
U.S. Justice Department, 109

Van Buren, Martin, 274
Vice Presidency, 273–75
Vietnam, 298, 303
Vietnamese Americans, 52
Vietnam War, 11, 38, 40, 68, 70, 71, 110, 124, 180, 298
  television and, 247–48, 277
Voting Rights Act of 1965, 176–77

Wallace, George, 41, 43–44
Wall Street Journal, 77
Washington Post, 242

Washington Week in Review:
  the beginnings of, 3–6, 10–11
  negative mail, 24–28
  Nixon administration and, 21–22
  popularity of, 6, 9–10, 23–25, 29–30
Watergate, 11, 22, 38, 79, 110, 167, 243, 249, 266, 277
Watson Research Center, Thomas J., 200
Watt, James, 16
Wattenberg, Martin P., 37, 47, 166
Watts riots, 40
Weinberger, Caspar, 70, 92, 95–96, 97, 152, 198–199, 216, 224
Welch, Joseph 248
West Germany, 217
WETA-TV, 3, 4
White, Theodore, 242

White Sands Missile Range, 209
Williams, Irving G., 273–74
Willis, David, 4
Wilson, Woodrow, 81, 273
Wirthlin, Richard, 113, 169, 279
World Bank, 312, 318
World Court, 72
Worrell, Eugene, 239–40
Wright, Jim, 176
Wright brothers, 198

Yates, Ronald, 299
Yazdi, Ibrahim, 287
Yeager, Chuck, 198
Yonas, Gerald, 204, 207, 209, 218–19
Yugoslavia, 292

Ziegler, Ron, 20

BOOKS OF DISTINCTION
by THEODORE H. WHITE

___AMERICA IN SEARCH OF ITSELF *(I37-559, $8.95, U.S.A.)*
(I37-560, $10.75, Canada)
This is the climax of White's famous series, THE MAKING OF A PRESIDENT. The author illuminates the story of Reagan's election, the explosion of events in Iran and their impact on Carter's election race. White also deals with the last quarter of a century: how television took over the political process, how the Great Inflation came into being and how it came to undermine all American life. Finally, White addresses several demanding questions: What kind of people are we? Who leads us? Where are we now? Where are we going?

___IN SEARCH OF HISTORY   *(I34-271, $5.95, U.S.A.)*
Available in large-size paperback (I34-270, $6.95, Canada)
This is a book about the people who, making history, have changed your life—and about a great correspondent who listened to their stories for forty years. Now he has woven all those stories into this splendid tale of his own. **"In Search Of History** is the most fascinating and most useful personal memoir of this generation." —*William Safire*

WARNER BOOKS
P.O. Box 690
New York, N.Y. 10019

Please send me the books I have checked. I enclose a check or money order (not cash), plus 50¢ per order and 50¢ per copy to cover postage and handling.* (Allow 4 weeks for delivery.)

_____ Please send me your free mail order catalog. (If ordering only the catalog, include a large self-addressed, stamped envelope.)

Name _____
Address _____
City _____
State _____ Zip _____
*N.Y. State and California residents add applicable sales tax.   42

The Best of the Business from Warner Books

___IN SEARCH OF EXCELLENCE
Thomas J. Peters and   *(K38-281, $9.95, U.S.A.)*
Robert H. Waterman, Jr.   *(K38-282, $11.95, Canada)*

Highly acclaimed and highly optimistic about the future of American management, this essential book proves that American business is alive and well—and successful! Subtitled "Lessons from America's Best-Run Companies," it reveals the secrets of the art of successful American management, the eight fascinating basic principles that the authors found hard at work at Johnson & Johnson, Procter & Gamble, IBM, Hewlett-Packard, Delta Airlines, McDonald's, and other well-run firms. Here are the native American policies and attitudes that lead to growth and profits—policies and attitudes that thousands of business people all over the country are now trying for themselves!

___MEGATRENDS
Ten New Directions Transforming Our Lives
John Naisbitt   *(I32-922, $4.95, U.S.A.)*
                                                      (I32-923, $6.50, Canada)
Hardcover: *(I51-251, $17.50 in U.S.A., $22.95 in Canada)*

Once in a great while a book so accurately captures the essence of its time that it becomes the spokesman for that decade. In 1956 it was *The Organization Man*. In 1970 it was *Future Shock*. In the 1980's it will be *Megatrends*, the only "future" book whose predictions for tomorrow are based on a dynamic analysis of what America is today. As Naisbitt details America's shift from industrial production to providing services and information, you can project your career and business moves. As you learn where the new centers of activity are developing, you can decide where you should live. If you have political goals, John Naisbitt's analysis of governmental trends can help you target your energies. This is the challenge, the means, and the method to better our lives . . . a must for everyone who cares about the future.

WARNER BOOKS
P.O. Box 690
New York, N.Y. 10019

Please send me the books I have checked. I enclose a check or money order (not cash), plus 50¢ per order and 50¢ per copy to cover postage and handling.*
(Allow 4 weeks for delivery.)

_____ Please send me your free mail order catalog. (If ordering only the catalog, include a large self-addressed, stamped envelope.)

Name _____

Address _____

City _____

State _____ Zip _____

*N.Y. State and California residents add applicable sales tax.

Books of Distinction
by EDWIN NEWMAN

—A CIVIL TONGUE *(Q30-758, $3.95, U.S.A.)*
(Q30-759, $4.95, Canada)

A witty and provocative appeal, by the author of *Strictly Speaking*, for direct, concise, and imaginative use of the English language. "For an informal, painless course in how to write concise, clear, straightforward English, it is recommended."
—*Library Journal*

—STRICTLY SPEAKING *(Q34-218, $3.95, U.S.A.)*
(Q34-219, $4.95, Canada)

One of broadcasting's most respected newsmen poses this question: Will America be the death of English? In this witty and refreshing treatise Newman points a wry, accusatory finger at fellow newsmen, sportscasters, politicians, and other public figures who trample on our language.

WARNER BOOKS
P.O. Box 690
New York, N.Y. 10019

Please send me the books I have checked. I enclose a check or money order (not cash), plus 50¢ per order and 50¢ per copy to cover postage and handling.*
(Allow 4 weeks for delivery.)

_____ Please send me your free mail order catalog. (If ordering only the catalog, include a large self-addressed, stamped envelope.)

Name _____
Address _____
City _____
State _____ Zip _____
*N.Y. State and California residents add applicable sales tax.

By the year 2000, 2 out of 3 Americans could be illiterate.

It's true.

Today, 75 million adults... about one American in three, can't read adequately. And by the year 2000, U.S. News & World Report envisions an America with a literacy rate of only 30%.

Before that America comes to be, you can stop it... by joining the fight against illiteracy today.

Call the Coalition for Literacy at toll-free **1-800-228-8813** and volunteer.

Volunteer Against Illiteracy. The only degree you need is a degree of caring.

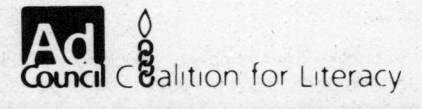

Ad Council Coalition for Literacy

Warner Books is proud to be an active supporter of the Coalition for Literacy.